Praise for *Your Voice, Your Vote: 2020–21 Edition*

"Burk is insistent and urgent when pressing the cause of gender equality. Part primer, part call to arms with its lessons on how politics work . . . valuable lessons for every voter: Take time to know what your candidates stand for, question and prod them beyond bromides and talking points, and hold them accountable."

—*The Washington Post*

"Martha Burk reminds us there is still work to do—and shows us a road to gender equality that goes straight through the voting booth."
—Susan Scanlan, chair, National Council of Women's Organizations

"Martha Burk is much more than simply an advocate for women's issues. Her broad range of experience and understanding of the political process make her uniquely qualified to outline what's at stake—not just for women, but the country as a whole—in the upcoming election. A timely and important call to action."

—Bill Richardson, former governor of New Mexico

"Whether you're a young woman worried about your future, an employed woman fighting to break the glass ceiling, a mom out of the paid workforce, a retired woman struggling to make ends meet, or a feminist activist trying to change the world, this book has the information you need."

—Eleanor Smeal, publisher, *Ms.* magazine

"A call to action and a resource for women who want to understand what's really at stake, and why women should view their political selves in a more powerful way. Burk's book is also a great primer on the issues that you think you know something about, but would like a little more background on without the spin of cable talking heads, like the

Affordable Care Act, why women voters should care about the mort-gage/housing crisis, foreign affairs, reproductive health, paid maternity leave, civil rights—you name it, she's got it in this valuable book."

—Joanne Bamberger, *The Huffington Post*

"This is a must have for every voter, not just women . . . the heart of this book is Burk's explanation of the issues. Read the book and then share with the women in your life. Or buy a few copies and start an election discussion group."

—Vivalafeminista.com

Your Voice, Your Vote:

2020–21 Edition

The Savvy Woman's Guide to Politics, Power, and the Change We Need

★ ★ ★

Dr. Martha Burk

Skyhorse Publishing

9759

Skyhorse Publishing books may be purchased in bulk at special discounts for sales promotion, corporate gifts, fund-raising, or educational purposes. Special editions can also be created to specifications. For details, contact the Special Sales Department, Skyhorse Publishing, 307 West 36th Street, 11th Floor, New York, NY 10018 or info@skyhorsepublishing.com.

Skyhorse® and Skyhorse Publishing® are registered trademarks of Skyhorse Publishing, Inc.®, a Delaware corporation.

Visit our website at www.skyhorsepublishing.com.

10 9 8 7 6 5 4 3 2 1

Library of Congress Cataloging-in-Publication Data is available on file.

Cover design by Tom Lau

Print ISBN: 978-1-5107-5253-5
Ebook ISBN: 978-1-5107-5254-2

Printed in the United States of America.

Table of Contents

Chapter 1

Change, No Change, or Short-Changed: What's at Stake for Women in 2020 and Beyond?

Elections are often characterized as the "election of the century," and billed as "the most significant election in our lifetime" for one group or another, including women. The last few US presidential elections were no exception, and indeed had high drama and high expectations. What made them so significant?

In this century, we've had three regime changes at the top, with the presidency going from Republican to Democratic and back again to Republican. The balance of power in Congress has changed as well. In 2010 House majority changed from Democratic to Republican control, and not for the better, insofar as women are concerned. It got worse in 2014, when Republicans (historically more hostile to women's rights) also took over the Senate. Even though the House once again went to the Democrats in 2018, the government remains all but paralyzed, and anti-woman legislation has been introduced time and time again at the national and state levels. That's why 2020 and beyond is so important.

Women's rights, for which we fought so hard, have recently been eroded. The first federal ban in history on an abortion procedure became law in 2007, and a woman-hostile majority on the Supreme

Court seriously curtailed our ability to challenge employment discrimination. Title IX, the law requiring equal educational opportunities for girls and women, has been weakened and remains under constant assault. In 2019 courts allowed a Trump administration rule banning federal family planning dollars from going to health care providers providing abortion services, also impacting cancer and HIV screenings, birth control, and preventive care.

In spite of the setbacks, there is much room for forward progress. The pay gap remains, we still lack pregnancy leave or paid family leave, and child care is a patchwork of "make-do" arrangements that leaves families struggling. There are many other pressing national issues we don't normally think about as "women's issues," but that is indeed what they are. Gun violence, the low-wage economy, the continuing assaults on Medicare and Social Security, ongoing and potential wars, and tax policies all affect women in different ways than they affect men, and all are growing concerns.

We must view these challenges not as obstacles, but as opportunities. *Women are the majority of the population, the majority of registered voters, and the majority of those that actually show up at the polls. That means we have the opportunity to take control and make the changes we need in every election.* But having the opportunity is not enough. We must have the will—firmly grounded in essential knowledge of the issues for a path ahead. That's what this book is about.

This book is *not* about individual candidates or one party or the other, though it does hold both incumbents and parties accountable for their records. It *is* about how we can reverse the losses since the turn of the twenty-first century, and once more go forward. But please don't think of this as just another "good citizens act, good citizens vote" sermon. Voting and taking action don't help, and indeed can hurt, if women and the men who care about them end up doing something against their own interests because they don't know the facts.

It is still true that knowledge is power. By the time you close this book you will know what's at stake for women as we navigate the most important opportunities for progress—or lack of it—in this election year and the years following. But knowledge won't bring change without action—that means holding candidates and elected officials accountable for long-term solutions.

The first action we must take is confronting those who seek our votes—incumbents and challengers of both parties—with questions not only about their voting records, but also their future intentions on our most vital issues. At the end of each chapter, you will find such questions. After all, there's a national election every two years, and every one is "the election of the century" for women. And when the election is over, the information here will help you hold candidates that got elected accountable.

Those who would roll back the progress we've made toward reaching economic, social, legal, and political equality have vast financial resources, are very well-organized, and are too often driven by a misogyny that borders on outright hatred of women. They are not prone to participate in rational and reasonable discourse. They will usurp control of social policy at every opportunity, and block any positive steps they don't agree with. And we know that that is no idle threat—women are currently suffering both attacks and setbacks. It's up to women, and the men who care about them, to stop it, and we must start *right now* in public discourse, election campaigns, and in the voting booth.

> We shall employ agents, circulate tracts, petition the State and national Legislatures, and endeavor to enlist the pulpit and the press in our behalf.

These words are contained in the final paragraph of the *Declaration of Sentiments* from the First Women's Rights Convention held in 1848. The ladies of 1848 were determined, and after seventy-two more years of struggle, they got what they wanted most—the vote. If they were alive to exercise that right today, they might put it this way:

3

Read their records. Go to town hall meetings and confront them. Call in when you hear them on the radio or see them on TV. If they don't mention women, ask why not. Spread the word when they say something about our issues, good or bad. Use all kinds of social media. Raise Hell, and if need be, Take to the Streets. Don't be captivated by fancy speeches or red-hot rhetoric. Arm yourself with knowledge and *vote your own interests*.

How to Read This Book

The essential background you need to make a difference is found in the first five chapters; we urge you to read them first. After that—well, women have differing concerns. So you'll probably want to read about the issues most important to you next. We do think there are eye-opening facts in every section, but skipping around won't hurt. It is not necessary to go straight through to get the most out of *Your Voice, Your Vote: The Savvy Woman's Guide to Politics, Power, and the Change We Need*.

When you're finished, pass this book along, or keep it for reference and encourage your friends to get a copy and read it too. After all, one woman *can* change the world—but it's easier when we combine our power into a force to be reckoned with.

Author's Note

Your Voice, Your Vote is documented with over three hundred endnotes—all referencing established and reliable sources. Why so many? In today's environment of "alternative facts" and ready labeling of disliked information as "fake news," we thought it necessary to show the reader where we got our "actual facts" and "real news."

Chapter 2

The Gender Gap—Women Can Control Any Election

The Long, Long Road to the Female Majority

When the Constitution was adopted in 1789, the ruling class was white, male, and land-owning. Rights of full citizenship were granted on that basis. While was never disputed that persons granted citizenship were understood to be white and male, the framers could not agree on whether land ownership should also be a requirement for voting. Unable to resolve the issue, they left voting requirements to the states. None of the states allowed Indians, Black men, or any women to vote.

The Fourteenth Amendment, ratified three years after the abolition of slavery in 1868, granted citizenship to "persons" born or naturalized in the United States, and the right to vote to non-white men, but to no women, white or non-white. It also guaranteed equal protection under the law to all persons.

The breathtaking hypocrisy of the federal government proposing a constitutional amendment guaranteeing equal protection for all citizens, while denying the female half the vote, was not lost on the suffragists. In the years before adoption controversy raged as to whether women should be included, with the formidable Susan B. Anthony on the side of women (Black and white) and the equally formidable Black leader Frederick Douglass against. Douglass's arguments were summed up by the influential newspaper editor Horace Greeley when he told the women:

> . . . hold your claims, though just and imperative . . . in abeyance until the negro is safe beyond peradventure, and your turn will come next. I conjure you to remember that this is the negro's hour, and your first duty now is to go through the State and plead his claims.[2]

Of course he meant "male" negroes. Ultimately the guys won (surprise!), introducing the word male into the Constitution for the first time, and enshrining in that document that race discrimination is more serious than sex discrimination—a strange and enormously harmful notion that continues to be upheld by the courts to this day.

Women would have to work another fifty-two years, until 1920, to pass a separate amendment to get equal voting rights. Carrie Chapman Catt, one of the movement leaders, told just how hard it was:

> To get the word male in effect out of the Constitution cost the women of the country fifty-two years of pauseless campaign . . . During that time they were forced to conduct 56 campaigns of referenda to male voters; 480 campaigns to get Legislatures to submit suffrage amendments to voters; 47 campaigns to get state constitutional conventions to write woman suffrage into state constitutions; 277 campaigns to get state party conventions to include woman suffrage planks; 30 campaigns to get presidential party conventions to adopt woman suffrage planks in party platforms; and 19 campaigns with 19 successive Congresses.[3]

There were too many arguments against women's suffrage to count, but a frequent one was that women did not need the vote because they would just vote the same way their husbands did anyway. Another argument posited the opposite outcome; anti-suffragists, far from believing women would be so apathetic, feared that women would take over the nation and its politics. As a matter of fact, neither happened. For the next sixty years, though not necessarily casting their ballots in the same way as men, women certainly didn't take over the country.

But the 1980 election brought the "perfect storm" in terms of the women's vote. Women now outnumbered men in the population, and that year they surpassed men in both voter registration and turnout. And for the first time in US history, women voted in a markedly different way than men.

The Equal Rights Amendment (ERA), granting equal constitutional rights to women, was pending before the states, and the right to abortion had been upheld by the Supreme Court through the *Roe v. Wade* decision only seven years earlier. Ronald Reagan, the Republican candidate, ran on a platform that included opposition to both abortion rights and the ERA. His opponent, Democratic incumbent Jimmy Carter, was pro-choice and a strong ERA advocate. Reagan won the election, but his support split along gender lines, with 54 percent of men voting for him versus 46 percent of women—a difference of eight percentage points.

This *gender gap,* named and identified by feminist political analyst Eleanor Smeal, has never gone away. Neither has women's majority in voting, and that's why change is possible.

Though it has never disappeared, since 1980 the gender gap has been larger in some elections than others. It was smallest in 1992 with women favoring Bill Clinton by 3 percent, when third party candidate Ross Perot siphoned votes from both major party candidates. The gap was largest in 2000—women favored Al Gore over George W. Bush by 12 percentage points—in a contested election that was awarded to Bush by the Supreme Court with a 5-4 decision.[4]

There was a 7 percent gender gap in the Obama election of 2008, and a 20 percent gap in 2012 (unmarried women, who made up a fifth of the electorate, went for him by a whopping 70 percent).[5]

The gender gap in the vote for president continued to break records in 2016. Women were widely expected to create a winning majority for Hillary Clinton—but it didn't exactly happen. Clinton won women by 12 points but lost men to Trump by 12—a 24-point gender gap. The majority of non-college educated white women (64 percent) voted for Trump, while only 35 percent backed Clinton. Black, Hispanic, and other non-white females backed Clinton in far greater numbers: non-college educated Black women by 97 percent over Trump, and non-college educated Hispanic women by 75 percent.[6] (Clinton won the overall popular vote by more than three million, but lost in the Electoral College when selected counties in a few crucial states defied all predictions and went against her. As of this writing, it is still unresolved whether Russian interference that is now well-documented made the difference.)

Women's votes have also been decisive in a number of close congressional elections, which can make a huge difference, since legislation benefitting or disadvantaging women can depend on which party controls Congress.

* In 2006 control of the Senate and the House turned over from Republican to Democratic because of Republican support for the war in Iraq. Eighty percent of women rated ending it very high as opposed to 71 percent of men.[7] Everyone also knew that if the Democrats won the House, the first woman in history would be Speaker—Nancy Pelosi of California. Women saw this as much more important than men (54 to 43 percent).[8]
* The Democrats achieved a filibuster-proof Senate majority in 2008 by picking up eight seats, seven of which had substantial gender gaps of 4 to 16 percent.[9]

* In the 2010 mid-term elections, the House again turned Republican, with a drop off in women's support for Democrats, almost all from white women. African American women voted for Democrats 92 percent of the time, and Hispanic women 65 percent.[10]
* In 2012 women's votes were again decisive in maintaining Democratic control of the Senate. One of the key Senate races with a gender gap of over 10 percent was in the election of Elizabeth Warren.
* Both chambers of Congress flipped to Republican in 2014, but not because women shifted their votes. The 10-point party gender gap was at least as wide as at any point over the last fifteen years,[11] but with the lowest voter turnout since 1942 at 36.4 percent of eligible voters.
* Even though Republicans retained their majorities in 2016, gender gaps persisted in both Senate and House races. Women were more likely than men to support Democrats for Senate by 3 to 16 percentage points. There was an 11-point gender gap favoring Democrats in House races.[12]
* Women's votes fueled a new Democratic House majority in 2018 along with a tsunami of new Democratic female members. The gender gap was 23 points,[13] and propelled Representative Nancy Pelosi into the Speaker's chair once more.

Women are Democrats, Men are Republicans

There are growing gender gaps in party identification. For a number of years, women have not only been voting in greater numbers than men, but choosing more Democratic than Republican candidates. Since 1972, both women and men have also switched to the independent category from one or the other parties. Men have migrated away from calling themselves Democrats, with more moving to independent than to Republican. Females have been more stable, with the majority identifying as Democrats since 1972, and fewer leaving either party to become independents.

As of 2016, there was a 14 percent gender gap in Democratic Party identification between women and men (40 percent to 26 percent). The gender gap between females and males identifying as Republicans was 8 percent (30 percent to 38 percent). Both parties have steadily lost members to the independent column over the years, though independent men switched to Republican identification in 2016.

However, since there are very few independent candidates on the ballot, voters of both genders are forced to vote for either Republicans or Democrats, explaining the difference in actual voting patterns versus party identification.

The table below shows us how party identification has changed over the years.

Year-by-Year Party Identification By Gender[14]						
Year	Male			Female		
	Dem.	Ind.	Rep.	Dem.	Ind.	Rep.
1972	44%	22%	34%	47%	17%	36%
1976	39%	38%	23%	43%	30%	27%
1980	42%	27%	31%	48%	24%	28%
1984	35%	29%	36%	41%	23%	35%
1988	33%	28%	39%	42%	25%	33%

Year	Male			Female		
	Dem.	Ind.	Rep.	Dem.	Ind.	Rep.
1992	34%	30%	36%	41%	26%	34%
1996	34%	29%	37%	44%	23%	33%
2000	33%	29%	38%	44%	25%	32%
2004	31%	29%	39%	41%	24%	35%
2006	32%	31%	37%	43%	23%	34%
2009	32%	34%	28%	41%	26%	25%[15]
2010	30%	n/a	23%	38 %	n/a	25%
2011	27%	n/a	26%	36%	n/a	26%
2012	27%	43%	25%	37%	33%	24%[16]
2014	24%	45%	26%	37%	35%	23%[17]
2016	26%	32%	38%	40%	27%	30%[18]
2018†	47%	–	51%	60%	–	39%

† Actual vote as per 2018 exit polls, party identification including independents not available.

Gender Gaps in How Congress Votes

Female elected leaders have also been responsible for making a difference in Congress on a variety of measures, from efforts to end the Iraq War, to pushing for more money for breast cancer research and combating violence against women. Women are often in solidarity across party lines, and differ with men within their own parties.

In the House of Representatives, Democratic women are decidedly more liberal than Democratic men,[19] and women of both parties will sometimes vote together in opposition to the male majority. In May, 2007, more than half of the female House members, regardless of party, voted against open-ended funding of the war, compared to only 29 percent of the male representatives.

Votes on social issues are even more telling. Sixty-four percent of the women in the Senate voted against the passage of the first federal abortion procedure ban in history, which became law in 2007, while 64 percent of the men in the Senate voted for it.[20] The women's vote did *not* split along party lines—both Democratic and Republican women voted against the ban. It is obvious that if there had been as many women in the Senate as there were men, the measure could have been defeated.

The same is true of the vote for the Stupak-Pitts amendment to outlaw abortion coverage in the health care overhaul that passed the House in November, 2009. The great majority of women from both parties voted against the restriction, but their numbers were not enough to prevail, since men constituted 83 percent of the House membership.

Republican and Democratic women also united in the Senate in 2009 to pass the Lilly Ledbetter Fair Pay Act, the first bill President Obama signed into law. All of the female Senators voted in favor of the bill. The men's vote split straight down party lines, with all of the Democrats supporting, and all of the Republican men voting no. Similar gender solidarity across party lines has been shown on votes for a military children's health program and ratification of the United Nations treaty on the disabled (though again the overall vote fell short).

Voting is not the only place where gender gaps have developed. Women and men differ substantially on many issues. You'll find examples throughout this book. Suffice it to say that if women did not vote at all or voted in lower numbers than men, different people would be elected, and different priorities would be emphasized by lawmakers.

These examples are just a small snapshot of why gender gaps do matter—whether in the voting booth or in the halls of Congress. If women want to make change, they must vote their priorities, regardless of party, and they must support leaders who share those priorities—again regardless of party. The good news is that women are now a permanent majority—in the population, in voter registration, and in voter turnout. That means women can control any election if they vote their own interests and vote together.

Wouldn't it be great if the fears of the anti-suffragists weren't so far-fetched after all?

Chapter 3

Who's in Charge? Why Should Women Care?

The Guy (or Gal) at the Top . . .

Throughout much of our history it has often seemed that control in Washington doesn't matter much. The government pretty much rolled along, regardless of who was in the White House or which party had the most members of Congress. After all, the federal government is a huge bureaucracy, each department has its mission, and it looked like not much changed from administration to administration.

But recent political climates have shown that that view is very wrong. Control matters enormously. Our government has been gridlocked to the point of being unable to make even the smallest decisions, much less fix the big problems. In 2013 and again in 2018-2019, Republicans shut down the government, risking financial default—because the president and Congress could not agree or compromise.

As we learned in civics classes, the federal government has three branches—executive (the president and his staff, including the cabinet, advisors, and other political appointees), judicial (courts and judges), and legislative (the Senate and House of Representatives)—and that the three have equal power and serve as checks and balances to one another. That's all true—up to a point. A lot depends on who's in charge of each branch at any given time.

In 2006, when answering a question about conduct of the Iraq War, President George W. Bush declared "I am the Decider." While pundits often made light of the remark, the fact is that it's true a lot of the time. And usually it matters a great deal who the Decider is.

Though the Constitution grants the power to declare war only to Congress, in reality it is presidents who decide. The president also gets to decide (with the advice and consent of the Senate) who will sit on the courts, and which individuals will head the cabinet departments.

Through these appointments, the president sets an agenda for the country, because appointees usually carry out their duties in accordance with the president's wishes. (The Supreme Court is sometimes an exception. While presidents mostly get the nominee they want—if not the first choice, then the second—justices can change their outlook over time. Of course they're appointed for life and can't lose their jobs.)

Consider some of the consequences—good and bad—of presidential agenda-setting and appointments in the last few administrations:

Ronald Reagan

* Anne M. Gorsuch, Environmental Protection Agency Director. A firm believer that the EPA was too big, wasteful, and too restrictive of business. Gorsuch cut the EPA budget by 22 percent. She boasted that she reduced the thickness of the book of clean water regulations from six inches to a half-inch.[21]
* Clarence Thomas, Equal Employment Opportunity Commission Director. Downsized the agency and all but eliminated class-action suits for employment discrimination. Declared that sexual harassment claims were not a priority for the agency.[22]

George H. W. Bush

* Clarence Thomas, Supreme Court. Voted with the conservative majority to uphold a federal abortion ban, curb women's employment rights, and outlaw using race as a factor in school integration plans.
* Antonia Novello, Surgeon General. First woman and first Hispanic to hold the position. Focused her attention on the health of women, children, and minorities.

William J. Clinton

* Donna Shalala, Secretary Health and Human Services. Raised child immunization rates to the highest levels in history; created national initiatives to fight breast cancer and violence against women.[23]
* Ruth Bader Ginsburg, Supreme Court. Consistent vote for the rights of women and strong believer in freedom of choice. Issued rare dissents from the bench in 2007 in the *Gonzales* federal abortion ban case, and in the *Ledbetter* case, which curbed women's employment rights.[24]

George W. Bush

* Eric Keroack, followed by Susan Orr, Health and Human Services Family Planning. Both opposed birth control, even though the office oversees $283 million in annual grants to provide low-income families and others with contraceptive services and counseling.[25]
* Wade Horn, Health and Human Services Assistant Secretary. Founded the National Fatherhood Initiative to promote marriage as the solution to poverty, then gave the group a $12.38 million contract. Openly stated his belief that "the husband is

the head of the wife, just as Christ is the head of the church."
Advocated that Head Start be available only to children of
married couples, not single parents.[26]

* John Roberts, Chief Justice, Supreme Court, and Samuel Alito,
  Supreme Court. Both credited with sharply turning the Court
  to the right, joining in several 5-4 majorities upholding a federal abortion ban without a health exception, and curtailing
  women's employment rights.[27]

Barack Obama

* Sonia Sotomayor, Elena Kagan, Supreme Court. Sotomayor
  was first Hispanic woman appointed to the Court. Both advocates for rights of minorities and women.
* Hilda Solis, Secretary of Labor. First Hispanic Secretary of Labor. Declared women's employment and pay equity a priority
  for the department.
* Hillary Clinton, Secretary of State. Elevated office of women's
  rights to ambassador status. Strong advocate for global wom-
  en's rights.
* Janet Napolitano, Secretary of Homeland Security. Pioneer
  in coordinating federal, state, local, and bi-national homeland security efforts, and presided over large-scale disaster
  relief efforts.
* Kathleen Sebelius, followed by Sylvia Mathews Burwell, Secretary of Health & Human Services. Presided over planning
  and implementation of the Affordable Care Act, the largest
  change in US health care in history.
* Janet Yellin, Chair of the Federal Reserve Board. First female
  chair, she pushed for more help for ordinary households, not
  just banks, in the economic downturn and financial crisis.

Donald Trump†

* Ben Carson, Secretary of Housing and Urban Development. Appointed despite having told President Trump he was not qualified. Found by Government Accountability Office to have committed a crime.[28]
* Wilbur Ross, Secretary of Commerce. Found by a federal judge to have broken several laws in overseeing the US Census.[29]
* Andrew Wheeler, EPA Administrator. Former lobbyist for the coal industry, he replaced Obama Clean Power Plan with eased rules for coal-fired generating plants.[30]
* Betsy DeVos, Secretary of Education. Rewrote Title IX rules for sexual harassment in schools, making it harder to prosecute and essentially putting victims on trial.[31]
* Brett Kavanaugh, Supreme Court. Credibly accused of sexual assault. Voted to allow a Louisiana law that would have left only a single abortion provider in the state.

These high-level and very visible examples are only a small fraction of the number of appointments each president makes. Presidents infuse all government departments with appointees that carry out their philosophy. If that philosophy is fairness and good government, then women win. If that philosophy is anti-government, punitive toward the poor, sympathetic to the religious right, the very wealthy and corporations, then women lose.

Majorities Matter—Congress and Its Committees

Most business in Congress is done through a committee system,

---

† Space does not permit enumeration of Trump appointees found to have committed documented crimes, malfeasance, or ethics violations. For a more exhaustive list see https://washingtonmonthly.com/2019/05/17/trump-has-assembled-the-worst-cabinet-in-history/.

meaning that members can't automatically bring bills to the floor of the House or Senate for a vote. Bills are introduced, then they go to a committee for consideration. This is far from an orderly process, and what happens next almost always depends on which party is in the majority. That's because seats on each committee are determined by which party is in control.

If the Republicans are in control of the Senate or the House, they will have the majority of seats on *every committee* in that chamber, and the chairperson of *every committee* will be a Republican. The opposite is of course true if the Democrats are in the majority. The chairperson and majority members have control, so they are the decision makers as to which bills the committee will consider (and which bills it won't—those will die in committee).

This is a shorthand explanation of the bill process, but it will give you the basics. Suppose a bill is introduced that would make new law, or overturn an existing law. The bill is immediately sent to a committee that deals with the topic the bill addresses (e.g. education or energy), where the committee chair is in charge of its fate.

If the committee chair does not like the bill, it is never scheduled to come up for discussion. If the chair of the committee likes the bill, and thinks it ought to go to the floor for a vote, he or she schedules hearings, where advocates and experts come and talk to the committee about the pros and cons. Then the committee takes a vote on whether to send the bill to the full body (House or Senate) for a vote.

But the struggle isn't over, because the next step is getting it on the voting calendar, which is essentially a priority list. And guess who decides where it goes on the calendar? *The leaders from the majority party*. If a bill is placed too far down on the calendar, the clock may run out on the legislative session before it ever comes up for a vote, meaning the whole process has to be repeated by the next Congress.

Committees have another very important function—oversight. That means if something is going on in the government that they believe bears investigation, they can call witnesses before the committee to talk about it, and place them under oath if they want. Or not. And the "or not" is sometimes the more important part of the equation.

For example, when it became public in early 2006 that President Bush was conducting a program of wiretapping conversations of US citizens without court warrants, the chairman of the Senate Select Committee on Intelligence, Senator Pat Roberts (R–KS) refused to hold hearings to investigate the legality of the program. When the Democrats gained power in the mid-term elections, the Senate Judiciary Committee issued subpoenas to the White House, Vice President Dick Cheney's office, and the Justice Department after what the panel's chairman Patrick Leahy (D–VT) called "stonewalling of the worst kind" against efforts to investigate the wiretapping.[32] Similarly, when the Obama Administration refused to hand over documents from the Department of Justice justifying the legality of drone strikes in 2013, the House Judiciary Committee obtained the material only after threatening a subpoena.[33]

The biggest fights over subpoena power in modern history have come during the Trump administration, in the aftermath of the Mueller Report, which investigated whether Russia had interfered in the 2016 election. The Democratic-majority House issued a number of subpoenas to institutions for records related to the Russia probe, to Trump financial transactions and efforts to add a citizenship question to the census, to several former White House staffers, to the Secretary of the Treasury, and to the former White House counsel. Trump ordered all to ignore the subpoenas, variously claiming executive privilege or "absolute immunity" (which does not exist) to prevent testimony before the House.[34] The standoff moved to the courts in 2019 as the conflict between the White House and Congress escalated to an impeachment inquiry. At this writing it is unclear when, or if, any of the recalcitrant persons will testify before Congress prior to the 2020 elections.

Committees can also call people other than government employees before them to explain things that impact the public health, safety, or well-being. An infamous example occurred in 2012 when House Republicans convened a hearing on whether contraception should be provided in insurance plans under health care reform, since Catholic bishops had objected to the requirement being placed not only on churches but also any institution loosely affiliated with a church (e.g. a university or hospital). Because the committee majority has final say over who the witnesses will be, in addition to whether to call a hearing in the first place, only men were allowed to testify. This caused a firestorm of protest from female committee members, and they walked out of the hearing.

An earlier (but still infamous) case is instructive. In 1994 the Democratic majority was investigating whether tobacco should be regulated as a drug. In an almost comical display, tobacco executives stood as a group before a congressional committee and swore under oath that they didn't believe tobacco was addictive. But before any action could be taken on regulation, control of Congress switched to the Republicans in the next election, and here's what happened: Since the 1994 tobacco hearings the Republicans have taken control of the government majority, and the committee that investigated the tobacco companies is now headed by Thomas Bliley, a Republican from Virginia and one of the industry's strongest supporters.[35] In the quarter century since, hearings have never been reconvened—and tobacco has never been regulated.

Size (of the Majority) Matters—A Lot

It's fair to say the US Congress has been gridlocked in most of the last decade. Gridlock can be caused by an imbalance of power (one party having the overwhelming majority), recalcitrance (either party not wanting the other to claim victory), or hostility of one party to the agenda of whoever is in the White House. Though neither party has had an overwhelming majority, the balance has been such that very little has been accomplished. And it can happen even if one party is in control of both Congress and the White House. Here's an example: The number one priority of women (and men) in the 2006 midterm election was ending the war in Iraq. According to all the polls, this was the main factor in changing both the House and Senate from Republican to Democratic majorities. (Several races that gave control of the Senate to the Democrats were clearly decided by the women's vote.)

But even though the Democrats now had control, they could not end the war because they did not have enough votes. You might be wondering why not—they had majorities in both houses, didn't they?

In the easiest case, for a bill to become law, it must pass each house of Congress by a simple majority, and be signed by the president. But if the president wants to veto a bill to prevent it from becoming law after the Congress passes it, the path to enactment can be much harder—and this is indeed a situation where size matters.

Why? Two reasons. First, not all members of a party can be counted on to vote together, so a few defections can make the difference between victory and defeat. Second, a simple majority is not necessarily enough anyway, because if the president vetoes a bill (or announces he is planning to do so) a much larger majority (two-thirds of both houses) is needed to override. Most of the time, if party leaders know they can't override a threatened or promised veto, they won't even bring a bill up for a vote. The exception is when they want to embarrass the other party or the president on a measure that is popular with the people.

In the Senate, there is an additional hurdle to bill passage that is not found in the House—the filibuster. While House rules determine the amount of time a bill can be debated before it must be brought to a vote, there is no limit to the time a bill can be debated in the Senate. That means a bill can be filibustered, or debated so long that the other side gives up (the bill is literally "talked to death"). Ending a filibuster requires three-fifths of the full Senate (sixty votes).

The filibuster threat was used by Republicans more during President Obama's term than at any other time in history—much of the time to block votes on legislation and nominees to judgeships and various other posts in the government. It was used repeatedly in the struggle over health care. Democrats needed sixty votes to overcome a threatened filibuster on a motion to begin debate (called *cloture*). In order to hold the party together and produce the winning majority, party leaders had to make some very expensive promises of federal dollars to the states of senators in their own ranks.[36] President Trump has said he wants to get rid of the filibuster altogether, or change the rules so that senators have to actually stand on the floor and talk, rather than just threaten to do so, but Congress has so far ignored his tweets on the subject.

All this means that just a few seats matter a great deal. If your incumbent "brings home the bacon" in road and bridge projects, but votes against your basic rights on abortion, you can't look the other way. If a candidate promises to solve the environmental crisis but stands against women's access to paid family leave, child care, or fair pay, don't ignore it.

Small majorities fail. Women must give pro-woman candidates a *mandate*—by electing them in large enough numbers to insure victory when it counts.

The (Almost) Last Word—The Supreme Court

The job of the Supreme Court is to settle arguments about the law. They may be arguments about whether something like flag burning or the right to abortion is protected under the Constitution, arguments about whether laws passed by Congress are constitutional, or arguments about how laws should be interpreted.

Supreme Court appointments are for life, and so they are extremely important. The decisions handed down by the Court are usually final, or at the very least can last for generations before new cases trigger revisiting a prior decision. Presidents typically appoint people to the Supreme Court who mirror the president's views about what the laws mean, or what they ought to mean.

Though everyone denies that litmus tests are used in appointments, this is simply not true. An anti-choice president is going to appoint anti-choice judges, and a pro-corporate president is going to appoint judges that he believes agree with him, whether or not the nominee is willing to say so publicly.

When it comes to women, past Supreme Courts have ruled that birth control is legal, that women have the right to abortion, that women have the right to equal educational opportunities, and that women have the right to be free from discrimination and sexual harassment at work, to cite just a few very important decisions.

But with new appointments of Justices Roberts and Alito to the Supreme Court under President George W. Bush, the tide turned against women (the Obama appointments did not change the conservative majority). The Trump appointments of Neil Gorsuch and Brett Kavanaugh further solidified conservative control. The greatest threats to *Roe v. Wade* which gave women the right to abortion in 1973 are now on the horizon, with conservative majorities in multiple states passing abortion bans in hopes that one will reach the Supreme Court and overturn *Roe* (see Chapter 10). The Supreme Court has already upheld a federal ban on one abortion procedure with no exception for health of the woman, and has also ruled that certain non-church employers can refuse to cover contraception in their insurance plans if the owners object on religious grounds.[37]

While the Supreme Court almost always has the last word, it can be overruled by Congress in some cases, usually those where the intent of a particular law is at issue. In reality, this happens very rarely—only twice in high-profile cases affecting women in the past fifty years.

Title IX, the law prohibiting discrimination in education if an institution is receiving federal funds, is instructional. When the law was passed in 1972, Congress intended it to apply across the board to all programs in an educational institution getting federal dollars, regardless of where the money was spent. So women in a university couldn't be kept out of the law school, for example, even if all the federal money went to the medical school.

But in 1984, in a case called *Grove City v. Bell*, the Court issued a narrow interpretation of Title IX that opened a loophole. The justices ruled that colleges could discriminate against women in some programs (e.g. sports) if that particular program did not receive federal money, even if the school as a whole did get federal dollars.

After intense advocacy by women's groups, Congress overturned the ruling four years later by passing a new law (the Civil Rights Restoration Act) explicitly stating that Title IX applies to all programs in any school receiving federal support, regardless of which department actually gets the money.

A similar fight was necessary to overturn the *Ledbetter v. Goodyear* decision in 2007, when the Supreme Court abandoned forty years of precedent and severely curtailed women's right to sue for sex discrimination in pay (see Pay Equity chapter for a full discussion). It took women's rights advocates two more years of lobbying Congress, and an election that produced a change in control of the White House, to get a new law passed that reversed the ruling.

But just because advocates succeeded after a several years of fighting in these extremely rare cases, don't believe congressional action is an easy or reliable safeguard against bad Court opinions. As we saw above in the discussion of majorities and overrides, there is no guarantee that this process can succeed once the Supreme Court makes a ruling—most of the time Congress doesn't even try. That's why it is crucial that pro-woman judges be appointed to begin with, and that the Senate has enough votes to confirm them.

Over the next four years, the president could appoint at least three and perhaps more Supreme Court justices, setting the course of law as it affects women for a generation or longer. Justice Ruth Bader Ginsburg, a champion of women's rights, will be eighty-seven in 2020, and Steven Breyer, who also votes to support women, will be eighty-one.

If new justices do not believe in the basic rights of women, the right to abortion will almost certainly be overturned, and other gains of the twentieth century, such as protection against discrimination in employment, education, pregnancy, and credit could be rolled back or eliminated, one by one.

It goes without saying that women must be the Deciders as to who will be in the White House making these appointments, and who will be in the Senate confirming them.

Chapter 4

What *Do* Women Want? What *Are* We Thinking?

Women and men often think alike, but when it comes to politics and priorities, the book title *Men are from Mars, Women are from Venus* is often accurate. That's because women's life experiences are different, and that causes them to see things in a different way than men. Gun control is a good example. When asked about how available guns should be, men might think of hunting, cleaning up Dodge City, or defending their households. Women think of getting raped at gunpoint or their children getting shot at school—a basic difference in point of view.

Even when women and men are on the same page, women may feel more strongly about an issue. For example, both sexes might rate something like Medicare solvency high on the list of priorities, but women are more passionate about it. And women and men often rank issues differently when it comes to what is most important.

We've already seen how gender differences play out in the voting booth. Looking at what women and men tell pollsters is one way to get behind the voting numbers and to see what drives the gender gap. It's also a way to get a good idea of the values and opinions that shape priorities, and how women and men might view the issues that should be addressed by elected officials and candidates.

How Do We Rate National Priorities?

How people rate national priorities depends on a number of factors, including what either the media or candidates are hammering on at the time of a given poll, how the questions are asked, what is included and in what order on lists of priorities that they are asked to rate. It is significant that asking people an open-ended question such as, "What do you think is the most important issue facing the country?" produces quite different answers than when people are presented with a "laundry list" and asked to rate each one in order of importance (see Chapter 6). Nevertheless, we can tell from polls what is on the radar at any given moment, and some issues rate high in both types of polls.

Not surprisingly, opinions about the importance economic issues in elections vary with state of the economy. Women's concerns about the economy since the turn of the century pre-date the Great Recession, going back at least as far as the 2006 election cycle, when there was an 11-point gender gap with men over the importance of the economy.[38] Economic concerns of both women and men went way up during the recession, with no appreciable gender gaps.[39]

By election 2016, with the recession in the rearview mirror, once again women's priorities diverged from those of men. When given a list, both genders rated the economy, health care, and jobs as the top issues (these were also the first three presented on the list). But women differed substantially from men on the importance of abortion, gender equality, family and medical leave, and gay rights. Even though President Trump had harangued on the issue incessantly, less than half of both women and men rated immigration as "very important"[40] and women rated gay marriage much higher in importance than men did.[41]

Women made the difference in the 2018 midterms[42] when the House flipped from Republican to Democratic, accounting for 53 percent of voters in preliminary exit poll results, voting for Democratic candidates by 60 to 39 percent. And there was a tremendous gender gap in views of president Trump's work in office with men dividing

50 to 49 percent on Trump approve–disapprove, reversing to 39 to 60 percent approve-disapprove among women. The Supreme Court also played into the election—57 percent of men approved of Brett Kavanaugh's confirmation, but only 43 percent of women agreed.

By 2019 the priorities had shifted somewhat. The economy and health care were still leading concerns, with immigration and poor leadership in the government gaining ground in the overall electorate (no gender breakdown available). Opinions during the 2020 election year will undoubtedly shift on issue priorities and voter preferences, but some things won't change. Women will still differ from men on key issues affecting their lives. Women will also be the majority of registered voters, and the majority of those that actually show up at the polls. Bottom line? Women can control *any* election.

Are Women (and Men) Feminists? Are You?

The answer to this question seems to depend on whether women are asked about the *word* feminist, or the *dictionary definition* of a feminist. When asked if they are feminists with no explanation—Do you consider yourself a feminist?—only about 38 percent say yes (22 percent of men).[43] But when asked the question using the definition of feminism—that it is a belief in political, economic, and social equality across genders—the response differs. After hearing this definition, 60 percent of women identify as feminists, and so do 44 percent of men. The numbers go even higher—above 80 percent for both women and men—when simply asked if they believe in equality across genders.[44]

Sharp party divisions on the need for more work to achieve equality for women emerged in the wake of the 2016 elections. Democrats are largely dissatisfied with the nation's progress on this issue—69 percent say the country hasn't gone far enough when it comes to giving women equal rights with men. Among Republicans, more than half (54 percent) say things are about right, while only 26 percent say the country has more work to do.[45]

Women believe strongly that the women's movement has made their lives better, with 65 percent agreeing. Men are about evenly divided on the question—maybe because some of them now have to wash more dishes. When asked *how* the women's movement has made their lives better, women cite better jobs, more choices, better pay, and more legal equality.

Perhaps more women would think there is still a need for a strong women's movement if they realized that women do not have equal rights in the Constitution (see Chapter 23). Nearly three out of four Americans (69 percent of women and over 75 percent of men) assume that the Constitution *already* includes that guarantee—and they're all wrong.[46]

At substantially higher rates than men on every measure, women strongly support policies aimed at providing women with equal opportunities, such as giving women the legal protections needed to get equal pay (77 percent), and making sure there are effective safeguards against discrimination in the workplace, including protections from sexual harassment (72 percent). These large majorities of women also say such policies are extremely or very important for Congress and the current presidential administration to take up (more than half the men are also strongly supportive, but by a smaller majority).

Women are also stronger than men in recognizing that there is still work to be done. In the wake of the #MeToo movement, a record-low 46 percent of women in the US are now satisfied with the treatment of women in society, even on the heels of some recent advances for women, namely a historic wave of women elected to Congress in 2018.[47] Women running at all levels in 2020 and beyond could use this wave of dissatisfaction to their advantage.

Women (and Men) Are Pro-Choice

Public divisions over access to abortion are long-standing, and have changed only slightly over the past four decades. There are gender gaps between women and men on abortion, and there are also divisions among women. Historically both pro-choice and anti-choice women have expressed significantly stronger feelings about the issue than men, and much more often said it could be a factor in their vote. Not so for men, many of whom have nevertheless said they would vote for a candidate who disagrees with them on choice, if they shared views with the candidate on most other issues.

Both women and men in the US are pro-choice, with only small gender differences. According to Gallup polling in 2019, extremely large majorities (74 percent or above) of both sexes say abortion should be legal in some or all circumstances. More women than men think abortion should be illegal (24 to 18 percent). And ominously, women's support for making abortion *illegal* in all circumstances went from 20 to 24 percent in the space of one year, 2018 to 2019.[48]

In a seeming contradiction, neither women nor men want *Roe v. Wade* overturned. A total of 77 percent of persons polled say the Supreme Court should uphold *Roe*, but within that there's a lot of nuance—26 percent say they would like to see it remain in place, but with more restrictions added; 21 percent want to see *Roe* expanded to establish the right to abortion under any circumstance; 16 percent want to keep it the way it is; and 14 percent want to see some of the restrictions allowed under *Roe* reduced. Just 13 percent overall say it should be overturned.[49]

Even after a conservative group released a doctored video in 2015 accusing Planned Parenthood of selling tissue from aborted fetuses, causing a national debate, 59 percent of those polled said they still had a favorable opinion of Planned Parenthood.[50] By 2019 when Planned Parenthood funding was under attack by the Trump administration, favorability had jumped to 70 percent among college women aged eighteen to twenty-four, the age group with the highest rates of unintended pregnancy and abortion.[51]

Women are More Supportive of LGBTQ Rights

After many years of advocacy, support for same-sex marriage by both women and men reached a majority in the US in 2011.[52] Women have been more supportive than men since 2001, and by 2015 after the Supreme Court declared gay marriage legal in all fifty states, women supported the right by 58 percent and men by 52 percent.[53] Today, a majority of Americans (61 percent) support same-sex marriage, while 31 percent oppose it. Support remains higher among women, with 66 percent supporting as compared to 57 percent of men.[54]

Extensive polling on LGBTQ issues was done in 2019 by Gallup in the run-up to the fiftieth anniversary of the Stonewall rebellion which sparked the modern gay rights movement. Results differed by both gender and political party. (Numbers indicate percentages approving of policy.)

	Men	Women	Rep.	Dem.	Ind.
Use of restrooms by gender identity	35	53	18	66	46
Transgender in military	64	79	43	88	78
Gay Marriage	66	61	44	79	68

Support for gay adoption has grown steadily over the past two decades. By 2014 (latest figures available) it had risen to 63 percent overall.[55]

Women and Men Differ on Gun Control

As the statistics on women and gun violence in Chapter 19 show us, gun control is very much a women's issue. Firearm murders by husbands, boyfriends, and other male partners surpasses the number of victims of mass shootings. And even though it's also a political party issue, women in both parties differ substantially from men. The table below from polls ahead of the 2018 mid-term elections, says it all.[56]

Gender and Party Differences in Support for Specific Restrictive Gun Control Measures						
Restrictive measure	Democratic Women	Democratic Men	Independent Women	Independent Men	Republican Women	Republican Men
Ban high capacity ammunition magazines	75	64	58	45	43	33
Require background checks	87	77	83	68	81	73
Ban assault style weapons	79	63	59	39	40	33
Prevent firearm sales to dangerous persons	85	77	80	63	80	69
Require three day waiting period	77	75	58	49	53	40
Prevent firearm sales to people convicted of violent misdemeanors	82	67	68	52	77	56

Source: Morning Consult + Politico National Tracking Poll #180339, n=1,997 registered voters, MOE +/- 2points, 29 March – 1 April 2018. Values reflect the percentages of men and women partisans who "strongly support" each restrictive measure.

Stopping gun violence is a major focus of women's groups such as Moms Demand Action, founded in the wake of the Sandy Hook elementary school massacre in 2012. And there's no doubt that women's votes made a difference in the 2018 elections when it comes to gun control, helping to overturn the House majority from Republicans to Democrats. Gun policy had become a top issue for voters, with polls showing those who favored stricter gun laws (majority women) were more likely than those who oppose them to say the issue of gun regulation was a very important voting issue.[57] Fully six in ten voters (61 percent) said candidates should give more attention to the gun violence prevention issue. This sentiment is especially strong among suburban women (72 percent), women over fifty (70 percent), women of color (75 percent), and white college-educated women (65 percent).[58]

Women and Men Are Mostly Together on Immigration

In the midst of a national humanitarian crisis at the US-Mexican border in 2019, the Gallup Organization conducted an extensive poll[59] on attitudes about immigration. At the time detainees were held in overcrowded and unsanitary conditions, sometimes without food or clean water, and some died in custody. Hundreds of children were separated from their parents for long periods ranging from months to years.

Gallup polled adults on many aspects of immigration, ranging from the effects on the US economy and culture to crime and whether immigration should be increased or decreased.

By huge margin (76 to 19 percent) respondents overall said immigration is a good thing for the country.

Women and men were usually very close together on various aspects of the immigration issue, with a few differences:

* Women were less likely than men (21 to 25 percent) to rate it the most important problem facing the US, and more likely (52 to 47 percent) to say immigration doesn't have much effect on crime.
* Women were also more favorable than men (59 to 55 percent) as to the positive effect immigrants have on food, music, and the arts, though more women than men (35 to 27 percent) said immigration makes the economy worse.

This chapter has shown us that not all women agree, and opinions can vary by political party. But it has also shown us that women often have very different priorities than men, and how important it is for women to make their priorities known at the ballot box.

Chapter 5

Where We Stand: We've Come a Long Way . . . and Yet?

There is no question that women in the United States, whether rich, poor, or in between, enjoy a relatively high standard of living compared to many women worldwide. But among developed nations, US women are far from being number one politically and socially. If we are to change things at the ballot box, we first have to know where we really stand in comparison to women in industrialized countries with economies and governments similar to our own.

The Global Gender Gap Index[60] ranks 149 countries on a combination of economic, political, education, and health-based gender gaps. We're fifty-first, just behind Mexico and just ahead of Peru. And we're *way* behind the top four—Iceland, Norway, Sweden, and Finland. Our neighbor to the north—Canada—ranks sixteenth. What's more, were not getting better. We've been dropping like the proverbial rock for the past few years—from seventeenth in 2011 to forty-ninth in 2017.

On the plus side, the US continues to rank in the top twenty on the Economic Opportunity and Participation subindex. But then we drop down to seventy-first in Health and Survival, and we sink to number ninety-eight in Political Leadership. Currently, our country has closed exactly 72 percent of its overall gender gap, a decrease of only 2 percent since 2015.

Below are a few fast facts. You will find many more you read the chapters that follow on specific issues.

Constitutional Rights:

* Women do not have equal rights with men under the United States Constitution, and only twenty-six US state constitutions have equal rights.
* Of the 197 constitutions in countries around the world, 165 have explicit guarantees for gender equality. Only thirty-two do not, and one is the United States.[61]

Political Participation:

* The US has never had a female president, vice president, chief justice, or Senate majority leader. The first female Speaker of the House (Nancy Pelosi) was elected in 2006, and the second in 2019 (again Pelosi). Other countries have had forty-six female prime ministers or presidents.[62]
* Even after a record number of women were elected to the House in the 2018 midterm elections, the US still ranked seventy-fifth in the world in the number of women in Congress (down from sixty-ninth in 2011), with 23.5 percent of the total seats.[63]
* Unlike the US, half of the countries of the world today use some type of electoral quota for their legislative bodies and the number is increasing.[64]

Earnings, Pay Gap:

* The US gender pay gap of 20 percent has been virtually the

same for over a decade. Women in Australia, Belgium, Italy, and Sweden reached that level as early as 2003.[65]

★ The poverty rate among women has been higher than that for men since 1968, and the gap is only slightly lower now than it was fifty years ago.[66, 67]

Workplace Protection:

★ US employers are prohibited by Title VII of the 1964 Civil Rights Act from discriminating on the basis of sex—but the burden of proof falls on the worker.

★ American women (and men) have no legal right to sick leave. This puts us in stark contrast to 145 other nations.[68]

★ While US law guarantees twelve weeks of *unpaid* family leave for birth, adoption, or family illness, there is no legal right for maternity leave, paternity leave, or paid family leave. Of 193 UN countries, only New Guinea, Suriname, a few South Pacific island nations, and the United States have no paid parental leave.[69]

Business:

★ Almost half (47 percent) of all US workers in 2020 are projected to be women, and the female workforce is growing faster than the male workforce.[70]

★ Nearly two-thirds (64.2 percent) of mothers are primary, sole, or co-breadwinners for their families. Black and Hispanic mothers make up a disproportionate share.[71]

★ Women-owned businesses get slightly less than 5 percent of federal contract dollars. Lockheed Martin and Boeing alone scoop up three times the amount going to all female owned businesses combined.[72]

Higher Education/Professions:

* Women now outnumber men in college enrollments, but they remain segregated by college major. Nine of the ten highest-paying majors are male-dominated, while six of the ten lowest-paying majors are female-dominated.[73]
* Women hold almost two-thirds of the country's $1.4-trillion student debt, and the student loan gender gap has nearly doubled since 2014.[74]
* Most business schools pay female faculty less than male counterparts, and the pay gap grows as academic rank increases.[75]
* The most common job for women majoring in engineering, computer science, economics, chemistry, and business remains K through 12 teacher.[76]

Child Care:

* Child care tends to be the first- or second-largest household expenditure. The average annual cost for an infant in center-based care is higher than a year's tuition and fees at a four-year public college in every region of the US.[77]
* Nearly one-third of US children under age eighteen live in a single-parent family, most with a solo mother.[78] Obviously access to child care is critical for these families.

Health Care:

* In the first five years after the Affordable Care Act passed, 7.7 million women gained coverage. An estimated fifty-five million women benefitted from preventive services coverage with no out-of-pocket costs.[79]
* The US spends more on maternal health than any other type of hospital care. Even so, US women have a higher risk of

dying of pregnancy-related complications than those in forty-nine other countries, and Black women are nearly four times more likely to do so than white women.[80]

Long-Term Care:

★ More than 80 percent of older adults requiring long-term care are able to live in the community, primarily because of informal assistance by women, approximately 66 percent of family caregivers.[81]

★ Women spend 50 percent more time giving care than men do, and are 2.5 times more likely to end up in poverty and five times more likely to depend on Social Security.[82]

Reproductive Rights:

★ The majority of Americans believe abortion should be legal in all or most cases, and the numbers have not changed since 2014.

★ The partisan divide on abortion has increased since 2014, with 70 percent of Democrats supporting legality, but only 34 percent of Republicans (55 percent of independents).[83]

Social Security Benefits:

★ In the US, Social Security benefits are based only on earnings of the worker (or if married, earnings of the spouse if the spouse's income is higher). There is no credit for time out of the workforce for caregiving.

★ In the UK, the number of work years needed for a full pension is reduced if the insured is caring for a child or an elderly or disabled relative.[84] In France, up to eight quarters of coverage may be credited to women for each child; and four of these quarters may be awarded to the father.[85]

Violence:

* The federal Office of Violence Against Women has published no new information since the Trump Administration took office. Nor has the Center for Disease Control conducted a new National Intimate Partner and Sexual Violence Survey. Figures below are from the 2015[86] survey (rereleased in 2018 but not updated), the latest information available from the government.
* Nearly 52.2 million women (43.6 percent) had experienced some form of contact sexual violence.
* Approximately one in six women experienced sexual coercion (e.g., being worn down by someone who repeatedly asked for sex, sexual pressure due to someone using their influence or authority) at some point in their lifetime.
* Ninety-two percent of all women killed with guns in high-income countries in 2015 were from the US.

Chapter 6

Health Care—On Life Support?

This may be the most important chapter in this book. Health care is the number one issue on the minds of most voters, and it's the number one issue candidates talk about—sometimes with a great deal of exaggeration and outright misinformation. So let's dive in and try to make some sense out of the rhetoric and explore what's at stake.

There is no single "health care system" that provides insurance coverage for illness in the US. There are several (one of which is none), depending on age, income, and job status. There are deep disagreements—about who should provide it, who should benefit, how much it should cost, and whether it is a right or a privilege. In a nutshell, here's what we have now:

* By far the most common health care in the United States is privately purchased by employers and individuals from for-profit insurance companies. (These plans were regulated by the Affordable Care Act (ACA), when implemented in the Obama administration, but less regulated under the Trump administration.)
* Traditional Medicare covers seniors (who pay monthly premiums going to the government's Medicare Trust Fund), with

the option of also purchasing a supplemental policy sold by private companies to cover expenses not paid by Medicare.

* Medicare Advantage (MA) plans must offer the same benefits as traditional Medicare, but are sold and administered by private insurance companies. The government pays a fixed amount per patient to the insurance company, and individual recipients pay premiums to the insurance company. Some offer more benefits than traditional Medicare, but most also limit choice of doctors and hospitals, and require permission to see a specialist or use out-of-network services.

* Medicaid is a federal insurance program administered by the states, covering very low income people. Medicaid rules on who is covered and what services are available can vary considerably from state to state. States contract with private providers to provide services.

* The Children's Health Insurance Program (CHIP) is a federal program administered by the states for uninsured kids whose families cannot afford insurance, but earn too much to qualify for Medicaid. CHIP contracts with private providers, and benefits can vary by state.

* Veteran's Administration Health Care is the federally run system for current and former members of the Armed Forces. Facilities belong to the federal government, and health care providers are employees of the federal government.

For more detail on these programs, see "Nuts and Bolts on Health Care" in Appendix I.

Private Insurance—The Affordable Care Act

When the ACA (dubbed Obamacare) finally passed in 2010 after much national debate, it brought sweeping changes to the private insurance market, which covers the vast majority of Americans. But contrary to red-hot rhetoric, it did *not* change the basic for-profit structure or in any way convert the system to a "government-run" one.

Below are the major provisions of the ACA as passed:

* Prohibited insurers from denying coverage to individuals due to pre-existing conditions.
* Required insurers to offer the same premium to all applicants of the same age and location without regard most pre-existing conditions (excluding tobacco use).
* Outlawed "gender rating" in insurance, the common practice of charging women more than men for the same coverage† (claiming women use more health care).
* Required small group and individual plans to cover ten essential health benefits including emergency, hospitalization, maternal and newborn, and mental health care.
* Required preventive care and screenings for women including approved contraceptive methods, sterilization procedures, and patient education and counseling for all women with reproductive capacity (religious organizations exempted).
* Banned annual and lifetime coverage caps on essential benefits.
* Prohibited insurers from dropping policyholders when they get sick.
* Banned co-payments, co-insurance, or deductibles for contraception and preventive care including mammograms, vaccinations, and medical screenings.
* Mandated that insurers must spend at least 80 to 85 percent of premium dollars on health costs; rebates must be issued to policyholders if this is violated.
* Implemented an "individual mandate" requirement that

---

† This was not because of maternity benefits. Most didn't offer maternity coverage at all. Senator Barbara Mikulski (D-MD) quipped during the health care debate that insurance companies had long ago declared being female a pre-existing condition.

people not covered by an employer sponsored health plan, Medicaid, Medicare or other public insurance programs buy insurance or pay a penalty.

★ Established health insurance exchanges (regulated marketplaces where all insurance companies must follow the above rules) in all fifty states, where individuals and small business can purchase private insurance plans.

★ Allowed states to expand Medicaid eligibility, with the federal government picking up 100 percent of the cost, gradually declining to 90 percent by 2020.

★ Permitted dependents to remain on their parents' insurance plan until their twenty-sixth birthday.

★ Maintained long-standing Hyde Amendment restrictions governing abortion policy, which prohibits federal funds from being used for abortions (except in cases of rape or incest, or when the life of the woman is endangered), and extended those restrictions to the health insurance exchanges.

★ Maintained federal "conscience" protections for health care providers who object to performing abortion or sterilization procedures that conflict with their beliefs. Prohibited discrimination against health care facilities and providers who are unwilling to provide, pay for, provide coverage of, or refer women for abortions.

★ Allowed insurers in state exchanges to cover abortion, but also allowed states to prohibit abortion coverage in qualified health plans offered through an exchange. As of July 2019, twenty-six states had done so. If insurance coverage for abortion is included in a plan in the exchange, a separate premium is required for this coverage paid for by the policyholder.

If the ACA is repealed, all of the above rules and policies except the Hyde Amendment will become moot or disappear.

President Trump campaigned on repealing the Affordable Care Act throughout 2016. By 2018 the Republican-controlled House had voted more than sixty times to repeal it. A repeal effort in the Senate in 2017 failed with the decisive vote cast by Republican Senator John McCain, earning President Trump's extreme animosity, which persists long after McCain's death in 2018.

President Trump has said Republicans are planning an ACA replacement that will be "far better than Obamacare" to be revealed *after* the 2020 election. In the absence of outright repeal, changes by Congress and the president have already weakened the ACA.

* Repealed the individual mandate,† meaning if people such as the young and healthier opt out in sizable numbers, the risk pool will be concentrated with heavier users of health insurance. Use of emergency rooms by sicker non-insured will increase, resulting in the cost of health care going up for everyone.
* Expanded loosely regulated health plans, also called nonqualified short-term plans (some just call them junk insurance) that are not subject to the ACA's requirements to provide free contraception, insure people with pre-existing conditions or include coverage for services such as prescription drugs, maternity care, mental health care, and substance abuse treatment.
* Allowed states to deny Medicaid coverage in a variety of ways, including implementing work requirements and requiring people in poverty to pay premiums. Pending proposals would deny coverage to legal immigrants and allow states to expand

---

† In 2018, a federal judge ruled that the elimination of the individual mandate penalty rendered the entire health care law unconstitutional. An appeal of that controversial ruling, which most legal experts expect to be overturned, was heard by the 5th US Circuit Court of Appeals in July, 2019. The losing side is expected to ask the Supreme Court to review the case, which could postpone a decision by up to two years.

coverage only to those below a new downward-adjusted poverty line.

★ In 2017, the Trump administration issued a new rule allowing
insurers and employers (including publicly traded companies)
to refuse to provide birth control if doing so went against their
"religious beliefs" or "moral convictions." The rule was struck
down in several courts, but the Trump administration has appealed. Like other ACA challenges, this one could take many
months or years to be resolved.

★ In 2019 proposed new rules denying ACA health care protections to LGBTQ individuals, and reaffirms the rights of
health care workers to deny care based on a religious or moral
objection, expanding rules issued earlier by Trump's health
department.[87]

In health care actions not related to efforts to repeal the ACA, the
Trump administration issued a rule change in May of 2018 that would
have forced pharmaceutical companies to include the wholesale prices
of their drugs in television advertising. The change was supported by
consumer groups and patient advocates, but was blocked before it
could take effect in 2019 by a federal judge as outside the regula-
tory power of the Department of Human Services.[88] The president
also signed a bipartisan bill to increase access to addiction treatment,
open more opioid recovery centers, and reduce opiate prescriptions,
though critics say it lacks enough money to curtail the epidemic.[89]
In any case, barring an election-year reprieve, the money runs out in
2020.

Why Women Needed (and Still Need) Health Care Reform

Health care was and still is a monumental concern for women. Before
the ACA became law, 82 percent ranked it very important, second

only to the economy and jobs. In contrast, only 72 percent of men said health care was very important—a 10-point gender gap. Sixty-four percent of men and women alike told pollsters that health insurance companies refusing to pay for medical treatments, even when doctors said they were necessary, was a serious problem.[90]

The burden of not being able to afford care has had a greater impact on women than men. In one study, over 50 percent of women delayed seeking medical care because they couldn't afford it (compared to 39 percent of men); and a third faced difficult decisions to pay for needed care, such as giving up basic necessities.[91]

Prior to passage of the ACA, the average cost of health insurance for an American family exceeded the entire yearly income of a minimum wage worker—and the majority of minimum wage workers are adult women. That's probably a big reason why forty-seven million people in the US had no health insurance, including almost one in five women. The numbers were terrible when broken down by race: 22 percent of African American women, 36 percent of Native American women, and a whopping 38 percent of Hispanic women were not covered.[92]

Before ACA, over 15 percent of women had no first trimester prenatal care,[93] and the vast majority of individual policies did not offer maternity benefits at any price.[94] Moreover, states could and did allow insurance companies to charge women more than they charged men for the same coverage (a practice known as "gender-rating") or to outright refuse coverage. According to a study by the National Women's Law Center a year before the ACA passed, 95 percent of the companies practiced gender rating on individual plans, and 60 percent of those charged a forty-year-old woman who didn't smoke up to 63 percent more than a man who did smoke for the same coverage.

Drugs were also a major health concern, as women between the ages of fifteen and forty-four spent 68 percent more on out-of-pocket health costs than did men, much of it on contraception. For young women, birth control was the single largest outlay, since insurance companies often refused to cover birth control pills (even though many covered Viagra-type drugs).

Far too many children in our country were going without health insurance as well. According to the government's own figures, more than one in ten US children were uninsured in the year before ACA passed,[95] and one in twenty had no usual source of health care. About 1.8 million kids every year were unable to see a doctor because the family could not afford it, and 12 percent of those without coverage had not seen a doctor in over two years (some had *never* seen a doctor). Not surprisingly, children in single mother families were the most likely to be unable to get health care when they needed it.[96]

While all of these problems did not instantly go away with passage of the ACA, the most discriminatory ones for women did. Gender rating was outlawed, and coverage for birth control (since weakened by President Trump) was mandated. Maternity and pre-natal care was also mandated, and subsidies for low-income households became available. By the fourth quarter of 2015, the percentage of uninsured Americans had already dropped to 11.4 percent, down from 18 percent when the ACA was implemented in 2013.[97]

The (Still Ongoing) Health Care Debate

For the years 2020 to 2027, national health spending growth is projected to average 5.7 percent, from 4.8 percent in 2019, and reach nearly $6.0 *trillion* by 2027.[98] Health care expenditures in the US are over 17 percent of the Gross Domestic Product (GDP) or about a sixth of the economy, well above the figure for any other industrialized country.[99] Every year over $3.65 trillion is spent in the US on health care—about $11,212 for every woman, man, and child in the country.[100] Even so, when we compare health outcomes—measurements such as infant mortality or life expectancy—the US trails other nations. Virtually every country in Europe has universal health care, as do Australia, Canada, and Japan.

Though the (somewhat weakened by President Trump) ACA is still the law, a ruling declaring it unconstitutional is still under review. The debate continues, with the president and many politicians vowing to eliminate or replace it as soon as they are elected.

Approaches to health care reform diverge widely. There are basic disagreements and differences in philosophy between the political parties, and they have not dissipated with the passage of time or changes in party control of the government.

In general, Democrats emphasize "universal coverage"—meaning everyone should have health insurance. Means of achieving the goal vary. Methods of paying the bill also vary, but virtually all Democratic schemes involved a partnership between employers, workers, and the government, with more help for people too poor to afford coverage.

Republicans generally argue that the medical system should be market-based, rely on individual responsibility, and not involve the government at all. Many refer to *any* government involvement as socialized medicine. (It is unclear whether they believe public schools are socialized education, and if so, whether it's bad for the US to have public education.) The schemes put forth that rely on the market involved further deregulation of the insurance industry, and leaving health care solutions up to the states instead of relying on a "one-size-fits-all, government-run system."

Decoding the Rhetoric

If you are confused by the terminology, mischaracterizations, accusations, and doomsday scenarios accompanying the health care debate, you're not alone. But if voters are to be actively engaged in the ongoing dialogue with elected officials, candidates, and parties about health care, they need to know what the terms being bandied about actually mean, and not rely on rhetoric that is often false or inaccurate. A few definitions:

Universal coverage means just that—everyone would have health insurance. Some through employers, some through individually purchased private plans, the elderly through Medicare, the very poor through Medicaid, and some low-income people through privately purchased plans that might be partially subsidized by the government through ACA or some other system if the ACA is replaced.

Universal coverage does *not* mean the government provides health care as a "welfare" or entitlement benefit to everyone regardless of income or employment status. Universal coverage was a goal of the ACA while maintaining private insurance along with instituting the individual mandate, with the for-profit insurance industry remaining in place and playing a primary role in achieving universal coverage. Choice of doctors and hospitals under universal coverage is the same as it was before the ACA—controlled by the type of plan the individual is covered under, and in no small part dictated by insurance companies.

Single-payer refers to a system where the government would be the insurer issuing the payments. Everyone's health care would be paid for out of one publicly administered trust fund, funded by taxes on both individuals and business, which would replace our current multi-payer (i.e. insurance companies) system.

Single-payer is what we have in place for seniors with traditional Medicare. Patients pay premiums to Medicare, and are free to use any doctor or hospital they choose. Medicare in turn pays the doctors and hospitals. (For extra services not covered by Medicare, private companies sell Medicare Supplemental policies, which the majority of recipients buy). Under universal single-payer, premiums to insurance companies would be replaced by premiums to a single government trust fund as in Medicare now, which is by definition not-for-profit. Countries with single-payer for everyone include Canada, Australia, and Japan.

While *single-payer would eliminate the role of for-profit insurance companies and the premiums paid to them*, the government would not be the primary *provider* of health care. It would just be the primary *payer*. There would still be freedom to choose doctors and other health care professionals, facilities, and services. Doctors would remain in private practice and be paid their fees from the government trust fund paid into by individuals and business. The government would not own or manage medical practices or medical facilities including clinics and hospitals, which would continue to be paid for their services. Again, the same system currently in place through Medicare.

Socialized medicine is distinct and different from a single-payer system. In a socialized health care system, the government *owns* health facilities, and health personnel work for the government and draw their paychecks directly from the government. This is the model used in the US Veterans Administration and the armed services, where the government owns the medical facilities and medical professionals are government employees. Unlike single-payer Medicare, VA health care actually *is* a government-run system. International examples of socialized medicine can be found in Great Britain and Spain.[101] Red-hot rhetoric notwithstanding, *neither political party presently advocates socialized medicine in the United States, nor did they do so during the debate over the Affordable Care Act.*

The Big Arguments Continue in 2020 and Beyond: What's Next? Who's Got a Plan?

Whether the ACA as we know it goes away through Supreme Court decisions or congressional repeal in 2020 and beyond, we know the debate won't go away as to the best way for health care to be provided.

So what have the parties proposed? In the Republican case, it's fair to say "nothing." President Trump has promised to reveal a plan *after* the 2020 election. In the meantime, below are a few of the schemes discussed by Republican legislators and right-leaning think tanks that are generally aligned with (and help shape) the party's positions. Most include giving states more control and sending them a fixed amount of money (block granting), relaxing federal mandates, and supporting the private insurance industry.[102]

* Allow states to alter several key ACA protections for those with pre-existing conditions. While it would still require insurers to provide coverage to everyone, states could adjust other rules, including weakening or eliminating the mandate that insurers cover pre-existing conditions. This has been approved by one court and is now in effect, though it could be overturned on appeal in the future.
* Allow states to change the pricing rules so that younger, healthier people could see their premiums go down, but those who need care and older Americans in their fifties and sixties could find themselves unable to afford policies.
* Allow states to revamp many of the ACA's financial protections, including those limiting how much people must pay for premiums and out-of-pocket costs each year, and how much of the tab insurers must pick up.
* Block grant federal funding for Medicaid expansion. States would receive a lump sum of money and would have a lot of leeway over how to spend it (or how not to) for those too poor to afford private insurance.
* Means-test Medicare, making it available only to the poorest elderly.
* Turn Medicare into a voucher system, whereby seniors would be given a coupon to shop for medical services on their own instead of receiving guaranteed benefits, as is currently the case. Some Republican lawmakers have openly gloated that the scheme would lead to the demise of Medicare altogether.[103]

All of these schemes are bad for women. Women are the majority of low-income workers, and women and children are the largest groups dependent on Medicaid. If Medicare is turned into a system for only the poorest elderly citizens (majority women), it will be quickly labeled "welfare" instead of what it is—a program paid for by payroll taxes. Experience shows it is much easier to cut welfare programs than to cut items such as corporate subsidies and defense contracts. As for the other "solution," if Medicare is turned into a voucher system, there is nothing to prevent health care providers from requiring huge supplemental payments in addition to the voucher amount.

If Medicare is eliminated or even significantly curtailed, families will have to take up the slack and pay for their parents' and grandparents' health care out of pocket. The program is very important for women, and female voters must ask the right questions before giving their support to any legislator or candidate.

When it comes to the Democrats, it's fair to say they do have a plan—in fact they have a variety of them—to replace or improve the ACA. Though all of these have been proposed by candidates and some members of Congress, there is nowhere near a consensus on which would be best or indeed most doable.

* **Medicare for All:** This means expanding the existing Medicare program to cover all citizens, not just those sixty-five and older. It would be financed as now, by payroll taxes, which would undoubtedly go up. But control by—and premiums paid to—for-profit insurance companies would go away. Medicare for All would by definition be a single-payer system with universal coverage for those not covered by other programs such as Medicaid, VA care, or CHIP. Proponents of single-payer systems, including many physicians and groups, such as Physicians for a National Health Program, cite huge savings from taking insurance companies out of the equation, since they spend billions on non-health care expenses such as agent commissions, advertising, legions of employees to review claims (often searching for reasons deny coverage), and lobbying in Washington.

- ★ **Public Option:** Create a federal health care plan, something like Medicare, but for persons under age sixty-five, which would be available for purchase as an optional alternative to private insurance. To avoid creating unfair competition with for-profit insurance, the plan would pay health care providers at negotiated rates, not at substantially lower Medicare rates. In some versions, the public plan would be available only to individuals who buy coverage on their own and to small businesses with one hundred or fewer employees.

- ★ **Medicare Buy-In:** Medicare buy-in (some bills have already been introduced) would let Americans age fifty to sixty-four buy Medicare plans through the Affordable Care Act exchanges. Enrollees would cover the premiums, so it would not require federal government funding. However, lower- and moderate-income participants could qualify for ACA subsidies to help defray their costs (if the ACA is still in effect).

The buy-in bills would retain the private insurance system—a source of controversy within the movement to expand coverage. As with Medicare, consumers would have to buy separate Part D plans to cover prescription medications or enroll in Medicare Advantage plans sold by private insurers that provide drug benefits. Enrollees would also presumably have to purchase supplemental Medigap policies to shield them against high out-of-pocket costs since, unlike the ACA plans, Medicare doesn't have an annual or lifetime cap.

Buy-in plans appear to assume continuation of the ACA since plans would be available to those age fifty-plus through the ACA exchanges. Supporters argue expanding Medicare access will strengthen the exchanges since older Americans, who are often sicker and costlier, will be shifted to Medicare. This should reduce premiums for those remaining in Affordable Care Act plans. Opponents say it would weaken for-profit insurance companies and create unfair competition.

It's difficult to say whether either public option or Medicare buy-in would help women, particularly if ACA is maintained with its various benefits for women. One would assume that if the Public Option is meant to be an alternative to ACA plans provided by private insurance, benefits for women would need to be maintained. It is an open question as to whether benefits such as contraception and maternity care would become an issue under Medicare for All and Medicare buy-in plans.

There is no doubt that we will continue to hear red-hot, red-meat rhetoric surrounding health care all the way until Election Day and beyond.

Here are some questions for candidates:

The Affordable Care Act

- Did you, or would you have, supported the Affordable Care Act?
- Are you in favor of repealing the ACA, and if so, what would you replace it with? Please be specific.
- If the ACA is repealed, we will lose protection from being dropped or excluded for pre-existing conditions, and once more face arbitrary caps and cessation of coverage by insurance companies. What would you do about that?
- If the ACA is repealed, insurance companies will be allowed to go back to the practice of charging women more than men for the same individual policies. Do you think this is okay?
- Some people say the Affordable Care Act is socialized medicine, though the government does not own or control health care facilities, treatment, or medical professionals as would be the case in a socialized system. Do you think the ACA is socialized medicine, and if so why?
- Our medical costs are far higher than those in other industrialized countries, and studies show our health outcomes are

not as good. How, specifically, would you improve health care outcomes and affordability in the US?

- Do you think birth control and mammograms should be covered without co-pays or deductibles? What about Viagra-type drugs?
- Knowing that abortion coverage is not part of health care reform, do you think businesses should be able to opt out of covering any other medical conditions or drugs because of conscience clauses?

Traditional Medicare / Medicare Advantage

- Do you support turning Medicare into a means-tested program? If so, do you still think workers should pay for it out of their monthly checks? How would such a Medicare program be funded?
- Do you support turning Medicare into a voucher program? If so, how would you keep the vouchers from becoming less valuable or worthless as health care providers raised prices?
- Do you think cutting the extra subsidies to Medicare Advantage programs was the right thing to do, since those subsidies cost the taxpayers much more than traditional Medicare?
- Do you think Part D drug programs should be better regulated? How?
- Do you think the government should be able to negotiate drug prices?

Veterans Health Care

- Do you think the Veterans Administration Health care is adequately funded, given that some veterans can't get care because of enrollment restrictions and long waits?

- Would you ease enrollment restrictions so that more veterans would be allowed into the program?
- Would you expand veterans' health care facilities so that geographic location is not such a hardship on veterans?

Chapter 7

Reproductive Rights—
The Perpetual Attack

Birth Control and Family Planning

Birth control has been under attack for much of US history, with the legal assault beginning in the nineteenth century. After Charles Goodyear developed the vulcanization of rubber in 1839, rubber manufacturers started supplying not just condoms, but douching syringes and "womb veils" (diaphragms and cervical caps), and what amounted to intrauterine devices (IUDs). By the 1870s, pharmacies were selling chemical suppositories, vaginal sponges, and medicated tampons. All of these contraceptives were widely promoted in advertisements that were often detailed and graphic, giving us a disconcerting idea of some of the objects that women were encouraged to insert into their bodies.

Anthony Comstock, a onetime salesman in New York City and the philosophical father of anti-choice zealots today, believed birth control encouraged prostitution and fed the vice trade by separating sex from marriage and childbearing. He recruited others to his cause, and in 1873 convinced Congress to pass a bill branding contraception as obscene, and prohibiting its distribution across state lines or through the mails. Similar laws were passed in twenty-four states; they came to be known collectively as Comstock Laws.

The Comstock laws did not do away with birth control—they merely led to marketing with the use of creative euphemisms describing "health devices," such as "married women's friends." Though courts and juries often looked the other way, the Comstock laws remained in effect until 1918, when the spread of venereal disease in the armed forces of World War I became a concern. A New York appeals court ruled that contraceptive devices were legal as instruments for the maintenance of health.[104]

After the decision, states repealed their Comstock laws, except for Connecticut. By the 1960s, it was the only state with such a law, although other states regulated the distribution of birth control devices or banned birth control advertising. The Planned Parenthood League of Connecticut had fought against the state's prohibition for decades, and in 1965 they prevailed in the Supreme Court, which ruled in *Griswold v. Connecticut* that the right to use birth control is protected as part of a right to privacy under the Constitution.

The federal government began to take an active part in providing birth control in 1967, when 6 percent of the funds allotted to the Maternal and Child Health Act were set aside for family planning. In 1970, President Nixon signed the Family Planning Services and Population Act (known as Title X), which established separate funds for birth control. Title X clinics offer low-income women voluntary contraceptive services, prenatal care, treatment for sexually-transmitted diseases (STDs), and other services, including abortion referrals.

In March of 2019, President Trump issued new final rules governing Title X clinics, dubbed "gag rules" by health and family planning groups. Widely seen as a way to defund Planned Parenthood (which operates 400 women's health clinics), the new rules ban federal family planning funds from going to health providers who perform or even refer patients for abortion services, and office space and examination rooms must be separated from physical facilities used to provide abortions. In addition, the rules direct family planning funds to anti-choice clinics that also oppose contraception.[105] In July, 2019, the US Court of Appeals for the Ninth Circuit allowed the rule to take effect while legal challenges work their way through the courts. The Trump administration announced it would immediately enforce the rule. In order to continue to provide abortion services, Planned Parenthood then announced it was leaving the Title X program. Loss of Title X funding resulted in the closure of several clinics. Trump's decision will remain in effect until resolved by an appeal to the Supreme Court. It is unclear whether the Court will hear the case in 2020. Meanwhile Planned Parenthood has pulled out of the Title X program, and been forced to close several clinics, depriving women of birth control and other reproductive services.

Medicaid, the nation's joint federal/state health insurance program for the poor, has specified family planning services as a mandatory benefit since the Nixon administration in 1972. According to the most recent data available (but prior to Medicaid expansion under the Affordable Care Act), women in their reproductive years (ages fifteen to forty-nine) accounted for 70 percent of female enrollment nationwide, and Medicaid provides more public dollars for family planning than any other federal program.[106]

Cost sharing by patients was prohibited until 2005, when Congress allowed states for the first time in more than thirty years to exclude family planning from some beneficiaries. Another provision caused brand name prescription prices for birth control pills dispensed on campuses to rise from about the $3 to $10 range per month to the $30 to $50 range, rendering contraceptives unaffordable for many. Congress reversed the 2005 changes, sweeping away exorbitant birth control co-pays for Medicaid recipients and women on college campuses with the Affordable Birth Control Act in March of 2009.[107]

The Guttmacher Institute, an organization researching reproductive health, says their data show that charging fees to poor women is a classic example of "penny wise and pound foolish." When women cannot afford co-pays, more will go without family planning services. To reduce both unintended pregnancies and abortions, programs should be expanded, not curtailed or eliminated.

California's experience is exemplary. The state's 2002 Medicaid family planning expansion is estimated to have prevented 213,000 unintended pregnancies, 45,000 of which would have been to teenagers. By preventing these pregnancies, the program helped women in California avoid an estimated total of 82,000 abortions, 16,000 of which would have been to teenagers. And that's for just one year.[108]

The influence of the US on birth control and family planning policies and practices reaches far beyond our own shores. Maternal mortality remains high in many countries and more than 200 million women want, but cannot get access to, modern methods of family planning. We are a major influence in what happens worldwide, including funding for birth control, accessibility of reproductive health services, and control of information about family planning.

International family planning has in fact become a "political football" in the US, with conservative Republican administrations cutting or eliminating programs altogether, and Democratic ones lending some support (see a full discussion under Global Women's Issues). President Obama overturned Bush era restrictions as one of his first acts in 2009. Barely two months after he took office, President Trump cut off all UN Population Funding (UNFPA)—the $32.5 million core contribution, plus $38 million for reproductive and maternal health services in humanitarian settings.[109]

Cutting Medicaid and the UNFPA are just two of the places where administrations can differ, and where party control of Congress can make a difference. Other areas are the Title X family planning program, providing information about condom use and efficacy on government websites, access to over-the-counter emergency contraception (commonly referred to as Plan B), and information about birth control in sex education classes.

While Democrats have historically been much stronger supporters

REPRODUCTIVE RIGHTS—THE PERPETUAL ATTACK

of family planning than Republicans, we should not believe that if Democrats are in control all the problems will be solved instantly. The anti-birth control forces are formidable, and they are able to influence politicians to vote against women's interests in this area, or at least to drag their feet or do nothing to overturn past harmful policies. The issues below are examples where nothing has been done, even with Democratic majorities.

Approval of over-the-counter emergency contraception was delayed until 2006, though the drug was approved by the FDA in 1998. It was approved without a prescription (but *behind the counter*) only for women 17 or older, who had to show a photo ID to the pharmacist.

Sixteen-year-olds and under needed a prescription. This effectively prevented access, since getting a prescription usually takes longer than the seventy-two hour window in which the drug is effective, even if a younger teen has insurance to pay for seeing a doctor and the wherewithal to do it. The rule also limited availability to immigrant women who may not have a government photo ID. The FDA approved the sale of Plan B to younger teens in 2011, but the US Department of Health and Human services under President Obama overruled the decision. The president claimed he had nothing to do with the ruling, but it was widely seen as political.[110]

In April of 2013, US District Judge Edward Korman blasted that decision as putting politics ahead of science and ordered the FDA to allow unrestricted sales of emergency contraceptives. The Obama administration lost a round in the appeals court, and the Food and Drug Administration approved unrestricted sales of Plan B One-Step, lifting all age limits on the emergency contraceptive.[111] If the new Trump rules (below) go into effect, Plan B will be affected, along with other forms of contraception.

Hospitals can (and many do) legally deny access to emergency contraception for rape victims. The Compassionate Assistance for Rape Emergencies Act would require hospitals receiving federal money to offer and provide emergency contraception to victims of sexual assault on request, but it languished in Congress when first introduced in 2003, and has not been re-introduced since 2012.

Another birth control issue that has surfaced in the last few years is pharmacists refusing to fill birth control prescriptions if they are opposed to contraception. This so-called "conscience movement" is supported by such organizations as the US Conference of Catholic Bishops and Pharmacists for Life International. Pharmacists who refuse say they have a "moral right" to refuse the prescriptions, and some go so far as to refuse to refer women to other pharmacies.[112] This obviously jeopardizes or eliminates the right of women to obtain drugs that are legally prescribed, not to mention allowing pharmacists to veto women's private choices. There is no question that refusal to fill emergency contraception pills leads to delays that can result in unwanted pregnancy.

The battle is being played out at the state level so far, with a few states having laws on the books that require the prescriptions to be filled, and another handful having laws that say pharmacists don't have to do so. No federal action has been taken yet. "Access to birth control" bills have been introduced in both the House and Senate, but have not gotten hearings. Since most of the activity on this issue is at the state level, it is particularly important that women ask any candidates running for state legislature where they stand on the issue. (And ask yourself: how much sense does it make for a person go to work for Kentucky Fried Chicken, then declare themselves a vegetarian and refuse to sell chicken—and still keep their job?)

One provision of the Affordable Care Act is that birth control is covered without deductibles and co-pays in the insurance exchanges. This has led to a firestorm of protest from Catholic bishops and evangelicals, and many candidates (including President Trump) are still running on promises to repeal the ACA.

Despite the general rule, the ACA exempted churches from covering birth control in their employee insurance plans if birth control is against their beliefs. But that was not good enough for the US

Conference of Catholic Bishops. In 2014 the Supreme Court issued a landmark decision in *Burwell v. Hobby Lobby* allowing closely held for-profit corporations to be exempt from a law should its owners religiously object to it. It was the first time that the court recognized a for-profit corporation's claim of religious belief. (I have never seen one get down on its knees and pray—have you?)

The Trump administration went a step further in November 2018, issuing a rule allowing more employers, including publicly traded companies, to opt out of providing no-cost contraceptive coverage to women by claiming religious *or moral* objections. In January 2019 a federal judge put a nationwide hold on the new rule. The Department of Justice did not say whether it would appeal, saying only that it will continue to vigorously defend religious liberty.

Conservative majorities and conservative leaders have shown in the past that they do not want to encourage birth control, and indeed in many cases would eliminate it altogether. And the future of domestic and international family planning programs, and therefore the fate of many women who may need birth control but cannot afford it, is still far from safe. Policies that influence women's choices and options are most definitely on the table in both state and federal elections.

Questions for candidates:

- Do you believe in an individual's right to access to birth control without interference from the government?
- Should hospitals receiving tax dollars be required to offer emergency contraception to rape victims?
- Do you support US aid to international family planning programs?
- Do you believe pharmacists should be able to refuse to fill legal prescriptions for any drug the pharmacy normally carries?
- Knowing that abortion coverage is not part of health care reform and religious organizations and businesses can now opt

out of birth control coverage due to "conscience clauses," do you think they should be able to opt out of covering any other medical conditions or drugs on the same basis?

Abstinence-Only Sex Education

Abstinence-only-until-marriage sex education refers to a government-mandated method of teaching sex education to kids in schools that accept federal money. As a practical matter, this includes virtually all public schools and some private ones. While abstinence-only sex education was not supported by the Obama administration, it had been supported under George W. Bush and continued to receive at least $25 million per year in federal tax dollars under Obama. It is a stark illustration of how the path to a misguided, and downright harmful national policy, can be very hard to change once it is begun, and it is also an excellent illustration of why control of Congress makes a big difference in outcomes.

The mandate for abstinence-only sex education began way back in 1981 when Ronald Reagan was in the White House. The Adolescent Family Life Act was crafted by conservatives to prevent teen pregnancy—by using government dollars to promote *only chastity and self-discipline*. In those days, the programs also had a strong dose of religion, before specific religious references and providing classes in church sanctuaries were outlawed in 1993.

But federal money for abstinence-only continued to flow, and was increased dramatically in 1996, when $50 million per year was added to President Clinton's high-priority welfare reform bill by conservatives. Funding for abstinence-only burgeoned under the Bush Administration, going from $60 million a year to $176 million.[113] By 2008 Congress had lavished over $1.5 *billion* in state and federal dollars on this ideologically driven and unscientific "sex education."[114]

The law, a provision of the Maternal and Child Health Block Grant, was groundbreaking, both for its funding level and also for its unprecedented, eight-point definition of abstinence education. In a nutshell, Title V mandated that schools taking federal money teach *only* abstinence as a way to avoid pregnancy, disease, and psychological and social consequences of having sex, *to the exclusion of* other programs, such as information about birth control methods. It further directed that students must be taught that marriage is the only appropriate context for sexual activity, also required states to provide assurance that funded programs and curricula *not promote contraception and/or condom use.*[115] That's it—no birth control or protection against sexually-transmitted diseases, no medically accurate information about reproduction and child-bearing, and no acknowledgment that not everyone will marry and have children.

Several attempts to end or cut back funding for abstinence-only education by the Democrats in Congress failed during the Bush administration, because they did not have veto-proof majorities in the House and Senate. Though Democrats passed a bill in 2007 that ended funding of the programs, the bill was vetoed by President Bush. A vote to override in the House failed by two votes, demonstrating once again that the size of the majority matters.

After a decade of extravagant and ever-increasing money injections, the government's own long-term research by the Department of Health and Human Services clearly demonstrated that abstinence-only programs do not delay sexual initiation, nor do they reduce rates of either teen pregnancy or sexually-transmitted diseases.[116] Moreover, the teenage pregnancy rate rose in 2006 for the first time since 1991, and the US led the industrialized world in teen pregnancies. Government officials were "surprised" but had "no immediate explanation." At the same time, sexually transmitted disease rates, including syphilis, gonorrhea, and chlamydia, had been rising.[117]

These results, along with tightening program requirements that included a new directive to indoctrinate adults up to age twenty-nine in community-based programs, contributed to a revolt in the states against abstinence-only sex education. The number of states that

YOUR VOICE, YOUR VOTE: 2020–21 EDITION

refused abstinence-only funding grew from one (California) in the first year to thirty-one by mid-2018, but nineteen states were still stressing abstinence-only requirements for teaching sex education in public schools.[118]

In his 2010 budget President Obama greatly curtailed funding for abstinence-only education, instead allocating $164 million for teen-pregnancy prevention programs that have been proven "through rigorous evaluations" to delay sexual activity, increase contraceptive use (without increasing sexual activity), and reduce teen pregnancy. An administration official said that no abstinence-only programs had met those standards.[119] And the numbers don't lie: according to the National Center for Health Statistics, the number of teens who have children decreased by 57 percent from 2000 and 2016, reaching a record low in 2016.[120]

Still, abstinence-only sex education is not dead, and like *Nightmare on Elm Street*'s Freddy Krueger, keeps coming back to haunt schools, students, and parents. The Trump administration attempted to cut $200 million from the Obama's Teen Pregnancy Prevention Programs, which would have caused funding to end in June of 2018 instead of the original end date of June 2020. However, the eighty-one organizations affected by this move sued the Trump administration and the courts ruled the funding cuts illegal, ensuring the funding until mid-2020.

Trump also appointed Valerie Huber, president an abstinence-only youth advocacy organization, as the chief of staff of the Department of Health and Human Services. The criteria for future grants from the Department of Health and Human Services emphasizes "sex risk avoidance" and, unlike the Teen Pregnancy Prevention Programs, removes any reference to LGBTQ youth and their sexuality education needs.[121]

Questions for Candidates:

- Do you support comprehensive, age-appropriate sex education in the public schools?
- How have you voted, or how would you vote, on providing public school money for abstinence-only sex education?
- Do you think our (state, school district, etc.) should take federal money for sex education if it restricts that education to abstinence-only and nothing else?

Access to Abortion

"For today, the women of this Nation still retain the liberty to control their destinies. But the signs are evident and very ominous, and a chill wind blows."
—Justice Harry Blackmun, 1989, in the *Webster v. Reproductive Health Services* Supreme Court decision opening the way for state restrictions on abortion.

(For a chronology of all important court decisions on abortion see Appendix II.)

Abortion was legal in the US from the time the earliest settlers arrived. At the time the Constitution was adopted, abortions before "quickening" were openly advertised and commonly performed. States began to criminalize abortion in the 1800s, and by 1910 all but one state had criminalized the procedure except where necessary, in a doctor's judgment, to save the woman's life.

The impetus for outlawing abortion was threefold. Some feared that newly arriving immigrants had birth rates higher than native-born white women, so outlawing abortion would up the birth rate of white women and therefore stave off "race suicide." Anti-abortion legislation was also part of a backlash to the growing movements for suffrage and birth control—an effort to control women and confine them to a traditional childbearing role. Finally, the medical profession wanted more control over women's health.[122]

Abortion was often performed by non-medical practitioners, including midwives, apothecaries, and homeopaths, thus competing with physicians for patient dollars. Physicians therefore sought to eliminate one of the principle procedures that kept these competitors in business. Rather than openly admitting to such motivations, the newly formed American Medical Association (AMA) argued that abortion was both immoral and dangerous.[123]

Since very few abortions could be certified as necessary to save a woman's life, women were forced into the back alleys. Criminalizing the procedure did not reduce the numbers of women who sought abortions. Although accurate records were not kept, it is known that between the 1880s and 1973, many thousands of women were harmed as a result of illegal abortion before the Supreme Court legalized the procedure. Estimates ranged as high as 1.2 million per year. Hospital emergency rooms treated thousands of women, many of whom died, and many of whom suffered lasting health effects.[124]

Beginning in the 1960s with the women's liberation movement, one-third of the states liberalized or repealed their criminal abortion laws. The right to an abortion for all women in the US was won in 1973, when the Supreme Court struck down the remaining restrictive state laws with its *Roe v. Wade* ruling. The ruling said that Americans' right to privacy included the right of a woman to decide whether to have children, and the right of a woman and her doctor to make that decision without interference from the state. It was not a ruling that granted wholesale "abortion on demand" to women. *Roe's* trimester-based analysis generally prohibits regulation of abortions in the first three months, allows regulation for protecting the health of the mother in the second three months, and allows for complete abortion bans after six months, the approximate time a fetus becomes viable (able to survive on its own outside the womb).

Immediately after the ruling, the anti-choice forces mobilized, and they continue to work to prevent state funding for the procedure for poor women, to eliminate abortion counseling at home and in other countries through withholding US family-planning funds, and to mount campaigns and lawsuits to make abortion very difficult to obtain. Many also picket abortion clinics. Some clinics have been bombed or burned to the ground. Doctors are routinely targeted for harassment, and some have been murdered.

Violence, harassment, disruption, and blockades are actions that amount to domestic terrorism against the clinics, doctors, and the women who seek their services. The May 2009 murder of Dr. George Tiller, owner of one of the few remaining late-term abortion facilities in the country in Wichita, Kansas, once again brought national attention to anti-abortion violence. Only after several years was the clinic reopened as the South Wind Women's Center under the auspices of the Trust Women Foundation.

Clinic violence occurs regardless of which party is in control of the government, and has continued to rise under Presidents Bush, Obama,[125] and Trump. In January 2019, the Feminist Majority Foundation released its 2018 National Clinic Violence Survey measuring anti-abortion violence, intimidation, and harassment of abortion providers nationwide. The overwhelming majority of clinics (87 percent) report experiencing some type of anti-abortion activity in the first half of 2018. The percentage of clinics that experienced the most severe types of threats and violence, including death threats, stalking, and blocking clinic access, remained high at 23.8 percent of clinics. Nearly half (45 percent) experienced at least one incident of severe violence and/or severe harassment, such as break-ins, robberies, and vandalism, in the first six months of 2018.[126]

Support for *Roe v. Wade* remains at the highest point in four decades, though there are differences based on gender, party, and religion.† A total of 77 percent say the Supreme Court should uphold

---

† For additional polling and statistics on abortion, see Chapter 4.

Roe; 26 percent want it to remain in place, but with more restrictions added; 21 percent want it expanded to establish the right to abortion under any circumstance; 16 percent want to keep it the way it is; and 14 percent want to see some of the restrictions allowed under *Roe* reduced. Just 13 percent overall say it should be overturned.[127]

Some people believe that those who advocate for women's right to make their own reproductive choices are pushing "abortion on demand" on women. This is not the case. The so-called "abortion wars" are about a woman's right to control her own body and her medical privacy. Abortion rights advocates want women to be able to choose abortion, or choose to carry a pregnancy to term, without the interference of the government. They also believe that legal abortion should be available to women in other countries, because where abortion is outlawed, death rates from self-induced and illegal abortions are high, just as they once were in the United States. Contrary to rhetoric from the anti-choice right wing, abortion rights advocates do *not* endorse abortion as a method of birth control. While many women would never make the choice to have an abortion, the abortion rights movement is about preserving their rights as autonomous human beings as well.

Anti-choice forces continue to mount concentrated legal attacks, passing restrictive state laws, including restricting pre-viability procedures, mandatory waiting periods, biased counseling, and parental involvement. Some legal entities, including the US Justice Department under President Bush and the Kansas Attorney General, have tried to force hospitals to release women's private medical records, saying they are needed to determine if a crime has been committed.[128]

Two laws passed in Oklahoma in 2009 are examples of ongoing attacks on women's privacy. One bill, thrown out by the courts, said women had to undergo an ultrasound using an invasive technique called a "vaginal transducer," and listen to a doctor's explanation during the process before she could get an abortion.

The other measure required women seeking abortions to disclose information that would be put on a state-run website. That information includes previous pregnancies and live births; previous marriages; previous induced abortions; how the abortion was paid for; the reason for the abortion; and information about the mother's relationship with the father, among other things. The law was declared unconstitutional and unenforceable in 2010, but anti-choice lawmakers vowed to rewrite both bills and resubmit them in future legislative sessions.[129] They tried to declare an embryo a person in 2012, but the Oklahoma Supreme Court struck it down as unconstitutional.

Even if state legislatures are not inclined to pass restrictive laws (and most are), anti-choice activists have shown they will use state ballot initiatives to outlaw or restrict abortion. Ballot measures are proposed state laws that must be approved or rejected directly by voters within states. They can be placed on the ballot by legislatures, citizen petitions, or other methods, and are most often held in conjunction with general elections.

The fight to keep abortion legal seems never-ending. Here are some eye-opening statistics as of 2019 from the Guttmacher Institute, and this list is by no means exhaustive.[130]

* Various laws that would ban abortion are in place in twenty-seven states if *Roe* is overturned.
* Twenty-one states require abortion facilities or their clinicians to have unnecessary and burdensome connections to a local hospital.
* Targeted regulation of abortion providers (TRAP) laws—medically unnecessary regulations designed to shut down clinics—are now in place in twenty-seven states.
* Eighteen states mandate that women be given counseling before an abortion, including erroneous information a link between abortion and breast cancer (five states), the ability of a fetus to feel pain (thirteen states), or long-term mental health consequences for the woman (eight states).

* Requirements for waiting period before an abortion in effect in twenty-seven states.
* Required abortion reporting to the state in place in forty-six states, including whether mandated counseling and parental consent requirements are met.
* More than a third of states have successfully passed what are termed "twenty-week abortion bans." These bans are based on the unfounded assertion that a fetus can feel pain at twenty weeks post-fertilization.
* So-called "fetal-heartbeat" bans, which outlaw abortions as early as five weeks, have been passed in at least nine states as stepping stones to overturning *Roe* (see below).

The result of all of this harassment, both legal and otherwise, is that while abortion remains legal in the US, it is increasing harder to obtain. Not only are the above restrictions in place in many states, but clinics have shut down due to harassment. According to the latest data available, 88 percent of counties in the US have no identifiable abortion provider, and the number rises to 97 percent in rural counties. That means one in four women have to travel over fifty miles, and 8 percent travel 100 miles or more.[131] With mandatory waiting periods and the inability of many women to miss work, this puts abortion out of reach.

It is uncertain whether *Roe v. Wade* will be overturned outright in the next few years, but it is looking increasingly likely with the new conservative Supreme Court majority against abortion rights. Those who think abortion will still be legal, only "just go back to the states," as many like to say, need to think again. The majority of states now have laws on the books that will restrict the legal status of abortion or outlaw it altogether if *Roe* is overturned.

And don't fall for the line that these are "old" pre-*Roe* laws that will never be enforced—only a few fall into that category, and there is certainly no guarantee that they won't stand up. In fact, anti-choice state legislators in many states can be expected to "stand guard" to see that these laws are not overturned. By way of example, a bill to abolish a 1969 law that will ban abortion in New Mexico if *Roe* is overturned was defeated in 2019, despite Democratic majorities in both chambers of the legislature and a newly elected Democratic governor.

The right to reproductive choice and medical privacy is the single biggest issue at stake for women's lives and health in the 2020 election and beyond. It is not only relevant to young women who may be faced with the abortion decision, but to all women who value their autonomy and privacy. As of summer 2019, there are at least twenty lawsuits, in various stages of judicial review, that have the potential to be decided in ways that could significantly change the rights laid out *Roe*.

Many of the new cases involve challenges to state laws restricting access to the procedure. In Indiana, for example, abortion rights advocates sued to block a measure signed into law by then-Governor Mike Pence (R) that required women to undergo an ultrasound, then wait eighteen hours before having the procedure. Many Trump nominees for lower courts are outspoken foes of abortion rights, and a few of their decisions have included coded anti-abortion language. In a ruling upholding the constitutionality of a Kentucky law requiring abortion providers to perform an ultrasound and make the fetal heartbeat audible to the patient, Judge John K. Bush referred to "unborn life" rather than fetus.[132]

But an even more frightening new trend has developed since the election of Donald Trump. "Fetal heartbeat bans," which outlaw abortions once a pencil-tip sized pulsing of cells that will later develop into a heart is detected, have passed in at least nine states (some with no exceptions for rape or incest) and are being pushed in several more. Doctors say such bans could be as early as five weeks into pregnancy, before many women know they are pregnant. These measures are a direct challenge to *Roe*, where abortion without restriction is allowed up to twenty-four weeks. Though the laws have been blocked from taking effect pending outcomes of court challenges, abortion opponents readily admit they hope one of the many such bills they advocate will make it to the Supreme Court and be upheld, overturning *Roe*.[133]

Not only do the zealots want to ban abortion, they want to criminalize it. One Alabama lawmaker proposed a bill that would make abortion a felony at any point during a woman's pregnancy, including in cases of rape and incest. But the most horrific bill of all was debated in the Texas state legislature in April, 2019. The bill defines all abortions as murder, punishable by death in Texas. These extreme bills are not passing—yet. But the numbers are frightening: 446 people testified in favor of the Texas measure, with only 54 standing against it.[134]

Because federal, state, and even city bans are on the rise, it is particularly important to confront candidates at all levels as to their views and intentions.

Questions for candidates:

- Do you support a woman's right to abortion as embodied in *Roe v. Wade*?
- Do you oppose appointments to the Supreme Court of people who would overturn *Roe v. Wade* ?
- Do you support any restrictions on the right to abortion? If yes, which ones?
- If *Roe v. Wade* is overturned, would you support a federal Freedom of Choice Act guaranteeing a woman's right to privacy in medical decisions, including whether or not to have an abortion?
- Do you support a ban on abortion before twenty-four weeks, which would be in direct contradiction to *Roe v. Wade*?

Chapter 8

Pay Equity: Show Me the Money!

The pay gap between working women and men in the US continues to be one of the highest-ranking concerns for women. It is also a priority for men, because when one earner in a family brings in less than she should, the family suffers overall.

Though "equal pay for equal work" has been the law since the 1963 Equal Pay Act was passed, disparities in pay between women and men for full-time, year-round work are not lessening substantially, and cannot be expected to go away naturally, as some conservatives claim (after all, it's already been fifty-seven years).

According to US Census Bureau figures for full-time, year-round workers, women's earnings for 2018 (latest figures available) are on average 80 percent of men's. The gap has been virtually the same for over a decade.

Earnings for women of color continue to be lower than those for white women, who earn 77 percent of men's wages overall. Asian American women make 85 percent. African American women come in at 61 percent of men's earnings, and for Native American women the percentage is 58 cents. Hispanic women are at the bottom with only 53 percent. Moms overall make 69 percent.[135]

Women face a pay gap in nearly every occupation. Here are a

few other statistics compiled by the National Women's Law Center in Washington, D.C:[136]

* There is a gender wage gap in 97 percent of occupations.
* Based on today's wage gap, a woman who worked full-time, year round would typically lose $406,760 over a forty-year career. This woman would have to work nearly ten years longer than her male counterpart to make up this lifetime wage gap. These lost wages severely reduce women's ability to save for retirement and threaten their economic security later in life.
* Mothers who worked full-time, year-round typically had lower earnings than fathers ($40,000 compared to $56,000)—mothers were paid only 71 cents for every dollar paid to fathers. Mothers of every race are typically paid less than white, non-Hispanic fathers.
* Women are nearly two-thirds of minimum wage workers and two-thirds of tipped workers. Women of color are 23 percent of minimum wage workers, compared to 16 percent of all workers. Thirty percent of working women—and 37 percent of working women of color—would get a raise if the minimum wage increased to $12 per hour in 2020.
* According to the most recent analysis available, women in same-sex couples have a median personal income of $38,000, compared to $47,000 for men in same-sex couples and $48,000 for men in different-sex couples. Transgender women make less after they transition. One study found that the average earnings of transgender women workers fall by nearly one-third after transition.
* As a result of lower lifetime earnings and different work patterns, the average Social Security benefit for women sixty-five and older is about $14,753 per year, compared to $18,918 for men of the same age.

But even these miserable facts don't tell the whole story. The pay gap gets worse for women over their work lives, including for college graduates in high-paying fields. For example, men and women with professional degrees have similar earnings in their twenties. The earnings gap widens over time.

The pay gap also widens greatly for women who drop out of the workforce, even temporarily. According to a study by the Institute for Women's Policy Research, a woman who takes off for a single year will likely *never* catch up. She will earn less for up to fifteen years after she returns to the workforce.[137]

What Causes the Pay Gap?

There are a number of reasons for the pay gap, including job segregation—meaning some jobs are mostly held by men, and others mostly by women. Women workers tend to be segregated into lower paying clerical and service jobs, while men dominate higher paying blue collar, management, and technical jobs. Increasing training and targeted recruitment for these better paying jobs would help narrow the pay gap. A few companies are adopting these practices, citing better retention and a more robust bottom line as reasons for their initiatives.

"Women's jobs" have traditionally been seen by society as less valuable than "men's jobs," though the jobs may require the same level of skill, effort, responsibility, and working conditions (e.g. shop foreman vs. clerical supervisor, or social worker vs. parole officer). But we've seen that even in job titles that are dominated by women such as teaching and nursing, *men in those fields make more.*

There have been many studies of the gender pay gap, with conservative groups claiming that women choose to make less because they don't want to work as much, drop out of the workforce, or want less risky or so-called "women's" jobs that pay less. But when all of these factors—and others such as education—are accounted for statistically, there is still a pay gap. *Experts agree that sex discrimination is the only logical explanation.*[138]

A compelling—and potentially damning—study in 2008 by University of Chicago sociologist Kristen Schilt and NYU economist Matthew Wiswall starkly shows that gender counts. They looked at wage trajectories of people who underwent a sex change. The results: even when controlling for factors like education, men who transitioned to women earned, on average, 32 percent less after the surgery. Women who became men, on the other hand, earned 1.5 percent more.

Many conservatives claim it is motherhood, not the fact of being female that causes the gender gap. But they do not say fatherhood causes lower pay, nor can they explain the pay gap for women who are childless, or no longer raising children. It is obvious that the pay gap presents many problems for women, whether they are married or single, and whether they are mothers or not. And it can become like a self-fulfilling prophecy.

If someone has to take off work to take care of a child or elderly parent in a two-earner family, it makes economic sense for the lower earner to do it, because the family will lose less income that way. And because the lower earner is almost always the woman, she usually is the one to take time off. This means she will fall behind others at her workplace and may be seen as an unreliable or less serious worker, damaging her opportunities for promotion.

Women without children may still be seen by management as "potential mothers" and therefore devalued at promotion time. Single mothers, of course, are at the worst disadvantage, having no partner to take up the slack when caregiving calls.

Court Battles to Close the Gap

Court battles around pay discrimination at all levels have been ongoing since 1963, but the US Supreme Court's most important recent pay equity decisions—in 2007 and 2010—demonstrated a bias in favor of corporations against women.

In a truly bizarre ruling (*Ledbetter v. Goodyear*), the Court said that a woman who believes she is being denied equal pay must file a complaint within 180 days after the first instance of discrimination occurs, even if it went on for years before she found out about it.

Prior to that ruling, the law had been interpreted to mean women had 180 days to bring action from the time they *learned about* the discrimination (e.g. they had been paid less than men doing the same work for years but didn't know it). The following letter excerpt from the plaintiff Lilly Ledbetter, says it all:

I'm a former employee of Goodyear Tire and Rubber Company. For close to two decades, I was paid less than my male coworkers—even though I was doing the same work they were, and doing it well. The company kept the discrimination quiet and I didn't know about the pay gap until I got an anonymous note about it. Seeking to rectify this injustice, I brought Goodyear to court.

A jury found that Goodyear had discriminated and awarded me more than $3 million in damages. But Goodyear appealed my case all the way to the Supreme Court and got a reversal of the jury verdict by one vote. The Court said I should have filed my complaint within six months of the original act of discrimination—even though at the time I didn't know the discrimination was happening, let alone have enough evidence to complain.

My case set a new and dangerous precedent. According to the Court, if pay discrimination isn't challenged within six months, a company can pay a woman less than a man for the rest of the woman's career. I wonder what other forms of discrimination the Supreme Court will permit in the future.

Sincerely,
Lilly Ledbetter

The Ledbetter case galvanized organized women's groups and members of Congress to try and overcome the ruling. The Ledbetter Fair Pay Act, restoring the original intent of law as it had been interpreted for nearly forty-three years, passed in 2009. Far from being an easy or quick fix, this was only possible after to two years of advocacy and lobbying, an increase in the Democratic majority in both houses of Congress, and a new president who supported its passage. While the statute will help women who learn they are being discriminated against in bringing legal action, it will do nothing to prevent wage discrimination in the first place—it just gets us back to where we were over fifty years ago.

In another landmark decision in 2010, the Roberts Supreme Court ruled in *Dukes v. Walmart* that although women in the company may have been denied pay and promotions because of their gender, they could not sue as a class. The Court ruled that giving discretion to individual store managers, which can result in discrimination, did not constitute a company-wide discrimination policy (even though discrimination was the clear outcome of such a policy). Only the company-wide written anti-discrimination policy counted.

The Court further ruled that the claims were not sufficiently similar to qualify as a class, since they came from different parts of the country and occurred at different stores. The decision has already had wide-ranging consequences, with many class-action suits being thrown out by lower courts, citing *Dukes,* even if the circumstances were not similar. *Dukes* has also had a dampening effect on attorneys' willingness to bring class actions, since they are often done on a contingency fee basis and can cost hundreds of thousands of dollars before a decision is rendered.

This does not mean that all lawsuits for pay discrimination are dead, but it does mean that class actions are harder to get certified by the courts. In the first case filed under the California Equal Pay Act in 2017, the Court dismissed a sweeping class-action case against Google, ruling that there was no single common pay practice affecting all women at the company.[139] In a motion filed in California in 2019, attorneys are seeking class-action status for more than 4,200 women at Oracle alleging that female employees were paid on average $13,000 less per year than men doing similar work, but the case has not yet been certified as a class action.[140] Four women have filed a suit against Nike, but the company is fighting class-action status, and that case also has not yet been certified by the courts as a class action.[141]

Inability to sue as a class severely limits women's options for redress from workplace discrimination. Each woman must go it alone or with only a small group of co-workers, hiring a lawyer for many thousands of dollars (class-action lawyers sometimes work *pro bono*, but lawyers handling small suits do not). Low-wage female workers cannot afford this, and without the protection of a group, individuals are much more likely to experience retaliation for complaining in the first place.

Proposed Laws to Close the Pay Gap

A number of legislative solutions to the gender pay gap have been proposed. One is to prohibit discrimination in jobs requiring the same levels of skill, effort, responsibility, and working conditions, even if the job titles and duties are different. To avoid potential legal liability, employers would need to conduct internal surveys of their workplaces, evaluate them accordingly, and adjust wages for the job categories that are dominated by women (or dominated by men) that have been undervalued.

In a school district, this might translate to cafeteria servers (mostly women) being paid the same as custodians (mostly men). Even though the actual duties are quite different, the required skill level and effort are about the same.

This approach is known as *comparable worth*, and it has been used successfully in Ontario, Canada, as well as the state of Minnesota (public employees only) to narrow the gender wage gap. Conservatives charge that it would lead to wage setting by the government, though there is nothing in the proposals that would require this, or even suggest it. Lowering wages for a given job category to make things equal would also be prohibited.

Comparable worth was introduced in every congress beginning in the mid-1990s by Senator Tom Harkin (D-IA) in his *Fair Pay Act* (a separate bill from the Ledbetter Fair Pay Act above) until his retirement in 2013, when the bill disappeared. An additional important proposal in Harkin's bill was a requirement that employers report pay statistics by gender, race, and job category.

There is another bill that has also been pending on Capitol Hill since the mid-nineties called the *Paycheck Fairness Act*. It finally passed the House in 2019 (HR7 with the Democratic majority being joined by a handful of Republicans). It would prohibit employers from paying different amounts to individuals in similarly situated job titles, unless warranted by "bona fide job-related factors." It also would change existing law by letting women alleging pay bias to sue for compensatory or punitive damages, and limiting the use of salary histories to set workers' pay. Its chances in a Republican-controlled Senate are close to zero, as it is very unlikely to even be heard and passed in committee and make it to the floor for a vote.

Provisions include:

* Prohibiting employers from using salary history to set pay, ensuring that prior pay disparities don't follow workers from job to job.
* Protecting employees from retaliation for discussing pay with colleagues, including stopping employers from being able to fire employees for sharing information.
* Ensuring equal pay for equal work by requiring employers to prove that any pay disparities between men and women are a business necessity and job-related.
* Equalizing discrimination claims based on gender, race, and

ethnicity, so plaintiffs filing claims under the 1963 Equal Pay Act have the same robust remedies as those who make claims under other laws.

* Support employers and employees to achieve fair pay practices, including providing technical assistance to employers, requiring the Equal Employment Opportunity Commission to collect some pay data (not public), and offering salary negotiation training programs, which would give women the tools to advocate for higher wages.

Since such legislation has not passed, despite over twenty years of effort by women's groups, and there is virtually no chance that new laws will actually be enacted over strong opposition from a Republican Senate, a more "doable" strategy in the short run seems to be through non-legislative measures. President Obama issued a memorandum in 2014 directing the Secretary of Labor to collect summary compensation data by sex, race, ethnicity, and specified job categories from mid- and large-sized businesses. The Trump administration scuttled the plan before it could be implemented, but was challenged in a successful lawsuit brought by the National Women's Law Center. Reporting began in September 2019. While it was a small step forward, the data collected is primarily for enforcement of (weak) existing law and most of it is not made public.† Trump subsequently announced that the mandated reporting would last one year only.

Another approach is through the contracting process, pioneered in New Mexico in 2010, which requires public pay equity reporting as a condition of bidding for state contracts (so far the only such state initiative in the country). The rationale for the requirement is

---

† None of the information on the EEO-1 is public, except from federal contractors with fifty or more employees, and then only by request on a company-by-company basis. Smaller companies (under one hundred employees) that are not federal contractors are not required to report. The Trump administration has announced that it still intends to drop the reporting rule after one year.

accountability and transparency in how tax dollars are spent, and ensuring that contracts are not being given to companies that are unfair or abuse workers or the law.

Contract dollars, whether federal, state, or local, are already subject to a wide variety of requirements, including such things as providing health insurance to employees as a condition of contracting. Adding pay equity reports to the list should be a priority for public entities spending public dollars. After all, employers already know who works for them, their job titles, and how much they are paid. (This solution does not, of course, affect those who do not accept tax dollars. But it would affect many, many, employers, particularly those with thousands of employees and multimillion-dollar contracts.)

Eliminating the Salary History Trap

It is well known that many employers use salary history to determine pay for new employees. This obviously disadvantages women, since they are much likelier than men to have been paid less on a previous job.

In the absence of federal legislation, a growing number of states, counties, and cities have prohibited the use of salary history in setting pay. As of mid-2019, eighteen states and seventeen local jurisdictions have banned use of salary history in setting pay. Methods and scope differ, but most prohibit asking applicants about salary history and prohibit seeking the information from outside sources. Some apply to all employers in the jurisdiction, others only to public employees. A few require pay scales for jobs to be posted.†

Raising the Minimum Wage

Low minimum wages contribute substantially to the pay gap. Because adult women are the largest group earning the minimum wage, they

---

† For a complete list updated regularly, the reader is referred to https://www
.hrdive.com/news/salary-history-ban-states-list/516662/

are also the largest group to benefit when the minimum wage is raised. Fifty-nine percent of workers who received the last (2009) increase to the current rate of $7.25 were women. Over 1.25 million single parents (mostly women) with children under eighteen benefitted.[142] The numbers would be even higher now—over a decade since the last raise.

While the minimum wage increase helped some at the time, it is clearly not enough now. At $7.25 per hour, a full-time worker who takes no vacation will still earn only $15,080 per year before taxes. Even if a worker's wages are so low that she doesn't owe income taxes, she still must pay payroll taxes. The minimum wage is not currently indexed to inflation, so women lose ground every year it is not raised. After adjusting for inflation, it is still less than the minimum wage through most of the period from 1961 to 1981.[143]

The Democratic-held House passed a bill raising the minimum wage in July 2019 (six Democrats opposed it, while three Republicans supported it). It would gradually increase the US pay floor to $15 by 2025, then index further hikes to median wage growth. It would also phase out lower minimum wage paid to tipped workers. The bill has zero chance of becoming law before the 2020 election, since Senate Majority Leader Mitch McConnell has no plans to bring it up in the Senate, and President Trump has said he would veto the legislation even if it did pass.[144]

Closing the Gap by Unionizing

According to the Economic Policy Institute in Washington, D.C., working women in unions are paid 94 cents, on average, for every dollar paid to unionized working men, meaning the pay gap is considerably smaller than for the workforce at large. Furthermore, hourly wages for women represented by unions are 23 percent higher than for nonunionized women, and unions provide a boost to women, regardless of their race or ethnicity. Unionized workers are also more likely to have access to various kinds of paid leave, from paid sick days, vacations, and holidays to paid family and medical leave, enabling them to balance work and family obligations.[145]

Some analyses indicate that the premium women see from joining a union is equivalent to the increase in pay from a year of college. And when it comes to benefits, unionized women are far more likely to have health insurance and retirement plans—the effect is even greater than having a four-year degree.

The union path is not open to everyone, however. In many workplaces belonging to a union is not an option, and where employees have tried to unionize, they often face retaliation, intimidation, and even firing. While women have become a larger share of the unionized workforce (now at more than 46 percent) the share of both female and male workers who are in a union overall has declined.

One reason belonging to a union may have such an impact on the wage gap is that pay tends to be more transparent. Many workplaces prohibit employees from discussing wages, but union pay scales are often published or available for inspection. As stated above, when pay information is available, it discourages employers from discriminating and empowers employees.

The Last Word on Equal Pay

Even if new laws are passed, the fight won't be over. Conservatives and corporations can be counted on to challenge every pay statute in the courts, and to keep doing so for years. With the Supreme Court already having narrowed women's options in fighting pay discrimination, the choices in future elections and Court appointments become extremely important, both for passing stronger legislation and for safeguarding women from decisions that will further roll back the few remedies available.

Questions for candidates:

- Do you support disclosure of pay statistics by gender, race, and job category? For all businesses? For businesses accepting taxpayer money?
- Do you support making it unlawful for employers to prohibit employees from discussing pay with coworkers?
- Do you support making it unlawful to ask a prospective employee for salary history or to seek that history from another source?
- Do you support new laws to ban discrimination in pay for jobs of equal skill, effort, responsibility, and working conditions, even if the jobs are different?
- Do you support raising the minimum wage, and indexing it for inflation?
- How would you increase women's access to non-traditional jobs?
- Would you support the nomination of a judge who was known for his support of corporations or opposition to workers in employment decisions?
- Did you, or would you have, voted for the Paycheck Fairness Act which passed the House in 2019?

Chapter 9

Hey Big Spender: The Economy

"It's the economy, stupid!" That was the rallying cry for the Clinton campaign in the 1992 presidential election. It could as well be resurrected today. Voters—women and men alike—tend to list it one of the top concerns in every election.

Just what the heck *is* the economy? For most people, *economics* is a word that either scares them or causes their eyes to glaze over.

Economists throw around such terms as *demand curves, elasticity,* and *marginal utility* that ordinary humans have no clue about. Because we seldom understand these terms and the economic theories they come from, we are left to sort out the rhetoric of experts (many self-appointed), candidates, and elected officials about what is best for the economy.

The discussion here won't make it into any economics textbook, and some economists would undoubtedly judge it too simplistic, but it will give you an idea of what the arguments are about when various proposals are put forward on how to produce a sound economy. And when you finish this chapter, you will have the background and details necessary to understand what's at stake for women every time decision makers take action to "fix" the economy, or fail to do so.

The Personal (Economy) is Political

A simple dictionary definition of the economy is this: *the structure of economic life of a country.*

That's the dictionary definition. But for most people, the definition of the "economy" is very personal. If you and your family are doing well—you have a job at a decent wage that allows you to buy the things you need, to save for retirement, and to educate your kids without being terrified of the future—the economy is pretty good.

On the other hand if you are unemployed, in constant fear of being laid off, or have a job that does not pay enough, so that you can't afford adequate housing, can't pay for gasoline and other basics, much less save any money—then the economy for you is pretty bad, regardless of what is happening on Wall Street.

Measuring How the Economy is Doing

The state of your personal economy depends on how the overall economy in the country is doing. If the national economy is *expanding*, it means there are enough jobs and more are being created, more goods and services are being produced, and people have the money to pay for them.

In an expanding economy, home ownership will be stable or on the upswing. Consumers can not only afford the basics, they will be able to buy extras such as a new television or a weekend vacation. This creates more jobs to produce these goods and services, resulting in more money circulating and continued economic growth.

Conversely, in a *shrinking* economy, job growth slows or employment actually declines, and layoffs will be on the rise. This results in less consumer spending as people tighten their belts in fear of, or in reaction to, job losses. As people buy less, demand goes down, so fewer goods and services are produced, which means lower business revenue and profit—leading to more layoffs and less personal and business investment.

The gross domestic product (GDP), a statistic issued by the Commerce Department, is the official measure of how well the economy is doing. The GDP totals up everything the economy has produced in the quarter, and tells how that figure has changed, on a percentage basis, from the previous quarter. A positive percentage change means the economy is expanding; a negative one means it's shrinking. An annual GDP growth rate of 3 percent or more is considered *robust*.

A *recession* is when there has been a decline in the GDP for two consecutive quarters. When there is a recession, or even talk of one, consumers may become more wary and stop spending—even if nothing has actually changed much in their personal situations. That in turn can contribute to decline.

The Eternal Debate—What Can Government Do? What Should the Government Do?

When the economy slips into a near-recession or recession as it did in early 2008, both political parties get nervous, and propose various "fixes" to get more money into circulation and stop the downward spiral. (It's unclear whether they're feeling the people's pain or feeling the pain of trying to get elected in a downturn.)

As unemployment goes up and production goes down, there is usually not much disagreement that a stimulus is needed to spur more buying and restore confidence—but there are serious and fundamental disagreements about what kind of fix it should be.

Debate over how to produce a healthy economy goes to the very heart of the liberal/conservative philosophical divide. Conservatives put their faith in the business sector and the wealthy, while liberals and progressives believe government has a more direct role.

Trickle Down, or Trickle Up?

From the day he took office in 2001, President George W. Bush had one solution to virtually every economic problem—tax cuts primarily benefitting the wealthy. President Trump's philosophy is the same, and is a simple-minded version of conservative arguments in general: if corporations and the wealthy individuals who fund them through investments pay lower taxes, they will invest those tax savings in ways that will create jobs, such as building new plants, acquiring new subsidiaries, or expanding product lines. Businesses will direct money to suppliers, contractors, and employees to accomplish these goals. Everyone will have more money to spend and the economy will grow.

This theory has been generally referred to as "trickle-down," or "supply side economics," meaning change made at the top of the wealth pile eventually makes its way to workers at the bottom. Corollaries are that private enterprise is always better than government spending, and the less government interferes in the "free market" through regulation, the better.† Trickle down sounds reasonable—if you believe the tax cuts for wealthy investors and corporations really will be spent on creating jobs instead of multimillion-dollar bonuses for CEOs, fines and legal judgments for various abuses, or fatter dividends for stockholders. As for the expanding facilities and building new plants, that *could* work as advertised—unless the facilities are already in China and the new plants will be in India.

Liberals and progressives believe that putting money in the hands of those that actually need it to live on is a better plan to keep the economy going—because they spend more of what they have instead

---

† The economist John Kenneth Galbraith noted that "trickle-down economics" had been tried before in the US in the 1890s under the name "horse and sparrow theory": if you feed enough oats to the horse, some will pass through [in horse manure] to feed the sparrows."

96

of just adding it to investment accounts. This was essentially President Obama's approach with the stimulus plan to pull the US out of the Great Recession that began in 2007, the final year of the Bush Administration. Low- and moderate-income people have to spend it all, every month, just to buy the basics. Those subscribing to this school of thought would *not* replace the private sector, and in fact would agree that stimulating business in ways that actually create jobs is good (e.g. eliminating the tax incentives that cause businesses to move jobs overseas).

Progressives also believe that the government can have a positive influence on economic growth through spending tax dollars. They would create some jobs by repairing infrastructure such as roads and bridges, funding green energy research and development, hiring more teachers, police, and firefighters, and restoring government services that have been cut. They hold the principle that in a recession, money should be injected into the economy as quickly as possible. Even if the trickle-down fantasy were to actually work, the "tax breaks for business and the wealthy" scenario would take too long to do any good.

The Difference Interest Makes

Conservative rhetoric about "intrusive government intervention" notwithstanding, actions taken or not taken by the government have a great deal of influence over the economy.

One such action is controlling interest rates, or how much it costs to borrow money. This is done through the Federal Reserve Bank (generally called the Fed), which can be thought of as a "bank for bankers." To keep the money supply flowing smoothly, the Fed loans money to other banks at a certain interest rate for short-term loans. This is the *rediscount rate,* often called simply the discount rate.

The discount rate that banks pay to the Fed influences the interest rate they charge their own customers. The discount rate is lowered from time-to-time to stimulate borrowing or raised to dampen inflation. As the discount rate goes up, banks have to pay more for the money they borrow from the Fed, and in turn they have to charge more to businesses and consumers who borrow from them. That means interest rates on business debt, mortgages, car loans, and credit cards will go up.

When borrowers have to spend more on interest, they have less to spend on goods and services. Conversely, if the cost of borrowing is cheap, purchases that are financed effectively cost less, so businesses and consumers are inclined to spend more.

Lower rates and a healthy economy can also increase banks' willingness to lend to businesses and households. This may increase spending, especially by smaller borrowers who have few sources of credit other than banks. In a shrinking economy, the idea behind lowering interest rates is to get both businesses and individuals to be more willing to borrow and spend, thus stimulating economic growth.

Lower interest rates enable businesses to borrow more to buy new equipment, open a new location, or upgrade their facilities. This creates new jobs, and if more people are working they have more money to spend. They in turn pay more taxes, so the government can function without incurring more debt. Lowering interest rates is also thought to instill confidence that "things are going to be all right," arresting downward slides that are triggered by fear or talk of recession.

On the consumer end, low interest rates may induce buyers to buy more goods or buy more expensive things, since the interest rate is a big determinant of the monthly payments on credit cards, mortgages, and car loans. A simple example: Suppose you can afford a $500 per month payment for a new car. With a 6 percent annual interest rate and a four-year loan, you can afford payments on a car costing $21,000. But if interest is only 4 percent, you can go up to $21,800 and add some accessories for the same monthly payment.

This is not necessarily bad, so long as interest rates remain stable. If you buy your car this year at the lower rate and the terms of your loan do not allow the rate to go up, then your rate is "locked in." If interest rates on new car loans go up next year, you won't be affected unless you want to buy another car.

But if interest rates on a loan you've already made are *adjustable* and they're raised, the payments may now exceed the amount you budgeted. And you may be in trouble. That is exactly what happened in the case of the mortgage crisis that is widely blamed for triggering the recession of 2007 to 2009. Lenders very aggressively marketed loans with initial "teaser" interest rates that were low enough for borrowers to afford, but were structured to increase greatly after a short amount of time. Huge mortgages were granted to people with incomes too low to sustain the payments, with assurances that they could refinance the loans or sell at a profit. First-time borrowers, those with limited English, and borrowers who did not understand mortgages were often targeted. In many cases house payments *doubled*.

Very large numbers of borrowers could not make the payments, so they defaulted on the loans and lost their homes. Paving the way for the economy to fall into recession, the number of *mortgage defaults through fall 2007 were up 94 percent over the previous year*, with entire neighborhoods virtually abandoned.[146] This in turn affected local and state tax revenues, forcing cuts in public services. Becoming more pessimistic, people curbed spending. "Recession talk" in the media increased greatly, prompting the Fed to lower interest rates in 2008 to raise confidence and try to put a stop to the slide. But it was not enough—by 2008 61 percent of the public said the economy was suffering through its first recession since 2001.[147]

A thorough discussion of the Great Recession would require a separate book, but suffice it to say that women suffered most at the time and in the aftermath. The comparison of stimulus packages below under two different presidents underscores the importance for women to act on their views and their self-interest.

★ The majority of lousy mortgages went to women. Even though their credit scores were, on average, roughly the same as those of men, they were 32 percent more likely than men to be steered into high-interest adjustable loans. Though this gender gap existed in every income and ethnic group, African-American women were hit especially hard.

* In the first short-term stimulus package passed under Bush to try and arrest the slide, federally-chartered mortgage companies were allowed to divert money away from less expensive housing in favor of very large mortgages known as "jumbos." This meant less help for women who would lose their homes in disproportionate numbers as the mortgage interest rates reset to levels they couldn't afford.

* Help for elderly poor living solely on Social Security (primarily women) and veterans was included in the stimulus. But in exchange for those concessions, Republicans were allowed to insert language prohibiting undocumented immigrants from receiving any benefits.[148]

* The failure to include an increase in food stamp benefits was also a loss for women. Nearly 70 percent of adult food stamp beneficiaries are female.

* Like men, women lost out in Congress's failure to include an extension of unemployment benefits. According to the US Department of Labor, 37 percent of jobless men drew benefits, as compared to 33 percent of unemployed women.

By January 2009, when Barack Obama was sworn in as president, the housing crisis had worsened. Unemployment was on the rise, and credit for consumers and businesses was very hard to get. The newly elected president and Congress knew another stimulus package was needed. Though very few Republicans supported the final legislation authorizing another stimulus, there was less wrangling in Congress because the Democrats now controlled both houses. President Obama signed The American Recovery and Reinvestment Act into law less than a month after his inauguration.

This time there were a number of provisions that did benefit women, particularly low-income women and those with children. A one-time payment for low-income Social Security beneficiaries (mainly female) was approved, as was money for increasing teacher salaries and unemployment benefits, an increase in the SNAP (food stamp) program (women and children are the majority of recipients), and increasing the number of people eligible for Medicaid (poor women and children are the majority of recipients).

Some of these benefits expired as the recession eased, and some were supplemented or continued by the states. Two important benefits for women were later made permanent: an expanded earned income tax credit (EITC) which provides money to low-income workers (majority female) and upping the child tax credit (many families headed by single mothers).

On the downside, most of the jobs created by the Obama stimulus package were in construction, historically male dominated. The jobs targeted in fields dominated by women (child care, health-related) are notoriously low paid. Though an effort was made to require affirmative action for women in the "shovel-ready" construction projects so widely touted as the backbone of the package, that effort ultimately failed.

Even though the economy was doing well and no stimulus was indicated by the time President Trump came into office in 2017, he decided a tax cut was needed anyway. His plan is detailed in Chapter 8. In short, the massive cuts passed by the Republican Congress and signed by the president benefitted the wealthy and corporations (including Trump business holdings) much more than the middle class. The few cuts the middle class did get will expire in 2025, but the corporate tax cuts are set to go on in perpetuity.

The Big Argument for 2020 and Beyond

Experts say uncertainty about future actions by Trump—and a cooling global economy—may lead to a downturn in 2020. JPMorgan Chase predicted in mid-2019 that there was a 45 percent chance the US economy would enter a recession in the next year, up from 20 percent at the beginning of 2018.[149] Just as economic slowdowns and recessions can be short-lived, they can also go on for many months or years, and there is no such thing as a recession-proof economy.

Deficits and What They Cost You

As we'll see in the chapter on taxes, when the government gets less money in taxes if it doesn't cut spending, it has to borrow money to keep spending like it did before the cuts. This is called *deficit* spending. Doing this year after year creates the *national debt,* which is the total of the borrowed money over time. It's the same as an individual putting more money than she can afford to pay on a credit card year after year, not only adding to the basic balance but adding interest as well. She will eventually accrue enormous debt that is very hard or impossible to overcome unless she takes in more money or drastically cuts her spending.

Deficit spending and the national debt it creates are part of the discussion in every election. As a country, we spend more than we raise in taxes. Members of Congress dubbed "deficit hawks" use deficits and debt to advocate cutting spending (but only on public services—not wars and tax cuts, two of the biggest drivers of deficit spending). Former President Eisenhower put it best:

Every gun that is made, every warship launched, every rocket fired signifies in the final sense, a theft from those who hunger and are not fed, those who are cold and are not clothed. This world in arms is not spending money alone. It is spending the sweat of its laborers, the genius of its scientists, the hopes of its children. This is not a way of life at all in any true sense.[150]

—Dwight D. Eisenhower,
former president and military commander

Besides the loss of life, the wars have been a major factor in the national budget deficit. Since 1970, the US has run a budget deficit every year except for the last four years of the Clinton presidency, when there were surpluses from 1998 to 2001. President George W. Bush took office in 2001 with a *surplus* of over $171 billion.[151] The budget *deficit* by the end of Bush's two terms was projected at $1,750 billion by the Congressional Budget Office. According to the Congressional Research Service, the estimated cost of the Bush wars in Iraq and Afghanistan was scheduled to reach $1.41 *trillion* by the end of fiscal year 2012.[152] This cost was very close to President Obama's 2012 projected overall budget deficit of $1.6 trillion, much of it due to the Great Recession.

President Trump is on track to preside over the largest deficits in history, with its attendant national debt. Since he cut taxes drastically, government spending has soared. The federal deficit for the first ten months of the 2018 fiscal year was up almost 21 percent from the same time in 2017. Trump also gave the US military an extra $82 billion in 2018, raising total spending to $716 billion for 2019.[153]

Even though war costs have been a big part of deficits (and the resulting national debt) for over a decade, there has been little mention of those costs in deficit-reduction plans and talks from either party. Most of the discussion has centered on cutting domestic programs such as Medicare, Medicaid, Social Security, and education, which will have a great effect on the well-being of US women and children.

Though there are some pro-war Democrats and a few anti-war Republicans, it's fair to say that the parties have opposite views on the need for continuing wars. Democrats in Congress wanted to end the war in Iraq long before a timetable for withdrawal was laid out. Republicans stuck with the Bush/Cheney doctrine in voting to continue the wars with no timetable for withdrawal. Even though it was officially over in 2011, residual costs continued to pile up until 2016, pushing the total to $1.06 trillion and adding $1 trillion to the national debt.[154]

The war in Afghanistan, launched in 2001 after the 9/11 attacks on the US, is now in its nineteenth year. But beginning as early as 2009 there was serious disagreement between legislators and parties about the need to continue it indefinitely, though the majority of the public said it was not worth fighting.[155] Republicans generally supported the 30,000-troop buildup announced by President Obama, though they opposed the announced 2014 date for withdrawal.

Democrats were divided, but most liberals opposed any buildup. The war is dragging on under President Trump, with the addition of 14,000 troops in 2017 in hopes of preparing the Afghans to take over. In late 2018, the president said the US would withdraw about half of those remaining troops, even as American airstrikes were at the heaviest they had been since the height of the war. But the drawdown has not yet started, and military officials have not clarified how many troops will leave the country, or by when.[156] Tellingly, in May of 2019 the US military announced it would stop releasing information on the progress of the war.[157]

Even if there is no active war (and will that ever happen?), it doesn't mean military spending will be cut. The impact of bloated military budgets, to the detriment of domestic programs that benefit women and children, puts much at stake in every election, because Congress has the last word on whether or not to fund military action or new weapons programs. Since 2010, when many deficit-cutting Tea Party members were elected to the House, we have seen ongoing "crisis" votes to keep the government operating, because they want to cut domestic spending—but not spending on the military.

What Tariffs Cost You

Since the day he took office, President Trump has been obsessed with tariffs and starting trade wars with other countries, especially China. Tariffs are a tax on imports, and the US imports *a lot* of goods from China. Defying economic expert opinion and centuries of experience, the Tweeter-in-Chief allowed in 2018 that "trade wars are good, and easy to win."

Though the president says China will pay for the tariffs he has imposed, analysts disagree, pointing out that US companies and consumers have already paid $3 billion a month in additional taxes because of tariffs on Chinese goods and on aluminum and steel from around the globe in 2018 alone. And the cost will continue to rise. Most of it will be passed on to consumers and will hit low-income households—many headed by women—the hardest. All kinds of products are affected, from cell phones to baby pacifiers to cars, washing machines, furniture, and many, many, kinds of food. The cost to consumers per year is estimated to be from $800 to $2200 per US household of three.[158]

The economy promises to be one of the most contested issues in the 2020 elections, from presidential, congressional, and gubernatorial races down to the local level. The fundamental differences between the parties, and liberal and conservative ideologies, remain as entrenched as ever. If hard-core conservatives increase their influence in Congress and a conservative president is elected, gridlock and brinkmanship issues that affect the economy will continue. Spending cuts on social programs will continue to be put forth regularly as the solution to our fiscal problems, and women will pay the price.

In the run-up to the 2020 election, President Trump put forth a budget proposal that cemented his vision for the United States that bolsters funding for defense and border walls, while severely cutting social programs for the nation's poorest. His $4.7 trillion 2020 budget, encompassing everything from funding for food aid, education, and health care to national defense, includes slashing $845 billion from Medicare (a program Trump notably promised to leave untouched), cuts to Medicaid through major structural reforms, and deep cuts to Social Security, SNAP (food stamps), and Temporary Assistance to Needy Families. These are all programs women depend on. The budget would increase the defense outlay to $750 billion, 5 percent more than the 2019 budget.

It is unlikely that Congress will approve every cut the president wants, or fund every item on his wish list at the level he wants. But it is obvious that both short-term and long-term economic fixes are at stake in 2020 and beyond. Whether the economy is great or not-so-good at any given time, women must hold candidates and elected officials accountable for long-term solutions—solutions that recognize specific outcomes for women that can be far different than those for men.

Here are a few questions to help do that:

- Did you, or would you have, supported the Trump Administration cuts to Medicare, Medicaid, and Social Security?
- Did you, or would you have, supported President Trump's cuts to food stamps?
- What would you do to help the long-term unemployed, specifically women of color, to find jobs?
- Both our deficits and debt are at all-time highs. What would you do to fix that?
- Do you think continued spending on wars is good for the US?
- Have you, or would you, sign a pledge never to raise taxes on anyone for any reason?
- If you would vote to give more tax cuts for the very wealthy, what programs, specifically, would you cut to pay for them?
- Do agree with President Trump that trade wars are good, and won't affect the American consumer?

Chapter 10

Taxes

Taxes are a continuing part of the national dialogue, and they are part of the debate in every election for good reason. Everyone pays taxes of some kind, whether they are rich or poor. But various taxes affect people in different ways, depending on income—and depending on gender.

Candidates and officeholders talk a lot about taxes and the role of taxes in our society.

Explaining tax policy would take a separate book, but this chapter will give you the basics.

Since most people are neither very poor nor very rich, they pay a combination of taxes, including payroll, income, sales, and property taxes (non-homeowners do not escape property taxes, as the costs are passed along by landlords as part of the rent). These taxes are assessed variously by the federal government as well as states, counties, cities, and school districts.

Tax fairness (or unfairness) varies with income. If you have a very low income, you might pay no income taxes, and in fact could get money back from the government in the form of the Earned Income Tax Credit (EITC), the largest federal anti-poverty cash assistance program. It is a tax credit designed to supplement the earnings of low-income workers by reducing or eliminating income taxes. Single mothers and children are the largest group of beneficiaries. When the EITC exceeds the amount of taxes owed, it results in a tax refund to those who claim and qualify for the credit. Recipients do, however, still owe payroll taxes (Medicare and Social Security).

If you are wealthy and live on investments with no salary, you do pay income taxes (and capital gains taxes if you sell any investments at a profit) but incur no payroll taxes at all.

Individuals are not the only source of tax revenue; businesses also pay taxes. Taxes, of course, finance the various government operations, provide for government services like police and fire protection, infrastructure such as roads and bridges, government benefits like unemployment compensation, food stamps, Medicare, Medicaid, and Social Security (all programs women depend on more than men). And of course, wars.

Taxes affect everyone, but they can have differential effects for women. A *regressive* tax is one that takes proportionately more, percentage-wise, from those with less ability to pay. Conversely, it takes proportionately less from those with greater means. The sales tax, for instance, is a regressive tax. Since women in general make less than men, taxes that are regressive take a bigger percentage bite out of their incomes.

Here's a simple example from Dr. Ralph Estes, a business professor emeritus at American University and scholar at the Institute for Policy Studies in Washington, D.C:

> Say your income is $20,000 a year, and you spend all of it on food, clothing, and other things subject to a 6 percent sales tax. So, you pay $1200 in sales tax for the year. That amounts to 6 percent of your income.
>
> Now take a wealthy family with income of $500,000 a year. They don't need all that money to live on, so say they spend $100,000 on things subject to the sales tax. They

would pay $6,000 in sales taxes. They would pay more in dollars, but remember they have a lot more dollars than you do.

Now as a percentage of income, they are paying only 1.2 percent. And that's less than a fourth of the percentage you are paying. So, the person with the lower income pays 6 percent of their income in sales tax, the person with twenty-five times as much income pays 1.2 percent. And that percentage continues to fall as income rises.

That is exactly what we mean when we say a tax is regressive. It takes a bigger percentage bite out of the total income of those with a smaller ability to pay.[159]

A *progressive* tax is one that is more proportionate to ability to pay. The income tax is an example of a progressive tax. Those with greater income pay proportionately more in the form of a higher percentage, which results in a higher amount because they make more, while those with lesser means pay relatively less. A quick example using the similar numbers to those above, adjusted for the Trump tax revisions (below) signed in December 2017:

> With no deductions, the family earning $19,000 a year would pay 12 percent, or $2,280 in income taxes. The family earning $600,000 would pay 37 percent, or $222,000 in income taxes, assuming all of that income was from wages (capital gains and other types of income are taxed at much lower rates). So, not only is the wealthy family paying a higher percentage, it is paying a higher dollar amount because more dollars are being taxed. Thus, the income tax is a *progressive* tax structure.

If $222,000 seems like a lot of money, it is. But that family still has $378,000 left to spend after taxes, whereas the low-income family has only $16,720. In addition, the wealthy family is much more likely to have deductions for a home mortgage (and a second home, which can even be a yacht or RV). They also do not owe payroll taxes on the portion of their income over $132,900, while the low-income family owes payroll taxes on the full amount of their income.

In general, conservatives believe in "less government," and keeping taxes low is a way to achieve that. If the government has no money, it has to shrink and cut services. This is often called "starving the beast," meaning cutting the taxes that feed social spending on programs like Medicare and Social Security.[160] Conservatives also believe everyone earning a wage or salary should be taxed at the same rate regardless of income (regressive taxation). In addition, they maintain that income from investments should be taxed at a lower rate than income from actually reporting to work and performing a job.

Liberals and moderates generally believe taxes are necessary to achieve society's mutual goals and provide for the common welfare. They would quote Oliver Wendell Holmes, "Taxes are what we pay for civilized society." They believe that those who are more fortunate should pay more, and progressive taxes are the fairest way to achieve this.

Just about everyone who studies tax policy, including Nobel economists, agrees that, to be fair and equitable, taxes should overall be progressive, not regressive.[161] However, many politicians disagree. One hundred percent of tax plans put forward by Republican presidential primary candidates in 2016 were regressive.

Are Taxes Too High?

Historically, the total US tax burden has been borne by both individuals and businesses in varying proportions. The corporate share is less than half of what it was sixty-five years ago. In 1955, corporate taxes accounted for nearly 30 percent of the total taxes collected, and individuals accounted for 58 percent. That balance shifted steadily over the decades. After the Trump tax revisions that took effect in 2018, individual payroll and income taxes now account for 86 percent of total revenue (up from 83 percent in 2017), while corporate taxes had dropped to a measly 6 percent (down from 9 percent in 2017).[162]

While we often hear that US corporate tax rates are "the highest in the world," this not true. The US top corporate tax rate of 21 percent (reduced from 35 percent by the Trump overhaul) is now the lowest since 1939, and *below* the worldwide average of 23 percent. Moreover, the *amount* corporations actually end up forking over to the government is much lower, sometimes even zero. This is due to a dizzying number of deductions, write-offs, and other accounting tricks that allow corporations to legally reduce their tax burdens.

A 2019 report from the Institute on Taxation and Economic policy found that after the Trump tax changes, sixty of America's biggest corporations zeroed out their federal income taxes and then some. Instead of paying $16.4 billion in taxes at the new, lower 21 percent rate, these companies enjoyed a net corporate tax *rebate* of $4.3 billion. In other words, they not only paid zero in taxes, they got money back. The list includes mega-profitable companies like Amazon, Netflix, Gannett, IBM, and General Motors.[163]

For individuals, US tax rates are also lower than the average for developed countries.[164] While income taxes are still progressive, the rate on the highest income brackets is much lower than it has been in the past. The IRS reports that in 2014 (the last year the agency reported on this), the 400 richest income tax filers paid just 16.7 percent of their adjusted gross income (AGI) in federal income taxes. That is down from 22.3 percent just since 2000 and, is a less than half of the income tax rate of 37 percent that they are now theoretically subject to. That's because more than 50 percent of the income reported by those 400 taxpayers consisted of capital gains and dividends subject to the preferential rates.[165]

Tax Cuts: Good for Women or the One Percent?

Tax cuts aren't the exclusive property of either party, though in the last twenty years, Congress has cut taxes more when Republicans held the White House. When President George W. Bush took office in 2001, tax cuts were high on his agenda. In his first three years taxes were cut in a number of areas—the most important lowered income tax rates, investment income, capital gains, and the estate tax.

While the Bush tax cuts provided modest benefits to low and middle-income families, they benefitted the rich disproportionately. Women are disproportionately not the rich. One example of the detrimental effects: The cost of the cuts exceeded the cost of the Affordable Care Act.[166] And according to the Center for Defense Information, even with the spending for the wars in Iraq and Afghanistan, the federal budget would be in surplus now if the tax cuts for the wealthy and elite had not been enacted.[167]

During the Obama Administration, Congress enacted economic recovery legislation that created the Making Work Pay Credit, which was in effect for two years (2009 and 2010) in response to the Great Recession. The same legislation expanded two important tax credits for low-income working families, the Earned Income Tax Credit (EITC) and the Child Tax Credit.

Congress also enacted the Affordable Care Act (ACA), which included several tax provisions, including two significant tax hikes for the rich—an increase in the Medicare payroll tax for high earners and a new tax on investment income for high-income individuals.

At the end of 2010, the Making Work Pay Credit was allowed to expire and replaced with a payroll tax "holiday," which reduced Social Security payroll taxes paid in 2011 and extended them through 2012. After a protracted debate, Congress and President Obama agreed at the beginning of 2013 to make most, but not all, of the Bush tax cuts permanent.

At the end of 2017, Congress and President Trump enacted the

Tax Cuts and Jobs Act (TCJA). This law added personal income tax cuts and estate tax cuts on top of those Bush-era provisions still in effect, and cut the corporate income tax as well. While named a "cut" in its title, how much it actually lowers taxes and for how long depends on how rich you already are. The TCJA is long and complicated, but here are the features that will affect ordinary taxpayers the most:[168]

* There are still seven income tax brackets, and tax rates are lowered temporarily. Rates go back up to previous levels in 2026.
* The standard deduction is doubled but, eliminates the $4,150 personal exemption previously allowed for each person claimed. As a result, some families with several children will pay higher taxes despite the Act's increased standard deductions.
* Most standard deductions are eliminated, and others are curtailed, such as the mortgage deduction on new homes. Interest on home equity lines of credit can no longer be deducted.
* Deductions for state and local income, sales, and property taxes, which were previously unlimited, are now capped at $10,000 ($5,000 if you use married filing separately status) through 2025, and taxpayers must now choose between property taxes and income or sales taxes. Under prior law both could be deducted.
* The Child Tax Credit is increased from $1,000 to $2,000. Even parents who don't earn enough to pay taxes can claim a refund up to $1,400. There is also now a $500 (non-refundable) credit available for each non-child dependent.
* The tax benefit for charitable deductions was cut back, meaning many will no longer receive tax deductions for giving to charities. As a result, cutbacks on charitable giving are estimated to be $22 billion per year.

Bottom line: If you have a very high income, the Trump tax cuts help you the most. The Tax Foundation says the richest 5 percent of taxpayers will see a 2.2 percent increase in after-tax income. Those in the middle of the income range will see a paltry 1.7 percent increase, and those in bottom 20 percent of taxpayers will benefit even less—a minuscule a 0.4 percent increase. One more thing: Twenty-three provisions from the Trump tax cuts relating to individual income taxes will expire in 2025, meaning most individual taxpayers will see a tax hike. Corporate tax cuts never expire.

Tax Flim-Flam

Red-hot tax rhetoric from candidates usually centers on "new" and "fair" tax plans. Some of these, such as flat taxes and value-added taxes, are radical departures from current tax policy. Others, such as eliminating estate taxes, are just drastic changes to tax programs or practices already in place. Here, briefly, is what each would likely mean for women.

Flat taxes

Under this scheme, everyone pays the same income tax rate, whether they make minimum wage or CEO-level megamillions. Flat taxes are by definition regressive.

In some flat-tax proposals, the taxpayer can be an individual or business, most deductions (e.g. mortgage, child care, charitable contributions) would be eliminated, and fringe benefits would be counted as income. In other schemes, a progressive surtax could be applied to higher income levels.[169] Flat taxes, or "fair taxes," as some politicians have taken to calling them, are usually sold on the basis of simplifying tax returns and making the system more equitable.

For women, already the lowest earners, it means paying the same tax rate as Morgan Stanley CEO John Mack, who earned $41.4 million in the same year his company agreed to a $46 million dollar settlement for sex discrimination in pay. On top of that, women would most likely lose the few deductions they have, and any fringe benefits like health insurance would be taxable.

National sales tax or value-added tax

This tax is exactly what it sounds like. A federal sales tax would be instituted on top of the various state and local sales taxes. (Value-added taxes amount to the same thing as a national sales tax, though they are "hidden" because they are added at each stage of production before the consumer sees the bill.)

These taxes would replace the income tax. Again, they are highly regressive, as the rich pay much less in proportion to their income, because they spend proportionally less of their total income on goods and services which would be subject to the tax.

Sales taxes are often implemented with certain categories such as medicine and food exempted, only to be added back as people later get used to the tax and the state needs more money. These taxes also begin at low rates such as 3 percent—a major selling point of those pushing them—and inch up gradually.

Since all poor (majority female) and most middle-income people spend all their money on necessities each month, virtually 100 percent of their incomes are already subject to sales taxes. But now they may get some (minor) relief in the form of income tax credits or deductions and refunds, which would be eliminated under value-added schemes.

Eliminating "double taxation" on corporate dividends

Arguments for eliminating taxes on dividends are based on an argument that it is "double taxation." The idea is that corporations pay taxes, so when they distribute a dividend to stockholders, the money has already been taxed once and should not be taxed again.

But any taxpayer could make this same argument about sales taxes or property taxes. You've already paid income tax on the money you spend at the gas station, so paying a gasoline tax is "double taxation."

The problem with eliminating any tax is that the revenue has to be made up from other sources—meaning other taxpayers—or services have to be cut to cover the shortfall. These tax "improvements" overwhelmingly favor the rich. (And guess which gender is overwhelmingly not the rich.)

Abolishing the "death tax":

"Death tax" is a term conservatives use to describe the estate tax or inheritance tax. The term refers to the federal tax on estates *over* $22.36 million for a married couple, or $11.8 million for an individual (after the Trump tax changes doubled the previous exemptions). But the tax doesn't apply to the whole estate: taxes are due only on the portion of an estate's value that *exceeds* the exemption level. That means the estate tax is not a factor at all to over 99.7 percent of all US estates.[170]

So, repeal of the estate tax is of no benefit whatsoever to virtually all Americans, because they are never going to reach the threshold for the tax in the first place. To the contrary, doing away with the tax for the few very rich who pay it will contribute to shortfalls for the majority—shortfalls that play out in such ways as cuts to Medicaid, the Special Supplemental Nutrition Program for Women, Infants, and Children (WIC), or children's health care appropriations, to name a few.

Positive Tax Changes for Women

Any plan that makes the tax system more progressive will benefit women, because women are the majority of the poor and the majority of minimum-wage and low-wage workers. Even at higher levels of income, women make less than similarly situated men (see Chapter 8).

But there are other ways the tax system disadvantages women, and these should be fixed. Here are a few suggestions from the Money column of *Ms. Magazine*.[171]

Get marital status out of the tax code:

The "household," which is the basic tax-paying unit in the US system, is specifically defined to mean legally married couples (now including same-sex couples) or single individuals. We should redefine the tax unit so that it does not depend on marital status.

The easiest and fairest way to do this would be to follow the model used in almost all other industrialized nations, where every taxpayer is treated as an individual, regardless of the type of household. Such a change would permanently eliminate the "marriage bonus," where some couples pay less than two similarly situated individual taxpayers, and the "marriage penalty," where married couples sometimes pay more when earnings from a second worker nudge the couple into a higher tax bracket. The marriage penalty has the practical effect of encouraging one spouse (usually the wife) not to work outside the home, which in turn lowers her lifetime earnings, endangers job prospects in case of death or divorce, and lowers subsequent Social Security and retirement income.

Increase the Child Tax Credit, and apply it to all families with a payroll tax liability:

Families can get a refundable tax credit of $1,400 per child under seventeen from their federal income taxes, no matter how many children they have. But the working poor (majority female) get very little help from the Child Tax Credit, because it is deducted from the amount they pay in income tax, which is low because their incomes are so low. Yet many still have significant payroll tax bills (Social Security, Medicare).

More than 95 percent of Americans in the bottom 20 percent of the population pay more in payroll tax than in federal income tax, so expanding the credit so that it could be applied against payroll taxes would benefit low income women.

Institute paid family leave funded by unemployment taxes, with incentives for men to also take it:

The US is the only industrialized country on earth without some form of paid family leave. We should not only have a national system of paid leave but, go a step further and emulate Sweden's system. In order to get the full benefit, each parent must take a turn at caregiving—the benefit doubles if the father takes his turn.

This of course would not help single mothers, but for married couples it would go a long way toward getting men to do their fair share, leveling the playing field at home and at work.

Remove the caps on earnings subject to Social Security taxes, and give a Social Security credit for caregiving:

Social Security is the primary source of retirement income for women. The cries that Social Security is going broke (it's not—see Chapter 14), and the ever-present push to "reform" it through privatization, would lessen if more money was coming into the system.

Beginning in 2019 earnings above $132,900 are not subject to payroll taxes, meaning the rich once again escape paying their fair share (a CEO pulling down $10 million pays the same amount as a mid-manager making $132,900). And just as income tax policies effectively punish second incomes through the "marriage penalty," thereby encouraging women to stay home and take care of kids or elderly parents, the Social Security system punishes them again by entering a big fat zero for each year spent at home. That means a more meager retirement.

As above, to get men to take their turn, the credit could be expanded if both spouses took caregiving time off.

Revoke favorable tax treatments for institutions that discriminate against women:

Courts long ago ruled that religious schools that bar Black people are not entitled to tax exemptions. Yet churches that openly discriminate against women enjoy billions of dollars in tax savings through exemptions from income and property taxes, not to mention benefitting from the largesse of contributors who get to deduct their contributions from personal income taxes. In turn these funds are used to undermine women's rights.

Case in point: The Catholic church is perennially one of the largest contributors to anti-abortion referenda. The US Conference of Catholic Bishops was widely credited with being instrumental in pressuring the House to pass the Stupak amendment in 2009, which effectively eliminated abortion coverage in both private and public health insurance under the Affordable Care Act.

The Bishops stepped up their attack on women in early 2012, campaigning hard to eliminate birth control coverage from insurance coverage at any institution remotely affiliated with a church. They later increased their demands to say any Catholic business owner should be exempt from providing the coverage, resulting in the Hobby Lobby Supreme Court decision, in which the justices ruled that "closely held" corporations do not have to offer birth control in their health care plans if it goes against the religious beliefs of the owners.†

Tax rules also underwrite sex discrimination by allowing deductions

---

† In 2017, the Trump administration expanded the exemption with a new rule allowing insurers and employers (including publicly traded companies) which receive billions in tax breaks, to refuse to provide birth control if doing so went against their "religious beliefs" or "moral convictions." The rule was struck down in several courts, but is being appealed.

for business expenses at places that discriminate against women. After a national controversy in 2003 over the exclusion of women at Augusta National Golf Club, where corporations spend millions entertaining clients at taxpayer's expense, Representative Carolyn Maloney (D-NY) introduced a bill in Congress to disallow such corporate write-offs. The bill (never passed) didn't say "private" clubs can't keep women out, or that corporations can't entertain at such places. It did say they couldn't force taxpayers to foot the bill by deducting the expenses.

If some of the changes we need seem far-fetched or impossible, remember this: there was a time when the income tax itself was highly controversial. The suffragists used "No Taxation Without Representation," as a rallying cry. It's time women in the twenty-first century did the same thing.

Here are a few questions for candidates to get the discussion started:

- Do you support a national sales tax? A VAT (value added tax)?
- Do you support a "flat tax"?
- Do you support a caregiver credit in Social Security?
- Would you raise the earnings cap on Social Security taxes so those with very high salaries pay more?
- Would you revoke corporate tax deductions for entertainment at places which discriminate on the basis of gender, gender identity, sexual orientation, or race?
- Would you revoke corporate tax deductions for businesses that deny certain health benefits based on gender, gender identity, sexual orientation, or race?
- Would you revoke tax exempt status for nonprofit organizations that discriminate on the basis of gender, gender identity, sexual orientation, or race?

- Would you increase the child tax credit, and would you apply it against payroll taxes as well as income taxes?
- If you believe taxes should be lowered generally, what programs, specifically, would you cut or eliminate to pay for tax cuts?

Chapter 11

LGBTQ Civil Rights

Seventy percent of Americans say they have a close friend or close relative who is gay or lesbian, and support for gay marriage stands at 63 percent nationwide. Nearly seven in ten Americans (69 percent) favor laws that would protect lesbian women, gay men, bisexual, and transgendered and queer/questioning (LGBTQ) people from discrimination in jobs, public accommodations, and housing. Support is reliably bipartisan, though the level of Republican support has declined since President Trump was elected.[172] Yet discrimination against LGBTQ individuals continues in the workplace and in public policies and programs.

After decades of advocacy and legal campaigning, the last few years have brought significant strides in LGBTQ civil rights. Progress has been made in the military, in civil and federal protections, and in the right to marry. It has not been easy or quick, and under the Trump administration there have been some setbacks from previous gains, particularly for transgender citizens.

The eleven-year battle over amending the law to protect LGBTQ people from violent hate crimes is a perfect example of why *elected* majorities matter. Though wide majorities of *citizens* have favored protecting LGBTQ people from violence by including them in the legal definition of hate crimes, it took over a decade to get a law in place. Hate crimes expansion was first proposed in 1998, the year Matthew Shepard, a gay college student, died after he was beaten and tied to a fence in Wyoming. The Senate passed a Hate Crimes Prevention Act (HCPA) in 2004, and it cleared the House in 2005. But the Republican-controlled Congress squashed the bill in negotiations. The House passed it *again* in 2007 with 55 percent (including twenty-five Republicans) voting for it, but it was not enough to overcome a threatened Bush veto.

After the 2008 election that brought Democratic control to both the House and the Senate and put President Obama in the White House, the Matthew Shepard and James Byrd, Jr. Hate Crimes Prevention Act, which added gender, gender identity, and sexual orientation to the definition of hate crimes, was passed by Congress and signed into law by President Obama on October 28, 2009.

In late 2010 President Obama signed a law repealing the Clinton-era "Don't Ask, Don't Tell (DADT)" policy, which had prevented lesbians and gays from serving openly in the military. This was particularly important for women, because though women comprised between 14 percent and 15 percent of US military personnel, they comprised more than twice that proportion (30 percent) among those discharged under DADT from 1997 through 2009, when female discharges reached a high of 39 percent.[173] American voters favored repeal of the policy (56 percent to 37 percent), including those with family in the military (50 percent to 43 percent).[174]

Proponents of gay and lesbian rights won another significant victory in 2013, when in *United States v. Windsor*, the Supreme Court struck down a provision of the seventeen-year-old Defense of Marriage Act (DOMA) that denied federal benefits—like Social Security or the ability to file joint tax returns—to legally married same-sex couples. Striking down that part of DOMA impacted around 1,100 federal laws, including veterans' benefits, family medical leave, and tax laws. There were about 130,000 married same-sex couples in the US who up to that point had been treated as unmarried in the eyes of federal law.[175]

After years of fighting the issue state-by-state, advocates celebrated another landmark change in June of 2015, when the Supreme Court legalized gay marriage nationwide in its *Obergefell v. Hodges* decision. The majority concluded that the right for same-sex couples to marry is protected under the Fourteenth Amendment, citing the clauses that guarantee equal protection and due process. At the time, support for gay marriage had reached an all-time high with the public at 60 percent.[176]

The ruling did not stop opponents from fighting, however. Some public officials refused to issue marriage licenses on the basis that their "religious freedom" was being violated because they were being asked to perform a service that went against their religious beliefs. The Supreme Court has ruled against such reasoning, and though more such suits may be brought, they are not expected to prevail. However, "religious freedom" is still cited as a reason to deny services to same-sex couples and is still touted by many candidates as a serious problem.

Public opinion on LGBTQ rights in other areas has changed rapidly in the last few years, with solid majorities supporting equal inheritance rights, health insurance and other employment benefits, and adoption rights.[177] Support spans both political parties and all religious groups, with 69 percent of Americans overall favoring LGBTQ nondiscrimination protections: 71 percent of white mainline Protestants, 65 percent of Black Protestants, 61 percent of other non-white Protestants, 60 percent of Muslims, 60 percent of Hispanic Protestants, and 59 percent of Orthodox Christians. Even a slim majority of white evangelical Protestants (54 percent), support laws outlined in the Equality Act (below).[178]

When it comes to LGBTQ rights, President Trump says one thing but does another. During the 2016 campaign he spoke against a North Carolina law forbidding transgender people from using restrooms consistent with their gender identity. At the Republican

National Convention in 2016, he said would protect the rights of LG-BTQ people. But once in office he packed federal courts with anti-gay judges, barred transgender Americans from military service, gave the green light to those who don't want to do business with gays citing religious beliefs, and in 2019 prohibited the rainbow flag from being flown over American embassies on the fifty-ninth anniversary of the Stonewall uprising.[179]

As a candidate in 2016, President Trump stated his acceptance of gay marriage as well as lesbian, gay, bisexual and transgender rights. But since he took office, the administration has delivered a series of policy decisions that LGBTQ advocates consider dangerous to their civil rights. The actions below are only a partial list from the National Center for Transgender Equality.[180] Find a complete accounting at: www.transequality.org/the-discrimination-administration.

* In 2017, the president announced on Twitter that transgender people would be banned from serving in the military.
* In one of her first acts as Trump's Secretary of Education, Betsy DeVos revoked Obama-era guidance that protected transgender students. She later confirmed that the Department of Education was no longer investigating complaints from transgender students regarding access to bathrooms and locker rooms, as well as a range of other complaints of anti-transgender discrimination.
* In 2018 the Department of Health and Human Services circulated a memo across departments seeking to narrowly define gender as a biological, immutable condition determined by genitalia at birth.
* In April of 2019, a policy requiring troops and recruits to use uniforms, pronouns and sleeping and bathroom facilities for their biological sex, even if they identify as transgender, went into effect.

★ In May of 2019 alone, the administration published a final rule encouraging hospital officials, staff, and insurance companies to deny care to patients, including transgender patients, based on religious or moral beliefs, announced a plan to gut regulations prohibiting discrimination against transgender people in federally funded homeless shelters, and announced President Trump's opposition to the Equality Act, the federal legislation that would confirm and strengthen civil rights protections for LGBTQ Americans and others.

President Trump has appointed two Supreme Court justices (Neil Gorsuch and Brett Kavanaugh) that advocates see as hostile to LGBTQ individuals. A test to the newly reordered Court was introduced in the spring of 2019, when the Supreme Court said it would examine three cases to determine if the Civil Rights Act of 1964, which forbids discrimination on the basis of sex, applies to gay and transgender people. The Trump administration has argued that it does not. A ruling is expected in June of 2020.†

Despite the turnaround in public opinion and significant progress for LGBTQ individuals (and in light of Trump administration rollbacks), there is still work to be done insofar as legal protections are concerned. In the absence of a federal law specifically prohibiting sexual orientation or gender identity discrimination, a few states have moved on their own. Twenty-one states have laws barring employment discrimination based on sexual orientation and twenty also include gender identity.[181] National legal recognition of sexual orientation in employment laws would protect individuals from discrimination in the workplace.

Employment is not the only area in which discrimination based

---

† The cases involve a transgender funeral home director who won her case after being terminated; a gay skydiving instructor who successfully challenged his firing; and a social worker who was unable to convince a court that he was unlawfully dismissed because of his sexual orientation.

on sexual orientation or gender identity is still legal. It is also true in access to public spaces, housing, education, jury service, and credit. The Equality Act would provide consistent and explicit anti-discrimination protections for LGBTQ people across these key areas. The Equality Act was first introduced in 2015 and passed the House in 2019. Though the bill was also introduced in the Senate (with only one Republican cosponsor), it is very unlikely to even get a hearing in until there is a Democratic majority.

Questions for those that represent you (and those who aspire to do so):

- Do you support the Equality Act?
- Do you support or oppose a constitutional amendment to outlaw same-sex marriage?
- Do you believe the *Obergefell v. Hodges* Supreme Court decision legalizing gay marriage nationwide was rightly decided?
- Do you support including LGBTQ citizens in laws that prohibit workplace and housing discrimination? Have you, or would you, co-sponsor the Equality Act to do that?
- Did you support or would you have supported overturning the "Don't Ask, Don't Tell" policy banning gay men and lesbian women from serving openly in the US military?
- Did you, or would you have voted for the bill that expanded hate crimes laws to cover sexual orientation and gender identity?
- Do you support President Trump's rollbacks of transgender rights in the military, in health care, education, and access to homeless shelters?

Chapter 12

Social Security: Will I Be Dependent on "the Kindness of Strangers" in My Old Age?

In the US, both women and men are eligible for Social Security at age sixty-two (reduced lifetime benefit) or sixty-six (full lifetime benefit). The full benefit age will gradually rise to sixty-seven for people born after 1959. Benefits are based on earnings of the worker (or if married, earnings of the spouse if the spouse's income is higher).

Social Security is one of the largest entitlement programs provided by the federal government. It is always an election year issue, because the money outlays are huge, the population is aging, and some politicians like to use "the Social Security crisis" as a fear-mongering tactic or a way to promote schemes that will undermine the program. Their ultimate goal is to privatize it so the big banks can invest the money, or eliminate it altogether.

Before we get to a discussion of "fixes" candidates and lawmakers propose, a few quick facts about Social Security:

* Social Security does *not* face an immediate crisis, although there is a significant, but manageable, long-term financing problem.
* Social Security is in no danger of "running out of money," The Social Security Trust Fund is currently running a surplus.

According to the Social Security Administration, with *no changes at all* Social Security can pay full benefits through 2035, and 75 percent of promised benefits until 2093.[182]

★ Social Security is not draining the economy, and is not one of the causes of either the deficit or the national debt. The trust fund is 100 percent solvent with income exceeding expenses by $9.2 billion in 2015, though the government does keep borrowing the money for other uses.[183]

★ Between 2012 and 2035 the baby boomers will cause a slight increase in Social Security outlays, after which costs will even out and resume a gradual and manageable growth rate.[184]

★ Social Security is extremely popular among Americans, who overwhelmingly favor strengthening the program as opposed to cutting it. Voters overwhelmingly support increasing Social Security benefits. Large majorities of Americans of all ages, genders, races, and political affiliations support expanding Social Security by asking millionaires and billionaires to pay more into the system, including 70 percent of eighteen to twenty-nine year olds, 65 percent of thirty to forty-five year olds, 76 percent of forty-six to sixty-five year olds, and 70 percent of Americans over sixty-five.[185]

Now let's look at a few quick facts about Social Security and its largest group of beneficiaries—women:

★ Women represent 55.6 percent of all Social Security beneficiaries age sixty-two and older and approximately 65 percent of beneficiaries age eighty-five and older.[186] In addition to providing benefits to retired female workers, Social Security provides dependent benefits to spouses, divorced spouses, elderly widows, and widows with young children.

★ For unmarried women—including widows—age sixty-five and older, Social Security comprises 45 percent of their total income. In contrast, Social Security benefits comprise only 33 percent of unmarried elderly men's income and only 28 percent of elderly couples' income.[187]

* The average annual Social Security income received by women sixty-five years and older is $13,891, compared to $17,663 for men—a gender gap of 22 percent.[188]

* Social Security is progressive—meaning it provides more generous benefits to lower lifetime earners for the amount of taxes paid in when compared to higher earners. Because women are still the lowest earners as a group, even when working full time and year round, they benefit from this distribution toward lower earners.

* Without Social Security, 15.3 million recipients (59 percent of them women) would live in poverty.[189]

* Social Security is particularly important for women of color. The average annual Social Security income received by African American men sixty-five years and older was $14,994, compared to $13,426 for African American women.[190] Hispanic women have a higher life expectancy than the majority of the population, and tend to be concentrated in low wage jobs which may lack private pension benefits.[191]

No one disputes that long-term financing for Social Security is something we must attend to as a nation, since it could eventually pay out more than it takes in unless some adjustments are made. Politicians and parties propose various solutions, and present a variety of scare-tactic arguments about bankruptcy of the system—or even bankruptcy of the country—if nothing is done. In fact, according to experts including President Trump's own US National Security Advisor John Bolton, threats to the economy from the deficit and national debt are far more significant than any impact from Social Security.[192] According to the US Treasury Department, after the Trump tax cuts corporate tax receipts dropped from $297 billion in fiscal 2017 to $205 billion in fiscal

2018, a decrease of $92 billion, or 31 percent. The $92 billion would account for 82 percent of the increase in the deficit.[193]

Fixing the Shortfall

Setting aside doomsday scenarios, both the government and a number of respected think tanks have put forth ways to close the gap between what Social Security takes in and what it will eventually have to pay out (called the "solvency target," or in plain English, the shortfall).

Beginning in 2019 earnings subject to the Social Security payroll tax ("the cap") are $132,900 per worker per year. Anything over that is not taxed, meaning the very highest earners, including billionaires and CEOs garnering multimillion dollar salaries and even bigger bonuses, pay nothing on their incomes over $132,900. According to the government's own figures, eliminating the cap while leaving benefits as they are would actually create a long-term surplus.[194] And, it would make the Social Security tax much fairer. (Both Social Security and Medicare taxes are highly regressive—see Chapter 14.)

Investing 15 percent of the Social Security Trust fund in stocks, instead of the Treasury Bills currently used, has also been suggested by experts and AARP as a way to close some of the shortfall. This is an approach used by many state pension funds. (Note: This is *not* the same thing as privatizing Social Security—see below.)

Increasing the payroll tax by 1.4 percentage points each for employers and employee contributions would extend full funding of the trust fund until 2092.[195]

Obviously the first alternative is the easiest, and by far the fairest. Yet conservative think tanks and politicians repeatedly insist that the only way to "save" Social Security is by cutting benefits, privatizing the system, or both. Privatizing Social Security means allowing individuals to divert part or all of the money they now put in Social Security into private accounts. The AARP and other experts have long agreed that privatization is not a solution, and would in fact make the projected shortfall in Social Security much worse.

The privatization scheme is particularly dangerous for women for a number of reasons. Women live longer, and cannot outlive Social Security benefits, which are guaranteed for life. As we saw in the 2008 recession, the stock market and other investments are risky and can be greatly diminished or wiped out completely in economic downturns. Even if such accounts should make money over the long term, women would have smaller amounts to invest, resulting in smaller payouts that might not last a lifetime. Brokers might not even want accept such small sums to manage.

Most importantly, Social Security provides benefits to widows and divorced spouses. There is no guarantee that a spouse would leave a private account to his or her widow, and it is almost certain such accounts would not be left to an ex-spouse. There is also no provision for division of private accounts in divorce.

Cutting benefits would also have a disproportionately negative impact on women because more elderly women than elderly men are already poor, and benefit cuts are opposed by AARP, as well as all of the major US women's groups.

"Means-testing" Social Security benefits is a scheme that surfaces every few years. It means eliminating benefits after income passes a certain (unspecified) cutoff point—essentially turning Social Security into a "welfare" program instead of an entitlement that everyone pays into and everyone draws from. Once a program is thought of as "welfare" it is much easier for lawmakers to cut it drastically or eliminate it altogether, since the public has basically been taught that welfare is bad.

Positive Social Security Changes for Women

In addition to strengthening the long-term outlook for Social Security, we need to be thinking of ways that the system can be strengthened and made fairer for women. (Social Security is intended to be gender neutral, meaning benefits of spouses, divorced individuals, and widows are available to both women and men on an equal basis. But since women are still by far the lower earners, these proposed improvements would provide a proportionately greater benefit to women.)

Some years ago the largest coalition of women's advocacy groups in the country convened a summit to talk about how to do this. They came up with a number of recommendations, all of which could be paid for through adjustments such as those above.[196]

Family service credit:

Currently those who drop out of the workforce to care for children or elderly parents get a zero in their Social Security account for each year spent caregiving. This brings down the level of benefits at retirement, because those "zero years" of earnings are averaged in. A family service credit would mean caregivers would be given credit—at the level of minimum wage—for years out of the workforce when children are under the age of six, or providing for some "drop out" years when elderly parents need a full time caregiver. (This system is operative in a number of other countries, including the U.K. and France.)

A more detailed proposal for caregiving credit would provide the most benefits to lower earners and those who don't work at all while caregiving, but also provide some benefit to those who combine work and caregiving. Credits during caregiving years (which are now zero) would translate to higher Social Security benefits upon retirement, even if the credits were at a lower level than those for normal earnings.[197]

Improve eligibility for divorced spouses:

Currently an ex-spouse can collect benefits based on a former spouse's higher earnings if they were married ten years or longer. Improving the eligibility criteria would mean dropping this requirement to seven years, or a total of ten years of marriage and work history combined.

Improve widow(er)s benefit:

Widows are the majority of the elderly poor, and their economic circumstances worsen as they age. Depending on their particular situation, widows currently collect half to two-thirds of the combined benefit when the primary earner dies. This benefit should be raised to 75 percent of the couple's joint benefit, to go no higher than the highest earner's maximum benefit.

What Politicians Say

After discussions that have spanned decades, a few candidates and members of Congress are finally talking about changes like those above, though many more are talking about cutting, privatizing, or some combination of the two. They will need a push from women if any positive changes are to become reality.

Over the past decades Donald Trump has zigged and zagged, sometimes sounding very supportive of Social Security and other times not so much. Since his election, President Trump has partially broken his campaign promise of not touching Social Security by proposing cuts to the Social Security Disability Insurance (SSDI) program. He proposed budgetary cuts to Social Security in both his 2018 and 2020 budgets ($26 billion reduction to Social Security over the next ten years). Although presidential budget proposals are more of a talking point than final-word legislation, it nevertheless demonstrates that Trump's current thinking likely aligns with the core Republican ideology of fixing Social Security's long-term problems by reducing expenditures through cuts to benefits.[198]

Questions for candidates:

- Do you support diverting part or all of Social Security contributions to private accounts?
- Would you remove the cap on earnings taxed for Social Security so that the very rich pay their fair share? If not, why not?
- Does your plan for "strengthening" Social Security involve benefit cuts?
- Do you think Social Security should be means tested?
- Do you support benefit cuts in Social Security while maintaining tax cuts for the wealthy?
- Does your plan help those with lower lifetime earnings, usually meaning women?
- Do you think we should strengthen benefits for widows, lower earning spouses, and divorced spouses? How?
- Do you support giving some Social Security credit for years spent caring for children or elderly parents?
- Do you think the government should stop borrowing from the Social Security trust fund for other purposes, which contributes to the idea that Social Security is going broke?

Chapter 13

Violence Against Women

Violence in US society is a problem for both women and men. While men are more often victims of physical violence, certain types of violence disproportionately affect women and children—domestic violence, stalking, sexual assault, sex trafficking, and abortion clinic bombings and harassment.

The US Office on Violence Against Women has published no new information since the Trump Administration took office. Nor has the Center for Disease Control conducted a new National Intimate Partner and Sexual Violence Survey. Here are a few 2015[199] facts from the Center for Disease Control[200] and the National Coalition Against Domestic Violence (rape rates by race):[201]

* One in five women have experienced completed or attempted rape in their lifetime. A majority first experienced such victimization early in life, with 81.3 percent (nearly 20.8 million victims) reporting that it first occurred prior to age twenty-five.
* Nearly one in six women (16.0 percent, or 19.1 million) in the US have been victims of stalking at some point in their

lifetime, during which they felt very fearful or believed that they or someone close to them would be harmed or killed.

* Rape rates in the US vary by race. Twenty-two percent of Black women have experienced rape at some point in their lives, white women 18.8 percent, Hispanic women 14.6 percent, American Indian or as Alaska Native women 26.9 percent, and multiracial non-Hispanic women 33.5 percent.

* Over one third of women (36.4 percent or 43.5 million) experienced psychological aggression by an intimate partner during their lifetime.

* More than half of female homicide victims were killed in connection to intimate partner violence, the vast majority being male partners.

* Black and indigenous women are slain, in general, at significantly higher rates than women of other races, followed by Hispanic, white, and Asian/Pacific Islander.

These few facts do not begin to describe the scope of the problem. There are many other equally shocking statistics on violence involving women and children. The reader is referred to the organizations cited above, as well as the American Bar Association, for information on statistics and other aspects of the issue, including details on the Violence Against Women Act discussed below.

Stopping Violence—What We Have

Our most comprehensive federal legislation responding to violence against women was introduced in 1990. The Violence Against Women Act (VAWA) took four years to pass, and was signed by President Clinton in 1994. Here's what VAWA did:

* Established discretionary grant programs for state, local, and Native American tribal governments, including aid law to

enforcement officers and prosecutors, encouraging arrest policies, curbing domestic violence and child abuse, training for victim advocates, counselors, and probation and parole officers who work with released sex offenders.

* Funded battered women's shelters, rape prevention and education, reduction of sexual abuse of runaway and homeless youth, and community programs on domestic violence.
* Mandated several studies of violent crimes against women.
* Made changes in existing federal criminal law, and created new penalties for stalking or domestic abuse in cases crossing state lines, or forcing a victim to cross a state line.
* Strengthened penalties for repeat sex offenders, required restitution to victims in federal sex offense cases, and allowed evidence of prior sex offenses to be used in subsequent federal sex crime trials.
* Set new rules of evidence specifying that a victim's past sexual behavior generally is not admissible in federal civil or criminal cases of sexual misconduct, and rape victims can demand alleged assailants be tested for HIV.

VAWA was reauthorized in 2000, 2006, and again in 2013 (extending it through 2018), retaining most of the original programs and creating new ones to prevent sexual assaults on campuses, assist victims with civil legal concerns, create transitional housing for victims of domestic abuse, and enhance protections for elderly and disabled victims.

In 2013 additional protections were added for Native American women on reservations, granting tribal jurisdiction over domestic violence. Previously, tribal courts could sentence Native American offenders to only one year in prison, regardless of the seriousness of the crime. And tribal courts had no authority to prosecute a non-Native American for domestic violence, even if he lived on the reservation, worked for the tribe, and was married to a tribal member.

While several extensions of authorization for VAWA were

provided through 2019, authorizations for appropriations for all VAWA programs have since expired. However, thus far it appears that the expiration of authorizations has not impacted the continuing operation of VAWA programs. The Trump administration has requested 2020 funding for all VAWA-authorized programs funded in 2019, but it is unclear whether new provisions already passed by the House (below) are supported.

The House passed a new five-year reauthorization of VAWA in early 2019 that includes improvements to data collection, assessing tribal jurisdiction over non-tribal members who commit VAWA-related crimes on tribal lands, new approaches for law enforcement in assisting victims, and enforcement of the federal prohibition on firearms for those convicted of a misdemeanor crime of domestic violence and those who are subject to a domestic violence protective order. The National Rifle Association and 157 of their Republican buddies in the House opposed the firearms portion (surprise!) and the Senate has yet to vote on the reauthorization bill.

The federal Debbie Smith Act passed in 2004 is a grant program designed to eliminate the "rape kit" backlog, by preventing states from diverting the funds for other kinds of DNA backlogs. The kits contain DNA evidence collected in rape cases, and could lead to the apprehension of rapists. Jurisdictions, however, were slow to respond to provisions of the act. By 2011, there were up to 180,000 untested kits sitting on shelves in police departments, some as old as ten years.[202]

The Sexual Assault Forensic Evidence Registry (SAFER) Act, passed by Congress as part of the 2013 reauthorization of the Violence Against Women Act, refocused the Debbie Smith grant program to end the backlog. State and local grantees must now use a greater percentage of Debbie Smith funds (75 percent, up from 40 percent) directly on analyzing untested DNA evidence, or enhancing the capacity of labs to do so.

To aid in the process, the SAFER Act provides state and local governments with funding to conduct one-year audits of the untested rape kits in their possession and upload data on every individual kit into a national web-based registry. The SAFER refocus is paying off. As of 2018, thousands of rapists had been identified and arrested from old cases, and had resulted in the identification of nearly 1,313 suspected serial rapists from three cities alone—Cleveland, Detroit, and Memphis.[203]

Stopping Violence—What We Need

Despite the fact that almost all of the money from VAWA goes to local resources and supports the National Domestic Violence Hotline located in Texas (where Laura Bush is reported to have been a donor at one time), conservatives continue to claim it is a handout for "national feminist groups." Some want to do away with VAWA altogether.

Women's advocates must constantly defend VAWA and the national statistics on violence that are its underpinnings. Even though most of the statistics come from the federal government, conservative advocacy groups actively try to "debunk" the numbers. As a result, funding for VAWA is under incessant attack, and has actually decreased in the last two reauthorizations.

One gap in VAWA is in legal assistance to victims of domestic violence, which the law does not address. Studies estimate that fewer than one in five low-income survivors of domestic violence ever even see a lawyer. Yet legal advice is key for these women as they seek help from the police or the court system. Often, stopping the violence hinges on the ability to obtain effective protection orders, initiate separation proceedings, or design safe child custody arrangements. Without legal knowledge, these options are not accessible.

In 2008, then-Senator Joe Biden introduced the National Domestic Violence Volunteer Attorney Network Act that would meet this demand for legal assistance by mobilizing 100,000 volunteer attorneys willing to work on behalf of survivors of abuse. The bill did not receive hearings, and has never been reintroduced. If such a measure should ever become law, it would give the National Domestic Violence Ho-tline funds to provide legal referrals to victims who call in requesting help.[204] Since 2008, other than VAWA reauthorization, congressional action on domestic violence has been limited to "supporting the goals and ideals of National Domestic Violence Awareness Month."

Human Rights Watch recommends that the Department of Jus-tice authorize comprehensive studies that more accurately track sexual and domestic violence in the US, especially among individuals who are least likely to be surveyed by the National Crime Victimization Survey that is conducted every two years.

Overhauling gun control laws would also cut down on violence against women. It's against the law for people convicted of domes-tic violence or subject to restraining orders to buy a gun. But even that paltry prohibition doesn't cover dating partners—federal law only protects women victimized by spouses or co-parents. And if someone already owns a gun when convicted, they don't necessarily have to surrender it. A lot of the time they get to keep it to use another day.

Stalkers are usually home free too, even if convicted. Only seven-teen states bar them from buying or owning guns, but details such as whether stalking is a felony or a misdemeanor in a given state means uneven levels of enforcement. There's no federal ban at all, despite the often increasingly violent nature of stalking behavior.

There have been bills in Congress such the Manchin-Toomey amendment to the "Safe Communities, Safe Schools Act of 2013" which would have required background checks for private-party gun sales in commercial settings, including at gun shows and on the inter-net. Manchin-Toomey was supported by Mayors Against Illegal Guns and a host of other groups. It had exactly three co-sponsors. The Safe Schools Act itself was filibustered by Republicans and not reintro-duced when they gained control of the Senate in 2015.

Questions for candidates:

- Do you support (or did you vote for) continued full funding for the Violence Against Women Act, as passed by the House in 2019?
- Do you support The National Domestic Violence Volunteer Attorney Network Act that would provide volunteer attorneys for low income domestic violence victims?
- Do you think the federal government should collect more statistics on violence against women?
- Do you support closing loopholes on gun ownership to prohibit convicted stalkers and dating partners from buying guns, and confiscating guns from convicted abusers if they already own one?
- Do you support a federal law banning gun ownership by convicted stalkers?

Chapter 14

Our (Sick) System of Sick Leave, Maternity Leave, and Family Leave

Paid Sick Leave

There are no federal laws guaranteeing sick leave for employees in the US. Whether sick leave is granted is entirely up to employers, except in eleven states (CA, CT, OR, MA, VT, AZ, WA, RI, MD, NJ, MI), Washington, D.C., twenty cities, and three counties where laws are on the books.[205] In 2015 President Obama issued an executive order requiring federal contractors to allow employees to earn up to seven days or more of paid sick leave annually, including paid leave allowing for family care.

Because there is no national requirement for paid sick leave, workers' access to benefits for self-care or to care for a family member varies widely by income. For the lowest-earning families (bottom quartile), 76 percent have zero paid sick leave. For families in the middle (next two quartiles), 32 and 20 percent, respectively, lack such leave. Even for families in the top fourth of the income bracket, 15 percent do without paid sick leave.[206]

Frighteningly, during the H1N1 flu pandemic of 2009, some 77 percent of food service workers had no paid sick leave, undoubtedly resulting in many of them reporting to work with the virus.[207] There are no statistics on how many sick children were sent to school and sick parents reported to work in the 2019 US measles epidemic, but it was surely greater than zero.

For those US workers lucky enough to have paid sick leave, the benefit is limited in how it can be used. A very high percentage of plans are limited to personal illness; employees can't use it to care for ill family members. This puts us in stark contrast to much of the world—145 countries provide paid sick days for short or long-term illness, and more than seventy-nine give twenty-six weeks of time off for illness, or provide leave until the worker recovers.[208]

State laws are not as much help as they could be. Only a few states require employers granting leave to give workers greater leeway in using their sick days (e.g. caring for sick kids). While these laws help, many apply only to employers choosing to offer sick leave in the first place—there is no requirement that companies must provide the benefit.

And there is a growing backlash from business interests. More than twenty states have passed laws that prohibit local governments from imposing their own mandates, and many of those laws were enacted in the last five years. New Jersey's statewide paid-sick-leave law, which took effect in 2018, pre-empted thirteen local ordinances banning sick leave that were passed before the state mandate.[209] Bans do not always reflect the will of the voters. Most notably, in Wisconsin Governor Scott Walker signed legislation repealing Milwaukee's sick leave law—even though it had passed by ballot initiative with 69 percent support—and prohibited local ordinances from requiring businesses to provide paid sick leave to employees.

A bill called the Healthy Families Act has been introduced in Congress in every session since 2004. If it ever passes, it will require companies with fifteen or more employees to provide minimum paid sick leave and employment benefits of: (1) seven days annually for those who work at least thirty hours per week; and (2) a prorated annual amount for part-timers working twenty to twenty-nine hours a week (or who work between 1,000 and 1,500 hours per year). The new law would not affect workplaces that already have more generous sick leave policies. As of 2019 only a little over one fourth of the members of the Congress had signed on to the bill, which was languishing in committee with no hearings scheduled.

Pregnancy Leave

Like sick leave, there is no federal mandate that companies grant paid pregnancy leave. Still, there is a little more legal protection for pregnancy compared to sickness.

The Pregnancy Discrimination Act (passed in 1978) says if a woman is temporarily unable to perform her job due to pregnancy, the employer must treat her the same as any other temporarily disabled employee (e.g. someone who is injured or has had a heart attack). So if the guys in the executive suites get leave time to recover from a coronary, the girls in the word processing department must be treated equally when it comes to pregnancy, since both conditions would be considered a temporary disability. But if employers opt not to provide any paid time off for temporary disability, both workers are out of luck.

By way of comparison, out of 185 nations cited in a 2014 report from the International Labor Organization, only two lacked some form of paid maternity leave—the United States and, Papua New Guinea.[210] Seventy-eight also offered paternity leave. Of the thirty-six Member countries of the Organisation for Economic Co-operation and Development (OECD), from North and South America to Europe and Asia-Pacific as well as emerging countries like Mexico, Chile and Turkey, the US *stands alone* with no national maternity leave.[211]

If the US ever gets paid maternity/paternity leave, obviously it will go a long way toward relieving some of the family and job stress associated with pregnancy and childbirth. (And we'd just incidentally catch up with the rest of the civilized world.)

Family Leave

The US has had *unpaid* family leave since 1993, when President Clinton signed the Family and Medical Leave Act (FMLA). It was the first major bill signed into law by the newly sworn-in president, after a long and bumpy ride to the Oval Office. FMLA was the result of eight years of Congressional debate, thirteen separate votes, and two vetoes by President George H.W. Bush.[212]

Basically, the FMLA grants twelve weeks of *unpaid* leave for workers (on the job at least a year) who work for a company with fifty or more employees and can satisfy other requirements concerning hours and earnings. This means less than a fifth of new mothers and only about half of the US workforce overall qualifies. It is different from maternity/paternity leave, and it is not ordinary sick leave—it can only be used for *serious* health conditions of the employee, care of a *seriously* ill spouse, child, or parent, or for care, birth, or adoption of a child.

But the key word here is *unpaid*. Even for those whose workplaces are mandated to grant the benefit, many (probably most) employees cannot afford to take it.

Once again, the US lags behind other countries. International studies generally define paid family leave as a period of longer-term leave available to either or both parents, to allow them to look after an infant or young child, usually after maternity or paternity leave (which is a separate benefit) expires. The US is the only developed country in the United Nations without a national paid parental leave law.[213] Sweden may be the most progressive. Parents share 480 days of paid parental leave per child, and the benefits amount to 80 percent of the stay-at-home parent's salary. There are extra incentives to encourage men to take their share.[214]

US business groups (and the lawmakers and candidates they support) generally oppose such legislation. They say it would cost employers too much. No one asks how much lack of paid leave costs families.

There is some relief from states and cities, but not much. The

District of Columbia and six states offer paid family leave: California, New Jersey, Ohio, Rhode Island, New York, Washington, and Massachusetts.[215] In 2018 the National Partnership for Women and Families estimated that some one hundred cities and a few counties had also instituted paid family leave, usually for municipal employees, though no national database is available.

A handful of large corporations—mostly tech companies—have also instituted paid leave. While it's good that states, cities, and a few companies are moving on the issue, a piecemeal approach is not the answer. Access to family leave should not depend on where one lives or works. We need comprehensive federal legislation.

Women are now half the workforce and in it to stay, and it is in the national interest to craft a system whereby both women and men can take care of children and elderly parents when an emergency arises—without losing their jobs or suffering setbacks at work. Because women are still the primary caretakers in society and still make less than men overall, lack of paid leave can mean giving up a job altogether. And while an increasing number of men are also taking on caregiving obligations, men who ask for leave time are often denied or penalized because of stereotypes that caregiving is only "women's work."[216]

The virtual lack of action in Congress since 1993 has changed recently with the introduction of the Family Medical Insurance Leave Act by Kirsten Gillibrand (D-NY) in 2019. It would create a system of paid family leave financed by a payroll tax evenly split between employers and employees. Both would pay into a giant insurance pool—much like Social Security—and the wage replacement would come from that pool when needed. A good idea—but for now, passage seems a long way off. Gillibrand's bill has just thirty-four co-sponsors. (Where are the other sixty-six members of the Senate?) Companion legislation has been introduced in the House. Both are languishing in committees.

Women and men alike support better family leave policies,

according to national polls. A national survey in late 2018 shows a whopping 84 percent of voters support a comprehensive national paid family and medical leave policy—and that support cuts across party lines. Seventy percent of voters overall said they were more likely to vote for candidates that support paid leave, and 64 percent were more likely to vote against candidates that didn't.[217]

The problems of work-family balance are not going to go away. Some lawmakers have recognized that and introduced legislation to help solve the problems. Candidates need to address them too. It is up to women to pose the hard questions and determine whether the person who wants their vote supports family-friendly workplaces or not.

Questions for candidates:

- Do you support paid sick leave for employees? Have you, or would you, co-sponsor one of the bills now in Congress to provide it?
- Do you support paid maternity and paternity leave for birth or adoption of a child? Have you, or would you, co-sponsor a bill to provide it?
- Do you support paid family and medical leave? Have you, or would you, co-sponsor a bill to provide it?
- Do you support a comprehensive national plan for paid sick days and paid family leave that does not depend on where an employee lives?

Chapter 15

Child Care

Child care is one of the most challenging financial and logistical hurdles facing US families today, whether they are two-parent families or single-parent families. And most families struggle with child care regardless of whether their incomes are low, medium or high. That's because we have a hodge-podge of arrangements, and the availability of good care depends as much on where one lives as on income.

A Brief History of Child Care Programs in the United States

Beginning in the 1930s, the US government provided a modicum of public support for child care by offering some "back door" child care assistance through public programs meant to allow women to stay home with their children in the absence of another breadwinner.

In the Social Security system, this was (and still is) in the form of survivor's benefits. If a mother with small children became widowed, survivor's benefits assured she could stay home and care for the children herself. (Though initially based on the father-provider-mother-caretaker model of the 1930s, the benefit is now available to either widowed parent.)

In 1935 another benefit was created: divorced or never-married mothers who were not widows were given entitlement to (far less generous) payments through the Aid to Families with Dependent Children (AFDC) program that came to be known as "Welfare." It was assumed that with these payments, poor mothers would also stay home and take care of their own children.[218]

Government policy changed briefly during World War II, when women were needed in the workforce. The government provided child care centers, some even open at night to accommodate shift workers. But at the end of the war, the centers were abruptly closed, female factory workers were fired, and the jobs were turned over to men.[219]

A modest federal tax break was enacted in 1954 for working parents with child care expenses. Programs that were viewed as educational or developmental gained support in the 1960s, when the Head Start preschool development program (usually half-day) was implemented for children from deprived backgrounds.

In 1971 Congress passed a federal child care bill, but it was vetoed by President Nixon who called it the "Sovietization of American children." President Ford vetoed another one in 1974.

Over the years, welfare programs changed to an emphasis on getting single mothers *into* the workforce, with some support for outside child care that continues to the present day. Child Care Development Block Grants to the states were created in 1990 to help low-income families and those receiving or transitioning from public assistance with child care.

Has Anything Changed?

Virtually nothing has changed in the twenty-first century. We still do not have a national child care program, or even a national plan. No programs (just a few modest tax breaks) exist for non-poor families, and the programs we have for low-income parents are meager.

While public child care funding goes mostly to poor families, the great majority of eligible children do not actually receive it. According to the latest data available from the US Department of Health and Human Services, only 16 percent of children eligible under federal rules and 26 percent eligible under state rules actually get subsidies.[220]

Funding levels for the Child Care and Development Block Grant have waxed and waned over the years, depending on the state of the economy and the federal budget. As a result of the Great Recession, President Obama requested increased money in the stimulus package, and both Head Start and the Child Care and Development Block Grant received boosts.[221] While this was good news, funds were cut anyway as the recession continued. At the end of 2011 the money had all but dried up, and states were cutting back by as much as 30 percent.[222] Some of the funds were restored in 2014 with an increase of more than one-third.[223]

Continuing the seesaw, by 2016, child care assistance plummeted across the country and the federal Child Care and Development Block Grant program served the fewest children in its eighteen-year history.[224] In 2018, President Trump signed into law a $2.4 billion funding increase for program, providing a total of $8.1 billion to states to fund child care for low-income families. He has proposed another one-time increase of $1 billion for 2020, but experts say it "is unlikely to pass the legislative body in its current form."[225]

The situation in the US differs markedly from other countries, where child care and/or early childhood education is viewed as a public responsibility. Many countries in Europe have some form of national child care. For example, almost 100 percent of French three-, four-, and five-year-olds are enrolled in the full-day, free *écoles maternelles*. All are part of the same national system, with the same curriculum, staffed by teachers paid good wages by one national ministry.[226]

While the US is a long way from such a system, advocates argue that we should be thinking about one where most, if not all, children in the country can be served, even if it is not through a universal and standard model like the one in France.

Why Don't We Have Child Care?

In the 1970s, feminists used to say "the personal is political." They meant that problems we often interpret as personal—to be solved on our own without society's involvement—are actually reflections of the political will of the country and its leaders. Some examples back then were lack of equal access to universities, employers legally refusing to hire women or firing them for being pregnant, and domestic violence—to name just a few. Thanks to the women's movement, consciousness was raised, and people came to see these as systemic problems that society as whole should deal with. New laws were passed and programs created to address these issues and others.

One place the message still hasn't gotten through is child care. Most families have been taught by the culture to believe that when it comes to child care the "personal is personal," meaning families are on their own and there's little that can be done about it.

In terms of national policy, the US government and families alike tend to view child care as a family problem, not a public responsibility. This is the opposite view from countries in other parts of the world that provide public child care. Whether child care *should* be a public responsibility is controversial in the US. (It's worth noting that at one time public schools were also controversial with the education of children viewed as a "family matter.") Except for a few children's advocacy groups, there is no organized lobby for a national child care system.

Conservatives believe women (not men) should stay home with their children, unless they are poor single mothers, who should definitely go to work. Liberals give lip service to child care as being in the public interest, but do little to make it a reality.

Costs of Child Care

As more and more women enter the workforce and families cannot afford for one parent—or the only parent—to stay home, the need for quality, affordable child care increases. The labor force participation rate (the percent of the population working or looking for work) for all women with children under age eighteen was 71.5 percent in 2018.[227] Nearly one-third (32 percent) of US children under age eighteen live in a single-parent family, most with a solo mother.[228]

US parents pay almost all of their child care costs without state or federal assistance, amounting to a large portion of household income. This is undoubtedly the main reason why enrollment in child care and early childhood education is lower in the US than in other industrialized countries. The Organisation for Economic Co-operation and Development estimates that the cost of center-based care for two children in the US amounts to over 25 percent of a two parent family's net income—more than double the cost in almost all other developed countries, where the average is 12.6 percent.[229]

Child care tends to be the first or second-largest household expenditure, with costs of center-based care averaging $11,666 per year ($972 a month), but prices range from $3,582 to $18,773 a year ($300 to $1,564 monthly), according to the National Association of Child Care Resource & Referral Agencies.[230] For an infant, it's even higher—$1,230 per month, and in a family child care home, the average cost is $800 per month.[231] For families with two children, the price of care can easily exceed rent or college tuition in many areas of the country. So even though the Trump tax changes in 2017 increased the yearly Child Tax Credit from $1,000 to $2,000 (and very low-earning parents can get a refund up to $1,400) it's barely a dent in the actual costs.

Opponents of any kind of government help with child care say countries with child care have higher taxes, and taxes would surely go up in the US if we followed suit. That is probably true. But if we view what families are paying now as a "tax" that is not shared by everyone, a modest tax hike for a better system that all families could benefit from does not look so bad. There is strong support among parents to provide increased funding to improve the quality of child care by paying $10 more in taxes each year (73 percent of all parents, 78 percent of parents with children under age five).[232]

The economists Suzanne Helbrun and Barbara Bergmann showed years ago how national priorities play into the debate. They did a cost analysis for a medium-level system that would provide affordable care of improved quality to families, including those in the middle class. Starting with national average fees for care of children aged zero to twelve, they estimated the annual cost of a mid-level program with affordable co-pays, including how much additional money would be needed over costs of low-income programs that were already in place.[233] For the price of the defense spending for *one year*, the national child care plan could operate for over sixteen years—the span of an entire childhood.

Availability

It goes without saying that the higher one's income, the greater their ability to pay—if there is a decent program to pay *for*. Private in-home care by a nanny is almost exclusively limited to high-income families, but even that does not guarantee the availability of a trustworthy and competent caregiver.

While child care and pre-kindergarten are not the same thing, expansion of pre-k programs would help ease the child care crunch. Pre-K programs are administered by the states, and they vary widely, both in availability and funding.

According to the National Institute for Early Education Research at Rutgers University based on 2017-2018 academic year, just a third of four year olds and 5.5 percent of three year olds are enrolled in public preschool programs—virtually no change in years. At this pace, it would take states nearly twenty years to enroll even half of all four year olds and it would take nearly a century to reach the 50 percent mark for three year olds.[234]

Though it varies by location, wages for child care providers are notoriously low—the average annual pay is $21,993 a year ($10.57 per hour)[235] for full-time workers, below the federal poverty line for a family of four, and barely above the poverty guidelines for a family of three. Benefits are also minimal. This can add up to standards being compromised in order to find workers, and there is a great deal of turnover.

The vast majority of these low-paid, low-benefit jobs are held by women, and in times of near-full employment fewer will seek this work over more lucrative jobs, contributing to existing shortages of child care facilities. This in turn lowers the ability to work for mothers with young children, particularly those with children under six (an effect that is not seen in men's labor force participation).[236]

Questions for candidates:

- What would you do to increase the availability and affordability of child care?
- Do you support public funding for universal pre-kindergarten for four-year-olds? For three-year-olds?
- Have you, or would you, sponsor any bills that would help working families with child care? What kind of bills specifically?
- What is the next step you will take to move toward universal pre-kindergarten?

Chapter 16

Long-Term Care

In the US, long-term care has historically been treated as a private problem, unless you are among the poorest. Even then, there are few government resources. Medicare, the nation's medical insurance system for those over sixty-five, does not pay for personal or custodial services or long-term care. Medicaid, which provides health insurance for those with very low incomes and few if any savings or assets, will sometimes pay for nursing home or home-based care. But services and benefits depend on the state where you live, and generally assets must be "spent down" in order to qualify. The Department of Veterans Affairs (VA) *may* provide long-term care for service-related disabilities or for certain eligible veterans (e.g. low income).[237]

Long-Term Care in Other Countries

The US is far behind other developed nations in long-term care policy and practice. Long-term and elder care varies in other countries, but many provide some assistance regardless of income.

Other countries began tackling the problem for their citizens *decades* ago, according to an article by Martin Tolchin in *The New York Times*. In Canada, eight of the ten provinces now provide some form of long-term care coverage for all citizens. The Netherlands provides long-term nursing home care for the entire population. In Japan, there are geriatric hospitals that resemble American nursing homes for those who need skilled medical care, and for which the government pays the entire bill for those seventy years old and above.[238]

The US briefly flirted with providing long-term care insurance with the Community Living and Assistance Services and Supports Act (CLASS), passed as part of the Affordable Care Act in 2010. The program was purely voluntary, paid for by insurance premiums, and open to all working Americans. It would have provided a basic lifetime benefit of a least $50 a day in the event of illness or disability, to be used to pay for even non-medical needs such as making a house wheelchair-accessible or hiring a home caregiver to assist with basic tasks. But it did not survive. Opposed by a bipartisan group of senators and declared untenable by the Obama administration in 2011, it was repealed as part of the American Taxpayer Relief Act of 2012, known as the Fiscal Cliff Bill. Since then, no national action has been undertaken.

A Women's Issue

Since the US comes up short not only on national policies but on programs as well, long-term care is an issue that most families must solve on their own. And it is very much a women's issue. Caregiving remains undervalued in US society, partly due to inequities experienced by women as both caregivers and care recipients. Gender disparities are often reinforced by the family (e.g., norms regarding who should provide care) and the labor market (e.g., undervaluing the dollar value of caregiving work).

The long-term care problem hits women "coming and going," so to speak. Women live longer and therefore need long-term care more than men, and women are still the overwhelming majority of caregivers, whether paid or unpaid. The MetLife Mature Market Institute projects that half of US adults will eventually need some kind of long-term care. Seventy-two percent of nursing home residents are female, and 90 percent of paid direct-care workers and 61 percent of family caregivers are women.

Nationally, turnover rates for clinical care in nursing homes range from 55 to 75 percent with Certified Nurse Assistants having turnover rates of nearly 100 percent in some cases, meaning patient care is uneven and unreliable.[239] According to the National Center for Health Statistics, over two-thirds of US nursing homes are owned by for-profit companies, many of them corporate chains paying notoriously low wages, which are undoubtedly a major contributor to this turnover.

Unlike workers in care facilities, home care aides have historically not even qualified for the minimum wage. A labor department rule dating back to 1975 had been used to classify these workers as "companions," a class of workers that did not qualify for minimum wage or for overtime. Overturning the decades-old exemption, the US Department of Labor under President Obama extended minimum wage (then, and now, a paltry $7.25 per hour) and overtime benefits to the mostly female and minority workforce of nearly two million home health care workers, effective January 1, 2015.[240]

Purchasing Long-Term Care

In 2019 long-term care expenses were reported to be over $100,000 per year in some parts of the country.[241] Obviously the majority of families find this far out of reach. Private long-term care insurance must be purchased on the open market from insurance companies, generally while the individual is still healthy—and preferably young—in order to be affordable. And private insurers continue to charge women more than men for the same coverage.

As a result, most long-term care services are either provided by unpaid caregivers (predominately female), or paid out-of-pocket. Caregivers, particularly women and members of low-income families, are faced with tremendous stress. Many get caught in a difficult spiral.

They are forced to take time off from work, forgo promotions, and maybe even drop out of the workforce altogether to care for elderly relatives. Consequently, they work less and earn less, which reduces the Social Security and pension benefits they receive. So women, who generally live longer than men, must stretch their meager resources much further.

The Affordable Care Act bars sex discrimination in health insurance plans, but the long-term care industry has long maintained that the rules barring insurers from charging women more than men don't apply to them. The nation's largest long-term care insurer announced in 2013 that it would charge women between 20 and 40 percent more per month. Industry experts predicted the practice would become a trend—a prediction that has proven true. Although the National Women's Law Center filed federal complaints charging sex discrimination in January 2014, insurers continue to "gender rate" women with impunity.[242]

Needed: Changes in Public Policy

Abuse in long-term care facilities has turned into a political issue in recent years. Before the Obama administration, regulators could use their discretion on whether or not to punish nursing homes when patients were harmed. Near the end of Obama's term, the policy was changed to requiring regulators to punish a facility every time a resident was harmed, instead of leaving it to regulator discretion.

Regulation of nursing homes has been weakened under the Trump Administration. It granted facilities an eighteen-month moratorium from being penalized for violating eight new health and safety rules, and also revoked an Obama-era rule barring homes from pre-emptively requiring residents to submit to arbitration to settle disputes rather than go to court. In an extensive analysis, an investigation for Kaiser Health found that financial penalties on nursing homes for putting patients in "immediate jeopardy" were issued in fewer cases under Trump. And when they were issued, the fines averaged 18 percent less than they did in 2016.[243]

Even though the CLASS Act was scrapped, some provisions of the ACA might apply to long-term care purchased on the private market. Outlawing "gender rating" for policies, meaning charging women more than men for the same long-term coverage is a prominent example. The National Women's Law Center has filed a lawsuit against several insurers, reasoning that because they offer long-term care policies through Medicaid partnership programs in several states, they receive federal assistance, meaning they cannot discriminate on the basis of sex under the ACA. Litigation could take several years, and women are out of luck until the issue is settled by the courts.[244]

While we clearly do not have the long-term care supports that we should have, the need for long-term care could be reduced with other changes in public policy. According to AARP, most older people and those with disabilities want to remain independent and get the assistance they require at home or in their communities, not in nursing homes. Providing care at home or in an assisted living facility can improve quality of life and provide better value for the dollars spent.

Many of the services elders need to stay in their own homes are not medical. Transportation, help with bill-paying, and help with shopping or daily self-care are all services for which there is presently little or no support.

Providing support for these services, even funding volunteer networks, could go a long way toward keeping elders in their own homes longer, at the same time providing a higher quality of life than nursing home care that is expensive and oftentimes below par.

Questions for candidates:

- Are you satisfied with the fact that the US lags far behind other developed nations when it comes to long-term care for the elderly?

- What would you do to ease the financial burden of long-term care on families?
- Do you think a federal or state program to provide affordable long-term care insurance is needed?
- Do you think Medicare should be expanded to include long-term care?
- What would you do to improve the standards for nursing homes and ensure that patients are cared for adequately?
- Do you think the government should support pilot projects in livable communities, with services that keep seniors in their own homes longer, to see what works best? How would you do this?
- Do you believe the provision in the Affordable Care Act that outlaws charging women more than men for the same services applies to long-term care insurance from private insurance companies having partnerships with Medicaid?

Chapter 17

Education and Title IX: Back to "Separate But (Un)equal"

"No person in the United States shall, on the basis of sex, be excluded from participation in, be denied the benefits of, or be subjected to discrimination under any educational program or activity receiving federal financial assistance."
—Title IX of the Education Amendments of 1972

With these few words added to our national body of laws, sex discrimination in educational institutions that receive federal funds became illegal. Because many private schools accept some federal money, the law covers them as well as public schools at all levels—from kindergarten through graduate school.

Title IX was needed because sex discrimination (overwhelmingly against girls and women) had always been rampant in many areas of education. Most people did not realize this, because in those days sex discrimination was viewed as "normal." It was "normal" that girls could not have school sports teams; it was "normal" that girls could not be crossing guards; it was "normal" that girls were barred from auto mechanics and boys were barred from cosmetology; it was "normal" that medical, engineering, and law schools could refuse to admit women or limit female enrollment with strict quotas. It was also normal for girls to be expelled for becoming pregnant, and pregnant teachers to be fired when they began to "show." And a little sexual harassment was normal too—after all, "boys will be boys."

There is no doubt that Title IX has been a success. The numbers bear this out:

* In 1971, women were 40 percent of undergraduates overall, but could still be barred from college altogether or required to score higher on admissions tests to gain entrance.[245] In 2020 women are projected to make up 56 percent of undergraduate enrollments.[246] Broken down by race, Black and Hispanic females have enrolled at higher rates than their male counterparts since the 1980s.
* In 1971 women were awarded fewer than 10 percent of medical and law degrees. By 2018 females were awarded 47 percent of medical degrees,[247] and surpassed men in law enrollments in 2016, according to the American Bar Association.
* In 1971, only 294,015 girls participated in high school athletics, according to the US Department of Education. In 2018, girls' participation increased for the twenty-ninth consecutive year and set an all-time record of 3,415,306. This has not taken away opportunities for males, who are still by far the majority (4,565,580) of high school athletes.[248]
* The Supreme Court has ruled that sexual harassment in the schools, either by peers or school personnel, is illegal under Title IX. Before, victims of harassment, including boys, had no clear way to stop it or seek justice after it happened.

Title IX and Sports

Though the word "sports" does not appear in the law, Title IX has become closely linked in the public mind with increased opportunities for girls in athletics. Conservatives have brought lawsuits, calling it a "quota system" and charging that it is detrimental to men in sports programs.

Nothing in Title IX requires schools to eliminate men's teams. Research shows that the biggest reason minor men's sports are dropped at the college level is the football budget, which takes the lion's share of athletic dollars.

Despite its obvious success, Title IX has been under constant attack since it was passed in 1972, and rules and enforcement have varied significantly depending on which party controls the government.

In 1984 during the Reagan years, the Supreme Court issued a ruling that severely limited the scope of the law for four years† —until Congress restored it with the Civil Rights Restoration Act of 1987. Another assault came in 2005, when the Bush Department of Education issued a Title IX "clarification," which allowed schools to refuse to create additional sports opportunities for women based solely on email interest surveys. According to the new interpretation, failure of a female student to answer an email survey could be counted by the college as a lack of interest in participating in sports (the email survey scheme did not apply to men). The rule remained in effect until 2010, when the Obama Administration rescinded it.

Title IX and Sex Segregation

Prior to Title IX, girls were seldom sent to flagship math and science acceleration programs or special "star" schools for high achieving students. These spots were tacitly (or sometimes openly) reserved for boys. The only single-gender girl's schools tended to be those for pregnant students—with far fewer resources than even the regular classrooms afforded. That changed during the first thirty-five years after the passage Title IX.

Because gender-segregated schools and classrooms before the law was passed had been a hindrance to equal opportunity for girls, single-sex classes and extracurricular activities were largely limited by

---

† *Grove City College v. Bell.* See Chapter 21 for a full discussion.

Title IX to sex education classes and physical education classes that included contact sports. But in 2002, President Bush also signed the No Child Left Behind Act (NCLB), a bipartisan bill which had passed both houses of Congress with large majorities. Through a little-noticed provision, NCLB called on the Department of Education to "promote" single-sex schools. In response, new Title IX guidelines were issued in 2006, allowing gender-segregated schools and classrooms for the first time since 1972. These changes were not made by Congress, but by the Bush administration's appointees at the Department of Education, underscoring once again the importance of which party is in power. School districts can now set up single-sex options as long as the other sex is offered something "substantially" equal. "Substantially" is not defined, nor is the method for measuring success of single-sex education.

Since the weakened the guidelines of Title IX were issued, sex segregated schools and classrooms have exploded, though there is no consistent evidence that kids learn better in these classrooms than they would in mixed-gender schools with the same resources.[249] In other words, if mixed classrooms had the same low teacher-to-pupil ratios, increased funding, and individual student attention afforded in the new segregated ones, it is likely that all the students would benefit. Indeed there is evidence that socioeconomic status, school size, selectivity, and school resources are bigger factors than gender in the success of graduates of all-female or all-male colleges. The trick is not to separate students by gender, but to give all students the best educational experience possible.[250] Parents who now support or are considering single gender schools and classrooms should study the conservative positions on Title IX and single sex education, as they generally promote sex-role stereotyping and lesser treatment for girls as students. Parents should also ask themselves what the term "substantially equal" means in the Bush-era regulations. The movement has brought a proliferation of sex role stereotypes back into the schools.

In 2012 the Dallas Independent School District made national news when it excluded girls from a field trip to see the movie *Red*

Tails, about the Tuskegee airmen in World War II. The trip for the boys cost $57,000. The girls were left behind at school, and "some" were shown a six-year-old movie *Akeelah and the Bee*. The district's justification was that theater space was limited, and school officials thought the boys would enjoy the *Red Tails* outing more than the girls. They added that gender-specific events are often held.

Another example: Livingston Parish, Louisiana announced a plan to compel gender segregation in all classes in a formerly coed school. In their plan, they cited an "expert" with no education credentials who contends that "boys need to practice pursuing and killing prey, while girls need to practice taking care of babies." The plan was dropped after the American Civil Liberties Union filed suit on behalf of a girl who resisted the forced segregation.

The reader can decide whether these situations are "substantially equal." There is no reason to believe that they were isolated cases—in fact it is likely that similar instances of "not substantially equal" have increased as sex segregation has grown. The stereotypes can hurt boys as well. In a California experiment with dual academies, boys were seen as "bad" and taught in a more regimented way, while girls were seen as "good" and taught in more nurturing, cooperative, and open environments.[251]

And just because a few schools have dropped gender stereotyped plans under threat of litigation does not mean that single gender education is dead—far from it. A comprehensive study by the Feminist Majority Foundation in Washington, D.C. found that single sex schools and classrooms have been instituted in all but a handful of states (though not statewide anywhere). Further, most are in violation of Title IX, which even under the relaxed rules still requires extensive documentation as to how such segregation contributes to the elimination of discrimination.[252]

While the Obama Justice Department filed an amicus brief in one lawsuit stating that there should be a specific appropriate justification for each sex-segregated class, it did nothing to enforce the requirement that institutions prove the need for such classes and schools, nor has the Trump administration addressed it.

Title IX and Sexual Assault

Title IX has played an increasingly important role in the past few years when it comes to sexual assault on college campuses (which also includes harassment). In addition to being against criminal law, sexual assaults are a violation under Title IX. The Obama administration issued a warning letter to educational institutions emphasizing this, and his Department of Education issued procedural requirements for schools to adopt and publish grievance procedures for prompt and equitable resolution of student and employee sex discrimination complaints.[253]

The biggest threat to Title IX in decades has come with the Trump administration. The president appointed Betsy DeVos, a billionaire who donated $9.5 million to his campaign, as Secretary of Education in 2017 (confirmed by the Republican Senate by means of a tie-breaking vote from Vice President Pence). DeVos has no education degree or teaching experience, has never attended a public school or sent her children to one, and is on record as advocating for the funding of charter schools and vouchers for religious schools over public education.

The Trump education department under DeVos has issued new proposed rules governing sexual harassment and sexual assault on campus that critics say will result in many fewer cases being investigated. Proponents say it will just grant due process and even a playing field that is tilted against the accused. They would point to at least one high-profile and blatantly unfair judgment against an accused, who lost both his academic career and strong future employment prospects, and had to fight for years to clear his name.†

---

† See Powell, Michael. "A Rising Star's Record is Clean, But Now He Needs a Job," *The New York Times*, June 2, 2019.

The proposed new rules under DeVos are extensive, but here is a summary from *The Chronicle of Higher Education*:[254]

* A person accused of sexual misconduct would be guaranteed the right to cross-examine the accuser. The questioning would have to be done in a live hearing by a lawyer or other adviser, but the parties could be in separate rooms, using technology if needed. (Sounds like putting the accuser on trial). The Obama-era guidance had discouraged direct cross-examination because of its potential to retraumatize victims.

* Responsibilities to investigate would be limited to cases where there are formal complaints that are made by an official who has the ability to remedy the situation (that doesn't include reports from professors, resident advisers, and others). And the alleged incidents must happen on campus or within an educational program or activity. Critics point out that many incidents of sexual misconduct happen at apartments and frat houses just off campus, and it's not clear those would have to be investigated.

* The definition of sexual harassment requiring colleges to act would be narrower. The new rules would define sexual harassment to include "unwelcome conduct on the basis of sex that is so severe, pervasive, and objectively offensive that it effectively denies a person equal access to the recipient's education program or activity." The Obama administration defined harassment as "unwelcome conduct of a sexual nature."

* Colleges would have the option of using a higher standard of proof in deciding whether sexual misconduct occurred. Obama-era guidance told colleges to adopt a "preponderance of the evidence" standard, which means that it's more likely than not that the misconduct had occurred. The new rules would allow colleges to apply either that minimal standard or the higher "clear and convincing evidence" before initiating action.

★ Colleges would have more leeway to use mediation and other informal resolution procedures. Previous guidance had said that mediation—versus a formal investigation and adjudication process—was not appropriate in cases involving an alleged sexual assault. The concern was that alleged victims might feel pressured by their colleges to participate and that the process could be traumatizing. The proposed regulations say colleges may opt for an informal resolution at any time, provided that both parties "voluntarily" agree to it.

As of early 2020 the proposed rules had not taken effect. Over 100,000 comments were submitted during the comment period which closed in February 2019, and the Department of Education is required to respond to each one. Experts say the process could take as long as a year.

Questions for candidates:

- Do you support the proposed Title IX rules from the Trump administration making it much harder to file complaints of sexual assault and sexual harassment on campus?
- Do you believe the Bush-era Department of Education regulations that weakened Title IX and once again allow single gender schools and classrooms should be overturned?
- Do you believe schools planning single-gender classes should be required to thoroughly justify such classes as to their effects in overcoming discrimination, as required by law?
- Do you believe all schools should have Title IX coordinators and should regularly conduct Title IX self-evaluations to ensure that they are complying with the law?
- Do you think high schools should be required to publicly disclose gender equity data about their athletic programs, including funding, facilities, and sports opportunities?

Chapter 18

Affirmative Action is Our Business (and Education Too)

Though many people don't know exactly what the term "affirmative action" means, it makes them nervous anyway. They think it means a preference for hiring unqualified people (usually Black or female) over more qualified applicants (usually white men), merely because of race or gender. They also believe it means that there are "quotas" for unqualified applicants that must be filled.

The term "affirmative action" actually describes a number of policies that actively seek to overcome discrimination in hiring and promotion, government contracting, and education. Affirmative action can also refer to the process by which the under-representation of certain groups, including women, in a given workforce is corrected. It has nothing to do with quotas (they are in fact outlawed), nor does it mandate preferences.

The rationale for affirmative action rests on the fact that white males have historically been hired and promoted in greater numbers than women and male members of minority groups, and further that women and minority men are channeled or segregated into certain job categories which often pay less and offer fewer opportunities for promotion. Looking at it this way, one could say that affirmative action is meant to overcome a system of preferences (unwritten of course) that has been in place for much of our history.

Affirmative action is a part of the anti-discrimination fabric of US law. Discrimination in employment on the basis of race, religion, color, national origin, or sex is illegal under Title VII of the Civil Rights Act of 1964. But while Title VII prohibits discrimination, it does nothing to change the systems that foster discrimination in employment and education in the first place.

Because of this shortcoming, in 1965 President Johnson signed Executive Order 11246, prohibiting discrimination on the basis of race, color, religion, and national origin by the federal government and private employers and universities holding federal contracts, *and* requiring them to establish affirmative action plans for hiring and equal treatment on the job. Sex was added in an amendment to the Executive Order in 1967.

The requirement for affirmative action plans at the federal level *only* applies to the government itself, and to businesses and educational institutions holding federal contracts or receiving federal money. The idea is that our tax dollars should not be used to underwrite discriminatory policies on the part of businesses or schools benefitting from those tax dollars. *Affirmative action does not apply to private business in general*, though many companies not receiving federal contracts have developed affirmative action plans because they value diversity and believe it is good for business.

Affirmative action was designed to break down the "old boys' club" by encouraging personnel and procurement decision-makers to look beyond personal acquaintances, golf partners, and other insider networks. This is very important not only to job seekers but to women- and minority-owned businesses, since there are also affirmative action requirements for spreading federal contracting dollars fairly.

Conservatives have always attacked affirmative action programs as "quotas," calling them "reverse discrimination" against whites, usually white males. As stated above, affirmative action does not require quotas—in fact, quotas are specifically prohibited. But unwritten "quotas" that disadvantage women and minority men have been in place for decades. Those *de facto* quotas enforce long-standing norms granting outsider groups only a small share of jobs at the top, promotions, and leadership opportunities—and they gave rise to affirmative action in the first place.

An affirmative action employment plan seeks to insure that a company workforce is representative of the population of workers in the surrounding area. In other words, a plan that produces the same workforce that would result if there were no discrimination.

In addition to general hiring goals, a good affirmative action plan also includes goals for specific jobs. That's because it's possible to have a workforce that technically represents the surrounding pool of workers, but is segregated by job category. An example would be a workforce where the total is 50 percent male and 50 percent female, but 98 percent of the managers are male and 98 percent of the clerical workers are female.

For most jobs, affirmative action does not mean the workforce must reflect the total population of minority or female workers in a given area, since all of them are not qualified for every job. The number of women and minorities in a given position need only reflect the number of *qualified, available workers in the general pool of workers from which a company is drawing.*

For example, if women constitute 45 percent of the available workers in a city, an affirmative action plan for hiring unskilled workers could reasonably have a goal of 45 percent women in unskilled positions, since all women in the general labor market are presumably qualified for unskilled positions.

For skilled positions, only the number of qualified women in the surrounding labor market would be used as a basis for hiring goals. If it is known that 22 percent of the graduates of area engineering programs are women, then a reasonable affirmative action goal is 22 percent women for entry-level hiring, and a mid-level engineering workforce that is 22 percent female in a few years.

A plan for reaching female and minority applicants to let them know about job openings is normally included in affirmative action, since word-of-mouth advertising of openings in predominantly white male companies yields predominantly white male applicants.

Civil Rights or Civil Wrongs?

While support for affirmative action from 1995 to 2007 was strongest among Blacks (93 percent—no gender breakdown available), support among white women (71 percent) and men (65 percent) was also quite solid.[255] By mid-2009, even as a controversial affirmative action ruling took center stage during the confirmation hearings for Supreme Court Justice Sonia Sotomayor, public support was still very high, with affirmative action programs for women drawing the strongest support (63 percent).[256]

Poll numbers dipped in 2013 to 2014 when the question was asked only in the context of racial discrimination, with 53 to 63 percent saying affirmative action is still needed, 37 percent saying it should be phased out, and 10 percent unsure. Gender was not included in the question for several years,[257, 258] but by 2019, support had bounced back above previous highs. Overall, 65 percent favor affirmative action programs for women; and 61 percent now favor it for minorities—both new highs. The increase is driven by increasing support from whites, but there are sharp differences depending on party identification: 82 percent of Democrats, but only 46 percent of Republicans, are in favor of affirmative action for women.[259]

Affirmative action has been litigated almost since its inception, and generally courts have upheld the legality, with some qualifications.[260] It was reaffirmed in federal programs by the Supreme Court in 1995.[261] After that decision conservative attacks shifted to the states, since many states have affirmative action goals of their own for state employment, contracts with private firms, and admission to state universities.

Attacks on affirmative action at the state level are mostly in the form of ballot initiatives to outlaw the programs. The highest-profile attack was Proposition 209, passed in California in 1996 with consequences still reverberating today.

Called the "California Civil Rights Initiative" on the ballot, Proposition 209 amended the California constitution to outlaw state affirmative action programs in public education, public employment, and state contracting. Although the constitutionality of the initiative was legally challenged, the US Supreme Court denied further appeal in 1997 and let Proposition 209 stand.

Since the California initiative, a few more state anti–affirmative action initiatives have been successful. These so-called civil rights initiatives are dishonestly named, as they are *anti* civil rights initiatives. Most voters see the titles and mistakenly believe they will increase opportunities for minorities and women, not do away with them. When the City of Houston changed the ballot description of a city initiative to make it clear that the measure would overturn affirmative action, it was soundly defeated.

Only two other affirmative action decisions have reached the Supreme Court since the 1997 ruling. Abigail Fisher, a white woman, claimed that the University of Texas-Austin unconstitutionally discriminated against her after the university rejected her application in 2008 under its race-conscious admissions program.† Fisher claimed the school discriminated against her on the basis of race while accepting less qualified minority students. After ruling the program was constitutional but sending it back to the appeals court on another

---

† It is ironic that a white female was used as the plaintiff in this high-profile lawsuit seeking to outlaw affirmative action programs in education, since white women have historically benefitted greatly from them, not only in education, but also employment and government contracting.

matter, the Supreme Court finally ruled in favor of the university for the second time in 2016.[262]

A case involving a charge that Harvard University has used affirmative action goals to unfairly discriminate against Asian-Americans was recently decided in Harvard's favor by a federal judge. Appeals could ultimately send the case to the Supreme Court, where the appointment of two new justices by President Donald Trump has affirmative action supporters concerned that affirmative action could be greatly weakened or outlawed altogether. The final ruling could work against public opinion that, for now, is solidly in favor of the concept of affirmative action for both women and minorities.

Such initiatives are predominately led by one man, Ward Connerly, an African American who is very closely affiliated with contractor groups that contribute most of the money to his organization.[263] In addition to his outright victories, Connerly's threat of an anti-affirmative-action initiative in Florida in 1999 prompted then-Governor Jeb Bush to ban "racial preferences" at public colleges and universities as a preemptive measure. Racial affirmative action has also been discontinued at individual institutions, such as the University of Georgia and Texas A&M University.

Publicity advocating for anti-affirmative action initiatives usually centers around "unfair" university admission policies, though the true target is believed to be government contracting. In one sense it doesn't matter—once the initiatives pass, they apply to schools, jobs, and contracts equally. And they apply to white women, as well as minority women and men. The results are stark:

* In the year after Washington State passed its anti-affirmative action initiative, the freshman class at the state university had 40 percent fewer Blacks and 30 percent fewer Hispanics than the previous class. And business dropped dramatically for firms owned by minorities and women that previously qualified for

set–asides.[264] A push to overturn the initiative was begun in 2019; the push to keep it in place is led by Ward Connerly.

★ The percentage of women employed in the construction industry dropped 33 percent after Proposition 209, despite an increase in construction employment overall.[265]

★ In the first six years after Proposition 209, contracts to women-and-minority-owned firms were cut in half. Many have struggled to stay in business, drastically shrinking the number of jobs they can provide.[266]

★ The effect of 209 was evident in the first year in its impact on admissions. At UC Berkeley Law School, admissions of Black students dropped by 80 percent and Hispanic students by 50 percent.[267]

★ Ten years after Proposition 209, only one hundred African American students (twenty were recruited athletes) enrolled at UCLA—2 percent of the 4,802 total students. It was lowest in more than thirty years, even though the percentage of African Americans meeting admission requirements for the UC system had risen steadily since Proposition 209. Critics labeled this "race-based exclusion."[268]

★ By 2010, UC Berkeley was one of the lowest in the nation among its peer institutions, with only 17 percent minority enrollment—despite its location in a highly diverse area. By 2013, minority enrollment had dropped to 15 percent.[269] The Director of Undergraduate Admissions blamed Proposition 209 directly.[270] In 2018 females were 52 percent overall (majority whites and Asians) but other minorities including Hispanics and Blacks (women and men) were still stuck at 26 percent.[271]

★ The University of California has also noted a significant decline in the number of female faculty since Proposition 209 was implemented.[272]

There is no question that affirmative action is still needed. The pay gap between women and men begins right after college and grows in succeeding years.[273] Job segregation remains the norm, with women concentrated in teaching, nursing, clerical and sales—relatively low paid positions when compared to "men's jobs" like technical, management, and skilled trades. Minority women are hardest hit by cuts in admissions to professional schools and also by loss of job opportunities.

According to *Fortune*, there are a mere thirty-three women heading Fortune 500 companies in the US—just 6.6 percent. (And that was touted in the press as a record high!) In 2018, women held only 25 percent of Fortune 100 board seats—women of color held a measly 5.8 percent.[274] (Counting the actual number of women rather than percentages would yield lower numbers, because many women serve on multiple boards, especially minority women.)

Women-Owned Businesses Don't Get the Business

Women in business have much at stake in the elections, particularly those who want to contract with the federal government. The US government spends over $200 *billion* per year contracting with private business for goods and services. It is the largest purchasing organization in the world. The bulk of these contracts go to large corporations such as KBR and Halliburton.

For many years women were not included in programs setting aside procurement dollars for small disadvantaged businesses, unless they were members of racial or ethnic minority groups. To remedy the situation, Congress passed a law in 1994 mandating a 5 percent set-aside for women-owned-businesses. The law—the Equity in Contracting for Women Act—was created to improve the track record of the federal government in awarding a fair share of annual procurement spending to women-owned businesses.

Six years later the goal had not been met, so in 2000 Congress ordered the Small Business Administration (SBA) to write new rules to ensure that women-owned businesses got the targeted amount. It took the Bush administration seven years after that to actually develop and publish the rules, and then only because the US Women's Chamber of Commerce sued the SBA to force the agency to follow the congressional mandate.

When the rules did come out, female business owners were outraged. Even though the SBA's own data revealed that women got a disproportionately low number of contracts in three fourths of the 140 industries in which the agency does business, it listed only four where women-owned businesses could be preferred. One of those was furniture manufacturing—primarily done offshore. Contracts awarded under the program were also tiny—held to $5 million or less for manufacturing and $3 million or less for other areas.[275]

In 2010 the 5 percent regulation that established a federal procurement program for women-owned small businesses was at last finalized. And in 2013, the Small Business Administration announced the removal of caps on the contract award size for which they had been able to compete.[276]

After almost two decades the federal government under President Obama finally met the 5 percent contracting goal for women-owned businesses as a share of all contracts. The SBA also added thirty-six new industry categories where women can now compete for set-aside contracts and sole-source awards.[277] No substantive changes have taken place under President Trump; the 5 percent goal was missed by a small amount in his first year in office.

Though progress is finally being made, it is likely to take years for women to catch up—and a lot depends on who's in charge at the top. The last two decades have shown that much depends on the administration in power, and its willingness to enforce (or impede) the law. Even though the number of women business owners is growing at twice the rate of other businesses, a large gap still exists in the share of federal dollars going to contracts with women-owned businesses.

Although it is clear that small businesses owned by women have made some progress in the federal marketplace, there are still areas for improvement. There is a high rate of turnover among vendors, as well as evidence of contractors falsely claiming to be female or minority owned when they are not. The National Association of Small Business Contractors has called for enforcement of fines and legal consequences for large businesses that misrepresent their use of small business sub-contractors or erroneously represent themselves as "small," "women-owned," or "minority-owned."[278]

Questions for candidates:

- Do you support or oppose affirmative action in education, employment, and contracting?
- How would you prevent the drastic drop in university admissions for minority students that has been shown to happen when affirmative action programs are eliminated?
- What would you do to eliminate the "glass ceiling" in earnings and employment opportunities for women, particularly as they try to move up the ladder?
- Do you believe in set-asides in government contracting for women-owned businesses?
- Would you limit these set-asides to disadvantaged women?
- How would you be sure the Small Business Administration complies with the mandate from Congress that women-owned businesses get 5 percent of contracting dollars?
- Would you increase the amount of dollars the government sets aside for these contracts? How?

Chapter 19

More than a Few Good Women— in the Military

Who are the Military Women? Fast Facts from the Service Women's Action Network[279]

* Since the end of the draft in 1973, the percentage of female active duty troops has increased dramatically from 1.6 percent in 1973 to 16.3 percent as of February 2018. Today over 210,000 women serve on active duty in the military services (Army, Navy, Marine Corps, and Air Force), and another 5,955 serve in the Active Coast Guard—part of the Department of Homeland Security in peacetime.

* Reserve and Guard components also have an increasing percentage of women in their ranks: 158,090 (19.8 percent) of all personnel serving in the six Reserve and Guard forces. Women number 1,067 (17.4 percent) of all personnel serving in the Coast Guard Reserve.

* About 61 percent of the enlisted women are minority, as are about 38 percent of women officers. The Army has the highest proportion of African Americans among its women and the Coast Guard the lowest (35.2 percent and 6.1 percent respectively).

* West Point graduated the largest class of African American women in history (thirty-four) in 2019.
* In recent years, the percentage of Hispanic service women has risen from between 12 to 13 percent in 2011 to about 17.8 percent today. The Marine Corps has the highest percentage (28.5) and the Coast Guard the lowest (13.9).
* Native American women comprise .01 percent of military women, Asian American women comprise 4.9 percent, and Pacific Island women comprise 1.3 percent.
* Gay, lesbian, and bisexual personnel begin serving openly in the military as of September 2011.
* About 19 percent of military women are officers, while about 17.3 percent of military men are officers. The numbers (female colonels and captains) are 10.6 percent for the Army, 11.6 percent for the Navy, 14.1 percent for the Air Force, and 11 percent for the Coast Guard. The Marine Corps lags behind the other services; only 2.3 percent of Marine Corps colonels are women.
* As of early 2018, there were sixty-three women admirals and generals on active duty in the five services—up from just over thirty in 2000.

An increasing number of female officers are serving in mainstream combat occupations. These include pilots, navigators, and other air crew in all services, surface and submarine warfare in the Navy, and long-range air defense in the Army. Women now command Air Wings and Naval Fleets, as well as combat vessels, long-range artillery battalions, air squadrons, and carrier strike groups. Female aviators, surface warfare officers, and long-range field artillery officers have been promoted to flag and general officers, and a few have attained four-star rank. As women progress through the ranks in recently-opened ground combat units and occupations, they are expected to reach command positions in platoons, companies, battalions, and brigades, right up through general officer ranks.

Despite recent gains, military women have traditionally faced a number of obstacles to full equality, including denial of combat jobs, rape and sexual assault, access to abortion, and equal treatment as veterans. Most of these barriers remain. This chapter outlines each of the problem areas, with information on what has—and has not—been done about them.

Denial of Jobs: A History

Although females have served in the US military since 1901, until very recently they were the only American women whose professional advancement was artificially curtailed by government laws and policies. In the last decade, laws banning women from serving on military aircraft with combat missions and aboard combat ships were repealed. But under the combat exclusion rule dating back to 1994, women were still barred from serving aboard submarines, in infantry, armor, and most artillery units, or in Special Forces units, even though military leaders themselves said these bans were increasingly artificial and meaningless given modern combat realities.[280] Their primary recommendation was opening combat jobs to women.[281] The public also supported—by a 66 percent majority—opening combat jobs to women.[282]

Despite the combat exclusion rule, women were in fact put in combat roles in Afghanistan and Iraq, through being "attached" to combat units. But they were sometimes dropped into those units without proper training, and they got no official credit for the combat experience, which is required for advancing up the ranks.[283] Four women who served in those theaters filed a federal lawsuit to end the ban on combat roles, maintaining that despite the fact that changes that opened more than 14,000 positions to women had been announced earlier in the year, females were still barred from 280,000 military jobs.[284]

After many years of campaigning by advocacy groups and women in the military themselves, the rules were finally changed. In January of 2014, the Pentagon announced that all combat roles would be opened to women. Over a number of objections in branches of the military (most notably the Marine Corps†) in 2015 Secretary of Defense Ash Carter announced that women can now enter any Military Occupational Specialty and serve in any unit for which they meet the standards.

Rape and Sexual Assault

Rape and sexual assault against women in the US military—by other soldiers, contractor personnel, and training officers—has long been identified as a serious problem. Air Force General William Begert, who investigated sexual assault in the military way back in 2004, uncovered scores of rape accusations, a rising trend of reported abuses, and the most basic shortcomings in tracking the crime and attending to its victims.[285]

By 2012, a damning report by the Pentagon revealed that sexual assault in the US Army had increased 64 percent since 2006, with 3,191 reports. But in announcing new initiatives to bring down the numbers, then–Secretary of Defense Leon Panetta said that, realistically, the estimate for assaults "actually is closer to 19,000."

According to the latest Pentagon report, sexual assaults have continued unabated in the last decade, up 38 percent from 2016 to 2018. All of the increase was due to assaults on women—rates for men did

---

† The Marine Corps had long claimed that integrating women into combat would erode morale and lead to more sexual assaults. But a Corps study leaked by a women's advocacy group in 2015 shows that is not the case. After months of testing mixed-gender combat units, troops reported morale equal to all-male groups and assault levels no higher than in the Marines as a whole.

not go up. Not surprisingly, the highest numbers were for the Marines, followed by the Navy, Army, and Air Force respectively.[286] The report came on the heels of a "rape list" scandal in the Navy, in which a sexually explicit list targeting female crew members surfaced aboard the service's second submarine to integrate women, resulting in the firing of a commanding officer and several other punishments.[287]

Women working for war contractors in Iraq have also been raped, with contracting companies such as Halliburton and KBR ignoring or covering up the allegations. These women have no access to the military justice system, and in the past have been required to sign pre-employment arbitration agreements cutting off their access to the US criminal justice system.[288] This was "sort of" remedied in 2009, when a bill was passed that guarantees such women a day in court by withholding contracts from companies that require binding arbitration in cases of sexual assault (thirty senators voted against it). However, the provision must be reviewed annually and the DOD can exempt contractors from complying in the name of "national security."

Sexual assault and rape in the military have drawn intensified scrutiny from Congress, particularly by women in the Senate. It has long been known that the main reason women are reluctant to report sex crimes against them is the structure of the reporting system. Women must report rapes and assaults to their commanding officers, who are more often than not also the commanding officers of the perpetrators.

Commanding officers have near-total authority over whether a case is prosecuted and in selection of jurors. In the small fraction of reported cases that are prosecuted, they can overturn convictions without explanation. Commanders also decide whether or not assaults go on the record, and (emulating the Catholic Church on pedophilia) can transfer perpetrators to other assignments without noting past history.

In 2014 and again in 2015 and 2017, Senator Kirsten Gillibrand (D-NY) put up a fight in the Senate with a bill to remove decision-making on prosecuting sexual crimes from the chain of command, putting it instead in the hands of military prosecutors. Her bill was never passed by the Senate.

Other bills have been introduced to tackle the problem. One would leave the chain of command intact, but eliminates the "good soldier" defense that takes irrelevant factors such as the service record of the accused into account. It also would require that in every promotion decision the commander's record on the handling of sexual-assault cases must be taken into account. It is unclear whether any of these provisions will ever actually become law. Until Congress gets the backbone to do something about it, the current system that greatly disadvantages victims will remain in place.

Access to Abortion

Despite the alarming rate of sexual assault in the military, which obviously can result in pregnancy, until 2013 US military women could not obtain abortions in military facilities unless their lives were endangered (no rape/incest exception), even if they paid for the procedure with their own money. Nor could military insurance cover abortions except in the case of life endangerment. That means military women did not have the same coverage provided to civilian women who work for the federal government, to women on Medicaid in some states, and those serving time in federal prisons.[289]

The restrictions were eased by a small amount with the military budget bill signed by President Obama in early 2013. Servicewomen and members of families covered by military insurance can now obtain abortions for rape and incest in addition to life endangerment. If an abortion is needed or wanted for any other reason, it cannot be obtained at a military facility, and cannot be paid for by military insurance, even if performed at a private hospital.

When deployed overseas, this extremely restrictive abortion policy creates major hardships—women must resort to unsafe local facilities, or petition for leave to travel to a safe hospital or clinic in another country. In many foreign countries, abortion is illegal, meaning nonmilitary facilities are not available, whether safe or not.[290] Obviously this situation is a danger to the health and well-being of military women and female members of military families covered by military insurance. While bills to overturn military abortion restrictions have been introduced in Congress, none have had committee hearings, nor have they attracted a critical mass of co-sponsors in the House or the Senate (another reason to elect more women).

Divorce and Child Custody

Women in every military branch are twice as likely to get divorced as men.[291] Divorces in the Army alone have doubled since September 11, 2001, with one in five couples separating within two years of one spouse's deployment. Critics charge that Congress has failed to appropriate adequate money for counseling and support services to help keep families together after the deployment has ended.

Additionally, there have been too many horror stories of women and men going away to combat, only to return and discover they have lost custody of children. This has happened because state family court judges have ruled that state family law takes precedence over the Servicemembers Civil Relief Act (SCRA), the federal law that protects members of the military from such events as property foreclosures while they are away, but does not safeguard them against loss of their children.

SCRA was completely overhauled in 2003, but it did not clearly spell out custody rights for service members deployed overseas. Advocates want to ensure that jurisdiction rests with the state where the child resided before the soldier deployed, to prevent non-custodial parents from moving children to more "sympathetic" states when seeking changes in custody orders. Though a bill to this effect was introduced in 2009, it never became law. Custody disputes involving servicemembers are still subject to a hodge-podge of state laws,[292] and many require the involvement of courts and attorneys—options not always available to those on overseas deployment.

Veteran's Services

The Department of Veterans Affairs (VA) projects that by 2045, 20 percent of veterans will be female.[293] Yet the VA seems ill-equipped to serve the needs of women. As military women return from fighting in hot spots around the world, they are finding that veterans' services aren't meeting their needs.

In a comprehensive 2018 report, the Disabled American Veterans organization found that female veterans have a unique set of circumstances and needs compared to their male counterparts. Women veterans tend to be younger, more racially and ethnically diverse, more likely to be divorced, have child care responsibilities, less likely to be married, and five times more likely to be in a dual-service-member marriage than men. All of this means that female veterans are less likely to have a family support system and often shoulder greater economic stress than male veterans.[294]

Due to a variety of problems, women are the fastest growing group of homeless veterans. According to the latest figures available from the National Center on Homelessness Among Veterans funded by the VA, the number of female veterans identified as homeless, or who accessed VA programs to end homelessness tripled to 36,443 in a five-year period ending in 2015. That figure is projected to rise by about 9 percent to nearly 40,000 by 2025.[295]

Many homeless female veterans are victims of military sexual trauma and tend to shy away from help because they feel they were betrayed in the past. According to VA's National Center for PTSD, data from VA's military sexual trauma screening program show that about one in four women and one in one hundred men respond "yes," that they experienced sexual trauma or assault while in the military.[296]

Health care from the VA is another huge area of concern for female vets. Women using the VA facilities cite sexual harassment by male vets while visiting VA medical facilities as an overarching problem. Women often have to wait longer for appointments than men, and the VA still does not provide on-site obstetric care. Dismissive treatment by staff is another problem—reflecting the belief that benefits are for men as embodied in the organization's motto "To care for him who shall have borne the battle and for his widow, and his orphan." (Changing the motto is the subject of current legislation.)

All told, while the VA is making some progress, it is not keeping up in accommodating the growing number of women needing its services. Reports indicate that in addition to more funding and perhaps some separate facilities dedicated to women's health, an "attitude adjustment" may be needed in the leadership of the VA.[297]

Clearly the US must do better by its women in the active military, and female veterans. Here are some questions for those in a position to make those improvements.

Questions for candidates:

- Do you support allowing women to hold all military assignments for which they are qualified?
- Did you, or would you have, voted for the Gillibrand bill removing jurisdiction over military sexual assault from the chain of command?
- What would you do to stop the epidemic of sexual harassment, rape, and sexual assault that military women are experiencing from other soldiers and contractors?
- Do you think women who work for contractors who are raped should have access to the US criminal justice system? The military justice system? Did you vote for, or would you have voted for, the Franken amendment guaranteeing such women their day in court?

- Do you support widening the availability of abortion services for women in the military beyond rape, incest, and life endangerment at military medical facilities? Have you, or would you, sponsor any bills to that effect?
- How would you help returning veterans with family problems of divorce and family violence that seem to be associated with deployments?
- How would you protect military personnel from losing legal custody of their children while on deployment?
- Would you support funding additional services to combat homelessness among female veterans?
- Do you think more money is needed for the VA to modernize and expand its medical facilities to accommodate the growing number of female veterans?

Chapter 20

Global Women's Rights

In the every election, candidates and voters have the opportunity to spur the US toward greater global leadership in improving the lives of women worldwide, especially in poverty-stricken regions, conflict areas, and emerging democracies. Our government has sometimes exercised leadership in bettering the situation for women around the world, but often the efforts have stalled, or in some areas gone steadily backward.

Reproductive Health and Family Planning

One of the longest-running and most contentious areas of US influence regarding women internationally has been international family planning. The United States began its involvement during the Nixon administration. Since then, it has become highly politicized.

The history of the United Nations Population Fund (UNFPA) is instructive as to how family planning has become a proverbial "political football." The UNFPA was created to support family planning and reproductive health services, including maternal and child health care, in low-income countries. The United States was UNFPA's largest contributor, and we matched all other contributions in the first several years of the program's existence.

Funding cuts began in the early Reagan years, and money was cut off entirely from 1986 through the end of George H. W. Bush's term in 1992. The justification was that the program did not comply with restrictions that had been passed by Congress in 1985, which bar US funding for any international organization that the *president certifies* "supports or participates in the management of a program of coercive abortion or sterilization."[298] It also prohibits granting US funds to any overseas health clinic unless it agrees not to use its *own, private, non-US funds* for any abortion-related services. This prohibition has been dubbed the "global gag rule," and is also known as the Mexico City Policy.

President Clinton restored funding to UNFPA in 1995. That year, representatives from 179 nations met at the UN International Conference on Population and Development in Cairo, to develop a landmark plan linking economic and social development with women's reproductive rights. They set a goal of universal access to reproductive health services by 2015, and pledged to invest $17 billion in population programs annually by 2000. The US Congress appropriated $50 million for UNFPA, but then withheld $10 million of it, stipulating that no US funds could be spent in China because of its birth limitation policies.

On his first business day in office, President George W. Bush again reinstated the global gag rule despite repeated appropriations from Congress—and several reports from government agencies—concluding that there is no evidence that UNFPA has knowingly supported or participated in a program of coercive abortion or involuntary sterilization in China.

Since the main work of many of these clinics is birth control information (obviously reducing the need for abortion), women in poor countries have suffered. Lack of funds has caused many clinics to close altogether.[299]

In keeping with the trend since UNFPA was put in place, President Obama overturned the gag rule as one of his first acts after he was inaugurated in 2009. The memorandum rescinding it also allowed the US Agency for International Development to once again provide millions of dollars to programs offering medical services, birth control, HIV prevention, and other care.

In May of 2011 the Republican-controlled House of Representatives voted to completely cut off federal family planning funds to Planned Parenthood (a major provider of reproductive health services in underserved countries as well as at home), because the organization also provides abortion services, though not with federal money. The bill was defeated in the Senate, but only because a threatened filibuster by Democrats made passage contingent on sixty votes. Underscoring the point that majorities matter (in this case a Democratic majority), the bill drew forty-seven votes, all Republican. Republicans gained majority control in the Senate in 2014, and cutting off funds for Planned Parenthood once again became a top priority. The Tea Party caucus in the House ousted long-time Speaker John Boehner in 2015, partly because he refused to go along with a threatened government shutdown unless Planned Parenthood was defunded. Even with Boehner gone, the Tea Party caucus was not successful in defunding Planned Parenthood.

On January 23, 2017, a mere three days after he took office, President Donald Trump reinstated and expanded the global gag rule in one of his first acts as president. As it stands currently, the rule targets international organizations that work on any programs funded by US global health assistance—including programs to expand access to contraception, prevent and treat HIV/AIDS, combat malaria, and improve maternal and child health.[300]

Women in US Conflict Areas

Afghanistan

As we all know, for almost two decades the US has been engaged in a war in Afghanistan. The war began in 2001, in retaliation for the

195

September 11 attacks on New York and Washington D.C. by Al Qaeda terrorists. Afghanistan was known to have sheltered the group and its leader, Osama bin Laden.

At the time the Afghanistan conflict started, women and girls were being persecuted by the Taliban, the militia then ruling the country. They were denied basic human rights: not allowed to work or go to school, forced to wear head-to-toe burqas with even the eyes covered by mesh, and confined to their houses unless accompanied by a male relative. Women were stoned to death in stadiums filled to capacity for infractions such as sex outside marriage.

President George W. Bush promised to liberate women from this tyranny, and some progress was made in the initial stages of the war. But over the years, as the Taliban gained back much of the strength they lost immediately after the start of the war, women and girls have been persecuted once more. Girls' schools were routinely burned to the ground (by one estimate, one per day), female teachers killed for "going against Islam,"[301] and in 2009 then-President Hamid Karzai signed a law that legalized marital rape, which included clauses allowing men to deny their wives food if they refused to have sex.[302] In late 2011, Karzai publicly approved a decision by the Afghan government to pardon a woman who had been imprisoned for adultery after she had been raped—but only if she agreed to marry the rapist.[303] Though President Obama verbally condemned the law, the US did not make overturning it a condition of continued military or humanitarian assistance.

Since the announcement of the US pullout planned for completion at the end of 2016 (which did not happen), violence against women has escalated, and women are back in the burqa in fear of their lives. US women's groups and women in the Senate are worried that a swift withdrawal from Afghanistan announced by President Trump will result in major setbacks for women, and women's rights have not been on the agenda for peace talks.[304]

Their fears are well founded. The Taliban now refuse to negotiate

with the Afghan government, and peace talks have been directly between the Taliban and the US. In April 2019 it was announced with
great worldwide press fanfare that women would be included in the
Taliban delegation for the first time in an upcoming peace conference.
The next day Taliban leaders said comments about women were "misconstrued," and "We still have a clear-cut policy that we wouldn't allow women to represent us in any capacity or work publicly when we
come into power" according to one Afghanistan-based commander
speaking to NBC News.[305]

During the same month, girls' schools were firebombed in western Afghanistan. Officials had been told earlier to fire all the male
teachers, because girls should not be taught by men. Though the Taliban who controlled the area denied responsibility for the bombings,
graffiti left behind on a nearby wall read, "Long live the Islamic Emir-
ate"—the Taliban's name for their movement.[306]

Iraq

Even though there was no evidence that Iraq was connected to Al
Qaeda in Afghanistan, once the Iraq War began in 2003 the country became a haven for terrorists from other countries. As husbands
disappeared or were killed in the fighting, women lost much of their
freedom to move about and hold jobs. Many turned to prostitution to
support themselves and their children.[307]

President Obama completed the process of withdrawing American combat troops from Iraq in December 2011. In his withdrawal
speech and ceremony, he did not mention Iraqi women or women's
rights. President Trump visited the 5,200 remaining troops in Iraq
there to "keep watch" in 2018, but also did not mention Iraqi women
in his remarks. A few days after the visit, The London School of Economics and Political Science highlighted the ongoing deterioration of
women's rights:

Gender inequality in Iraq is high, and discriminatory laws and practices in the legal system show no sign of changing. The growth of militancy and extremism and the deterioration of economic and social conditions since the 2003 intervention led to further increases in violence against women and the restriction of women's freedom of movement in public places. This is despite the gains women made in political participation and local campaigns for women's human rights and gender equality.[308]

Sexual Violence

Civilians in conflict zones—particularly women and children, but also men—are often vulnerable to sexual violence, including rape, mutilation, and sexual slavery. This violence is carried out by government security forces and non-state actors including, rebel groups, militias, UN peacekeepers, and criminal organizations.

While such abuses are by no means limited to Africa, weak institutions in many African states can mean that victims have little redress; in addition to health and psychological consequences, survivors are also often shunned by their families and communities. Congress has repeatedly expressed interest in bringing attention to the issue and support for programs to address it through legislation and hearings.

Former Secretary of State Hillary Clinton took the lead on the Obama Administration's initiative to address sexual violence through speeches, official travel, public remarks, writings, and actions at the United Nations. Despite the efforts of Clinton and numerous congresses over the years, the issue of sexual violence in conflict is complex, and seemingly intractable. It has implications for international programs and policies related to health, humanitarian relief, global women's issues, the justice sector, the security sector, and multilateral activities. Potential issues for Congress include the authorization and appropriation of targeted assistance programs, oversight of programs already in place, and urging of allies to participate.

Under the Trump Administration, the US has backtracked on international women's issues. In its annual human rights reports issued by US State Department in 2018 and 2019, the section that previously reported on women's reproductive rights, including rates of preventable maternal deaths and access to contraception, was excised.

On April 23, 2019, the UN Security Council held an open debate on conflict-related sexual violence. In the final stages of negotiations around the text, the US threatened to veto the resolution unless it completely removed references to sexual and reproductive health. Even after a compromise was reached—one that omitted the language around sexual and reproductive health, but referenced a previous resolution that does—the US refused to accept any language that recognized that victims of rape in war should have access to sexual and reproductive health services, because the Trump administration believes it implies access to abortion. The resolution was ultimately adopted without any language on access, a victory for the Trump administration and a major blow to the global women's rights movement.[309]

International Treaties

The Women's Human Rights Treaty: CEDAW

The major worldwide treaty guaranteeing the rights of women worldwide is known as CEDAW, which stands for Convention on the Elimination of all Forms of Discrimination Against Women. To shortcut the unwieldy name, it is often simply called the women's human rights treaty.

CEDAW is the most authoritative UN instrument protecting women from discrimination. It is the first international treaty to comprehensively address fundamental rights for women in politics, health care, education, economics, employment, law, property, and marriage and family relations. The US is the only industrialized country in the world that has not ratified CEDAW. By not ratifying, the US is in the company of Iran, Sudan, Somalia, Palau, and Tonga.

The CEDAW treaty was actually signed by President Carter in 1980, and sent to the US Senate for ratification. To be ratified after the president signs it, a treaty must be reported out of the Senate Foreign Relations Committee and scheduled for a vote on the Senate floor. Once on the floor, it must pass by a two-thirds majority.

This is another case where committee control is important, because the committee chair can schedule hearings and committee votes to send legislation to the floor, or bottle it up without a hearing for many years.

Both Democrats and Republicans have at various times been in control of the White House and the Senate since President Carter signed the treaty. But the Senate Foreign Relations Committee has failed to act under both parties. Hearings were not held until 1990, a full ten years after Carter signed the treaty. In 1993, sixty-eight senators signed a letter asking President Clinton to support ratification of CEDAW. After a 13-5 favorable vote by the Foreign Relations Committee in 1994, a group of conservative senators then blocked a Senate floor vote.

Eight years later during the George W. Bush administration, Senate Foreign Relations Committee Chair Joe Biden held hearings in June 2002. The Committee voted 12-7 in favor of sending CEDAW to the full Senate for ratification. Bush was against it, and time ran out on the congressional session before a floor vote could be scheduled, meaning the process would have to be repeated by a new Foreign Relations Committee.

Even though President Obama declared CEDAW a priority and his Secretary of State Hillary Clinton advocated for it, the treaty never advanced higher than two subcommittee hearings in 2010 and 2014, and it never came up for a vote in the Senate.

President Trump took direct aim at CEDAW less than a month after he took office in his Draft Executive Order on International Treaties issued at the World Trade Organization conference in New Delhi in February 2017. In the first paragraph, he repeated the decades-old canard that the treaty would "prohibit the celebration of Mother's Day and require the decriminalization of prostitution."[310]

Conservatives do not want the US to ratify CEDAW. In addition to the Mother's Day claim, they say that it is a "global Equal Rights Amendment." Progressives, human rights, and women's rights groups urge that it be ratified, arguing that the US cannot occupy the moral high ground in global women's rights until our country signs the treaty. If the US does not sign, it encourages other nations to ignore the provisions of the treaty, and thus slow or stop the progress of women worldwide.

CEDAW has been used as a basis to advance women in the countries that have signed it, in areas such as providing education for girls, access to health care, political equality, the right to inherit property, and spousal rights in property ownership. All of these have helped in alleviating global poverty for women.[311]

Other Treaties Affecting Women

The 1995 United Nations Fourth World Conference on Women adopted what is known as the Beijing Platform for Action for Women. One provision is the recognition that women and children are particularly affected by the indiscriminate use of land mines, and the Platform urges ratification of international treaties that would prohibit them.

In December 1997, the treaty banning the use, production, trade, and stockpiling of antipersonnel mines was signed in Ottawa, Canada by 122 nations. Twenty two years later in 2019, more than 80 percent of the world's states had ratified the treaty, including most members of NATO. Thirty-two countries worldwide have not yet joined—including the only two in the western hemisphere, the United States and Cuba.[312]

The Convention on the Rights of the Child is the most widely accepted human rights treaty. Adopted by the United Nations in November 1989, the four core principles are nondiscrimination, devotion to the best interests of the child, respect for the views of the child, and the right to life, survival, and development. The treaty protects children's rights by setting standards in health care, education, and legal, civil, and social services.

The Convention on the Rights of the Child (CRC) has been ratified by *all* governments except one: the United States of America.[313] Although signed by the Clinton Administration, the treaty has never been submitted to the US Senate for consideration. The Obama administration said that it intended to submit the treaty to the Senate, but did not do so.

President Trump explicitly disavowed the treaty in his Draft Executive Order on International Treaties (above), writing that the treaty would "prohibit spanking," and that it is one of the treaties that "force countries to adhere to often radical domestic agendas." The Trump administration has also flaunted protections accorded refugees in the CRC, most likely because the US has not ratified it, even though our country is a signatory. As pointed out by the AMA Journal of Ethics, failure to ratify has had profound effects on refugees attempting asylum in the US since Trump's election.

By failing to ratify the CRC, the United States not only abdicates moral leadership, but also invites other nations to emulate its lack of care for children. Most pernicious, US policies employ children as weapons of deterrence on the theory that if we treat children poorly, parents fleeing persecution will not seek safe haven at our borders. Based on a purported border crisis, federal policies have led to separation of families, mass detention of children and families, and accelerated removal, broadcasting worldwide the United States' disregard of the child and family rights under the CRC.[314]

Questions for candidates:

- Do you support US aid to international family planning programs? Have you, or would you, vote to fund these programs in full?
- Would you support repeal of the "global gag rule" on organizations that provide legal abortion services overseas?
- Would you vote to continue full funding to the United Nations Population Fund and remove the president's discretion in withholding funds?
- Would you be in favor of withholding military or humanitarian aid from any country that does not grant full rights to women?
- Women are being persecuted in both Iraq and Afghanistan, and not allowed basic human rights by the religious police. What would you recommend the US do now to help women in those countries?
- Would you make adherence to international human rights principles for women in Iraq and Afghanistan a condition for those countries receiving continued US monetary and military assistance?
- What can the US do to ensure the rights of women as new governments are formed in the Middle East?
- Do you think the US is doing enough to protect women in African and other conflict areas from sexual violence?
- Do you support the ratification of CEDAW by the United States? What would you do to see that the treaty comes up for a vote?
- Do you support the anti-land mine treaty, and the international treaty on the rights of the child?

Chapter 21

The Last Word—Equal Constitutional Rights

Much of this book is about threats to the rights granted to women under various laws and Supreme Court decisions, such as Title IX (prohibition of discrimination in educational programs) Title VII (barring discrimination in pay and employment), *Roe v. Wade* (establishing the right to abortion), and the continuous assault on such laws by conservatives.

One reason that women must be constantly vigilant about protecting their rights under statutes and regulations is that women do not have *fundamental equal rights with men* in the US—meaning equal rights under our Constitution.

Although polls show that most people believe otherwise (see Chapter 2), women are *not* explicitly guaranteed equal rights with men under the United States Constitution. Without having equal rights constitutionally protected, women must rely on a patchwork of laws (e.g. Equal Credit Act, Pregnancy Discrimination Act, Equal Pay Act) that can be repealed or weakened at any time by acts of Congress, or in some cases by regulations and presidential executive orders.

Additionally, courts can and have narrowed protections originally guaranteed by statute or earlier court decisions, resulting in women having to wage long campaigns with new bills in Congress to restore what's been taken away or weakened.

Title IX is a case in point. The law was passed in 1972. It prohibited discrimination against women and girls in educational institutions receiving federal funds. It was challenged, and the *Grove City v. Bell* decision in 1984 declared that only *individual programs* receiving federal funds were subject to its requirements, not institutions as a whole. (So, for example, if the medical school got federal funds but other programs didn't, discrimination was barred only in the medical school.) Women's groups had to mount a four-year fight to pass legislation overturning *Grove City* and restoring the original intent, meaning Title IX applies institution-wide.

More recently, in 2007, the Supreme Court reversed forty years of precedent by negating a major portion of Title VII of the Civil Rights Act, which had protected women from pay discrimination (see Chapter 13). It took intense lobbying and a change in party control of Congress and the White House from Republican to Democratic in the 2008 elections to pass the Lilly Ledbetter Fair Pay Act in 2009, restoring the law to its original interpretation.

Without a constitutional amendment guaranteeing equal rights for women, these types of battles are likely to continue as Congress and the courts become more polarized.

Because equal rights are not explicitly protected in the US Constitution, the rights of women also often depend on the state in which they live. For example, until it was outlawed by the Affordable Care Act, women paid higher rates than similarly situated men for the same health coverage in all but a handful of states. It is still legal (and very common) in the great majority of states to charge women more for other types of insurance.

Similarly, state courts have ruled that state Equal Rights Amendments protect women's rights to reproductive services under Medicaid, but women whose states do not have ERAs are not protected.

The proposed Equal Rights Amendment is not complicated. The entire text is only fifty-two words:

> Section 1. Equality of rights under the law shall not be denied or abridged by the United States or by any state on account of sex.
> Section 2. The Congress shall have the power to enforce, by appropriate legislation, the provisions of this article.
> Section 3. This amendment shall take effect two years after the date of ratification.

The Equal Rights Amendment embodies a simple concept that had the blessing of both political parties until the Republicans struck it from their platform in 1980; they have never restored support. The Democrats followed suit in 2004, but restored platform support for the ERA in 2008 after outcries from women's groups. (See the latest platforms of both parties in Appendix III.)

For an amendment to become part of the Constitution, it must be passed by a two-thirds majority in each chamber of Congress, and then sent to the states for ratification. Each state votes on ratification separately, and an amendment cannot become part of the Constitution unless it is ratified by three-fourths of the states.

The Equal Rights Amendment was first introduced in Congress in 1923, on the heels of ratification of the Nineteenth Amendment in 1920 giving women the right to vote. The ERA was finally passed out of Congress and sent to the states in 1972, with a seven-year deadline for ratification, later extended three additional years. (The deadline is not in the amendment, but in the preamble, causing some scholars to make the argument that the time limit is non-binding, meaning that even today, only *one* more state would be needed for it to be ratified.)

The original ratification drive succeeded in thirty-five states, but thirty-eight were needed for it to become part of the Constitution.

After decades of inaction two more states ratified in 2017 and 2018. Votes in both Virginia and Louisiana that would have made either state the thirty-eighth to ratify failed in 2019, with some legislators claiming passage would mean overturning state abortion restrictions. In Virginia, the ERA was stopped by just one vote, and advocates are hoping to elect a new pro-ERA state legislature and make Virginia the final state to ratify in 2020.

The ERA has been reintroduced in every Congress since 1972, but has never again been put to a vote, although there was a (mostly symbolic) hearing in the House Judiciary Committee in 2019. Sponsors in the current Congress are Representative Carolyn Maloney (D-NY) in the House and Senator Robert Menendez (D-NJ) in the Senate. Companion bills removing the ratification deadline have been introduced in the House by Representative Jackie Speier (D-CA) and Senator Benjamin Cardin (D-MD). Though both have a high number of co-sponsors, no committee hearings (which could lead to floor votes in Congress) have been scheduled.

Conservatives argue that equal constitutional rights will result in "abortion on demand" and "unisex toilets," though the amendment mentions neither. When they're not raising the specter of unisex toilets (guess they've never been on an airplane), conservatives also argue that a new amendment isn't needed because the "equal protection under the law" clause of the Fourteenth Amendment already guarantees equal rights for women.

That is not true. The Fourteenth Amendment was passed to protect African American men from discrimination. It specified equality for male slaves—female slaves were excluded along with all women, regardless of race. Courts have consistently failed to find sex discrimination as serious (what lawyers call *level of scrutiny*) as race discrimination under the Fourteenth Amendment.[315] As recently as 2010, Supreme Court Justice Antonin Scalia publicly stated that the Fourteenth Amendment does not prohibit against sex discrimination. The

Equal Rights Amendment would require courts to apply the highest level of *strict scrutiny* in judicial review.

The result has been that many discriminatory practices such as establishing boys-only public classrooms and schools, openly discriminating against women in insurance programs, and until recently barring women from certain military jobs—just to name a few—are still legal.

Women in the US lag far behind women in the rest of the world when it comes to constitutional equality. Most individual countries in Europe have formalized equal rights for women in their constitutions, and equal rights are included in the Treaty of Lisbon, which amounts to a European Union constitution. Women have had equal constitutional rights in Japan since 1946, and the constitutions of many other countries worldwide declare women as legal equals to men.

Since the 1990s, new constitutions in countries like Mozambique, Namibia, Ethiopia, Malawi, Uganda, South Africa, Rwanda, Burundi, and Swaziland have included nondiscrimination or equality provisions, prohibiting customary practices if they undermine undermined the dignity, welfare or status of women.[316]

With one of our two major parties (Republican) not having equal constitutional rights for women in their platform, it is especially important to confront candidates in every election as to their intentions regarding the Equal Rights Amendment.

States That Have Not Ratified the Equal Rights Amendment:

Alabama, Arizona, Arkansas, Florida, Georgia, Louisiana, Mississippi, Missouri, North Carolina, Oklahoma, South Carolina, Utah, and Virginia.

Questions for candidates:

- Do you support the Equal Rights Amendment to the US Constitution?
- Do you believe the ERA will become part of the Constitution if one more state ratifies?
- Have you, or would you, co-sponsor the amendment in Congress?
- Would you push for hearings and a congressional vote on equal rights for women?
- Do you think equal rights for women should be a part of your party's platform?
- Until equal rights for women are in the Constitution, will you pledge to work to eliminate unequal treatment of women in all forms, all domains, and all legislation?

Appendix I

Nuts and Bolts of US Publicly Funded Health Care Programs

Traditional Medicare

While most health insurance in the US is provided through private employer or personal funds, we have a few significant publicly funded medical insurance programs that are important to women. The largest is Medicare, which is for people sixty-five and up and certain disabled people under sixty-five.

Though most of Medicare is paid for by the federal government, it requires a monthly premium from recipients.

Medicare is especially important to women, because they outlive men and will need health care coverage for a longer period of their lives. Women are also less likely to have private pensions that cover some medical needs like drugs, or provide supplemental coverage.

Medicare Part A covers only hospitalization or brief follow up care in a nursing facility. The vast majority of recipients meet eligibility requirements that do not require a payment for Part A.

But Part A does not cover doctor visits, diagnostic tests, medical equipment, and the like. So most recipients also buy a second Medicare policy, Part B, to cover these shortfalls. A third, private, supplemental policy (generally dubbed Medigap) can cover everything the first two do not, such as deductibles, is also purchased by most Medicare recipients from private companies. By government regulation, Medigap policies are standardized across insurance companies. Benefits are clearly spelled out and do not vary from company to company, though the price of a given level of coverage may vary.

People insured under traditional Medicare plans have complete control over their choice of doctors, hospitals, and specialists, though a very small percentage of facilities and doctors do not take Medicare. As explained in our Health Care chapter, Medicare is a single-payer system—and the government is that payer. That means people on Medicare do not have to file claims or hassle with insurance companies.

In 2019, Medicare Part B costs $135.50 per month (with a $185 deductible and high-income recipients paying slightly more). A mid-priced supplemental Medigap policy (e.g. one that would cover deductibles but only part of any treatment in a foreign country) runs about $300 per month, depending on age and state of residence. Medicare premiums are rising rapidly, as are the costs of Medigap policies which must be purchased from private insurance companies. This is particularly relevant to older women, because their retirement incomes are lower than those of men, and women are less likely to get help with Medigap from former employers.

Drug coverage under Medicare (Part D) became operative in 2006. Though Part D plans are approved and regulated very loosely by the Medicare program, they are actually designed and administered by private health insurance companies, unlike Medicare Parts A and B. Part D is completely optional.

Without question seniors needed some kind of drug coverage under Medicare, but Part D has come under much criticism from advocacy organizations, senior citizens, and members of Congress (though they're the ones that passed it). The biggest problem was a coverage gap, known as the "donut hole." Coverage is suspended each year when drug costs paid by you and your insurance company reach a certain amount ($3,820 in 2019) and doesn't resume until costs reach a higher amount ($5,100 in 2019), even though seniors continue to pay Part D monthly premiums. This means many people pay 100 percent of their drug costs for part of the year, plus premiums. For the average senior, this is about 3.5 months, over one quarter of the year. Before Part D was passed by Congress, Senator Lautenberg (D-NJ) offered an amendment that would have required Medicare beneficiaries to sign a disclaimer that they understood, in plain English, the coverage gap in their plan before they could enroll in it. The amendment was defeated 43-56, with every single Republican in the Senate voting against it.

However, the problem will be solved with the ACA (assuming it's not repealed), albeit slowly. It closes the "donut hole" over time. Unfortunately, several other serious problems remain. One of the biggest is that *the federal government is prohibited from negotiating with drug companies for the lowest drug prices.* Congress prohibited such bargaining when it passed the Bush-era Medicare drug benefit in 2003, and the prohibition was kept in the Affordable Care Act in order to get large drug companies to support the legislation. Studies have shown that prices charged by Medicare Part D drug plans are 46 percent higher than those paid by the Veterans Administration, which does negotiate with the pharmaceutical companies.[317] The inability of the Medicare system to bargain with big pharmaceutical companies for better drug prices keeps prices high. For older women on fixed incomes, higher prices can cause cutbacks on needed drugs, or hard choices between medicine and food or heat.

Unlike Medicare supplemental plans, Part D plans are not standardized and are extremely confusing. Companies can change the drugs covered or drop drugs from coverage altogether, meaning people must shop all over again each year for a plan that covers the drugs they take. Plans can also raise the co-pays and premiums at will, and most have done so in great leaps.[318]

There are also problems for low-income people who previously had their prescription costs paid by Medicaid. Part D replaced that coverage, and most of these recipients were automatically assigned to a Part D plan without any evaluation of their necessary prescriptions. Co-pays were instituted as well.

Medicare Advantage

A relatively new alternative to traditional Medicare is known as Medicare Advantage. Though HMO-type managed care programs have been available to enrollees under Medicare since 1997, they were greatly expanded in 2006 when the old plans were renamed Medicare Advantage, and incentives were created to induce for-profit HMOs run by insurance companies to participate.

Medicare Advantage plans are required to offer basic Medicare services and drug coverage under Part D. Beyond that, the government does not regulate them. That means that they can impose traditional managed care restrictions, such as limiting choice of doctors and hospitals, and denying coverage for services or treatments (they also get to rule on any appeals you make when they deny coverage). Medicare sends the HMO a check every month on the patient's behalf, but the plans can set premiums and co-pays at any level they like.[319]

There have been many reported abuses in the selling of Medicare Advantage programs by insurance companies, including agents telling seniors they are "from Medicare," and the use of very high-pressure sales tactics. Medicare Advantage programs have also been shown to be ripe for defrauding the government, and in 2016 alone a government audit found that Medicare overpaid Medicare Advantage plans by approximately $7 billion.[320] Critics in Congress say the plans are nothing more than a subsidy for private insurers—at a time when some of their colleagues propose cutting physician fees for traditional Medicare enrollees.

The ACA as passed cut more than $200 billion in excess subsidies from the Medicare Advantage program ($136 billion directly and another $70 billion indirectly), phased in over time. Cuts to Medicare Advantage do not cut benefits under these programs (though the plans themselves may do so), the cuts do curb the excess subsidies to private insurers. The savings will be used to increase services under traditional Medicare, and to close the "donut hole" in drug coverage. In late 2019, President Trump signed an executive order once again increasing payments to Medicare Advantage plans. It is unclear whether these increases will have a negative impact on traditional Medicare funding.

Medicaid

Medicaid is a state administered health insurance program for the poor that is paid for in large part by the federal government through block grants (lump sum payments given to the states to spend under their state rules.)

The majority of those enrolled in Medicaid are female. Women have lower incomes overall and are also the most frequent custodial parents of children who are on Medicaid. Many enrollees are women in their reproductive years. Medicaid provides coverage for a range of services, including preventive services such as pap smears and mammography, family planning, and pregnancy-related services. Medicaid is the primary source of insurance in 43 percent of childbirths, and that percentage is much higher the younger the mother is, according to the latest numbers from the Centers for Disease Control and Prevention.[321] Abortions are not covered by Medicaid except in extremely narrow circumstances (danger to life, rape, incest), but some states opt to use their own funds for Medicaid recipients.

Even though states have leeway in crafting their Medicaid programs, they must comply with federal standards to get the federal government's money. Nevertheless states were generally free to set their own eligibility criteria for recipients until 2007, when the Bush administration imposed restrictions on the states' ability to expand Medicaid coverage to more low-income families. With the economy in crisis in 2009 and many more people unemployed, the Obama administration increased Medicaid payments to the states. In order to qualify for the increases, states had to roll back any cuts that had been made after July 1, 2008. Unlike previous Medicaid coverage, it now covers adults without dependent children (more men) and childless adults, greatly expanding the number of people covered. Initially the federal government planned to withhold existing funding if states didn't expand their programs, but the requirement was dropped.

Like almost every other provision of the ACA, expanding Medicaid was mightily resisted by those who opposed the law in the first place, and challenged in court as part of a lawsuit by attorneys general from several states. When the Supreme Court upheld the expansion in 2012, it included a critical caveat: The federal government may not threaten the states that don't comply with the loss of their existing funding. As a result, the Medicaid expansion is now optional for the states. As of 2019, thirty-three states (including D.C.) had opted to expand their programs, three more were expected to expand by 2020, and fourteen had said no to expansion.[322] Failing to expand the Medicaid program appears to be mostly on the part of states controlled by legislatures or governors that oppose the ACA, since the federal government picks up 100 percent of the cost of expansion for the first three years, phasing down to 90 percent in 2020 and all subsequent years.

Children's Health Insurance Program (CHIP)

The Children's Health Insurance Program is a government funded program to provide health insurance for low-income children who are not covered under Medicaid. It was created in 1997—passed by a Republican Congress and signed by a Democratic president. According to the Commonwealth Fund, a private foundation working for better health care, "the program represents a fine balance, designed to maintain equilibrium between states and the federal government, as well as between political conservatives and liberals."[323]

Like Medicaid, states have flexibility in designing benefits for CHIP, with the federal government paying an average of 92.5 percent of the cost and the states 7.5 percent as of 2019. But also like Medicaid, the states must comply with federal requirements to get federal money.

In the original CHIP bill, children in families making up to 200 percent of the poverty line could be covered. The poverty line was then $21,200 for a family of four. When the program came up for re-authorization in 2007, Democrats in Congress tried to raise the level to 300 percent of poverty. President Bush vetoed the bill, saying it would be "an incremental step toward the goal of government-run health care." (His spokeswoman had charged the week before that it would be "socialized-type medicine.") Both statements were inaccurate, as the program is administered by private insurers and delivered by private nurses and doctors.[324] Under ACA, federal funding was extended from 2013 to 2015 and the federal match was increased for the years 2016 through 2019.

ACA also prevented states from restricting CHIP eligibility standards, methodologies, or procedures from enactment until September 30, 2019. President Trump's 2020 budget proposal would eliminate the CHIP's Child Enrollment Contingency Fund (for use in case states face higher enrollments than anticipated) in fiscal year 2021 and replace it with a new vaguely defined Shortfall Fund.

Veteran's Administration Health Care

The Veterans Administration (VA), had traditionally provided VA health care to all veterans, with co-pays for those veterans considered to be "non-poor." In 2003 the Bush administration ordered a halt to the enrollment of "non-poor" veterans, citing not enough capacity. Not all VA health care benefits are available to all veterans. The VA maintains a

priority system, with the most benefits going to those with the greatest health or financial need. The recent history of the VA health system
is not a pretty picture. Here's a short timeline.

* A Harvard research team estimated that 2,266 US military veterans under the age of sixty-five died in 2008 because they
  lacked health insurance and thus had reduced access to care.
  That figure is more than fourteen times the number of deaths
  suffered by US troops in Afghanistan in the same year, and more
  than twice as many as had died since the war began in 2001.[325]

* In 2009, new regulations were put into effect by the VA. Income restrictions on enrollment for health benefits, while not
  eliminated, were relaxed. Consideration was also given to geographic area, recognizing that the cost of living in some parts
  of the country is higher than in others.

* In 2014 a national scandal erupted over veteran deaths because
  of delays in diagnosis and treatment at VA hospitals. Thought
  the VA promised reforms, as of early 2015 government data
  showed that the number of patients facing long waits at VA
  facilities had not dropped at all.[326]

* The ACA left veteran's health coverage essentially unchanged,
  though many vets previously uninsured got coverage under
  the ACA's Medicaid expansion. While women are a small percentage of veterans, they are especially vulnerable to cuts because of their lower incomes and longer lifetime needs for
  health care.

The problems continue. The General Accounting Office (GAO) des-
ignated VA health care as a high-risk area in 2015 due to five areas of concern regarding VA's ability to provide timely access to safe,
high-quality health care for veterans: (1) ambiguous policies and in-
consistent processes; (2) inadequate oversight and accountability; (3)
IT challenges; (4) inadequate staff training; and (5) unclear resource

needs and allocation priorities. In 2017, GAO reported that while VA had taken some actions to address these issues, little progress had actually been made.

Since GAO's 2017 High-Risk Report, VA has worked to address each of these areas, but still has not made sufficient progress to address the concerns. GAO has found, for example:

* VA medical center officials did not always document or conduct required reviews of providers in a timely manner when allegations were made against them. As a result, VA medical center officials may have lacked the information they needed to ensure that VA providers were competent to provide safe, high-quality care to veterans.

* VA lacked complete, reliable data to systematically monitor the timeliness of veterans' access to care. Veterans referred to the Veteran's Choice program for routine care could wait up to seventy calendar days for care (as allowed by VA's policies), rather than the thirty days required by law.

* VA's data on employee misconduct and disciplinary actions were unreliable and could not be accurately analyzed. VA also did not consistently ensure that allegations of misconduct of senior officials were appropriately reviewed, or ensure that these officials were held accountable.

* VA's suicide prevention media outreach activities declined in recent years due to leadership turnover and reorganization.

* VA needs to further develop its capacity building initiatives and establish metrics to monitor and measure its progress in addressing high-risk areas of concern.

* VA needs to continue to implement the health care recommendations GAO has made. As of December 2018, more than 125 recommendations remain unaddressed, including seventeen older than three years.

APPENDIX II

Supreme Court Decisions on Reproductive Rights

1965: *Griswold v. Connecticut* Supreme Court decision strikes down a state law that prohibited giving married people information, instruction, or medical advice on contraception.

1972: *Eisenstadt v. Baird* Supreme Court decision establishes the right of unmarried people to use contraceptives.

1973: *Roe v. Wade* Supreme Court decision strikes down state laws that made abortion illegal.

1991: *Rust v. Sullivan* upholds the constitutionality of a 1988 "gag rule" prohibiting doctors and counselors at clinics giving patients abortion information from receiving federal funding.

1992: *Planned Parenthood of Southeastern Pennsylvania v. Casey* reaffirms the "core" holdings of *Roe* that women have a right to abortion before fetal viability, but allows states to restrict abortion access so long as these restrictions do not impose an "undue burden" on women seeking abortions.

2000: *Stenberg v. Carhart* (Carhart I) rules that the Nebraska statute banning so-called "partial-birth abortion" is unconstitutional for two independent reasons: lacks of a necessary exception for preserving the health of the woman, and targeted procedures prohibit abortions in the second trimester, creating an "undue burden" on women. Ruling effectively invalidates twenty-nine of thirty-one similar statewide bans. In 2003 a federal ban on the procedure is passed by Congress and signed into law by President Bush. The National Abortion Federation immediately challenges the law in court and is successful in blocking enforcement of the law for its members. Two other legal challenges (Carhart II, see below) were also mounted.

2006: *Ayotte v. Planned Parenthood of Northern New England*, challenged New Hampshire's law requiring doctors to delay a teenager's abortion until forty-eight hours after a parent was notified, but lacking a medical emergency exception to protect a pregnant teenager's health. In a unanimous decision, the Court reiterated its long-standing principle that abortion restrictions must include protections for women's health.[327]

2007: *Gonzales v. Carhart* and *Gonzales v. Planned Parenthood Federation of America*, (Carhart II) After three lower courts struck down the Bush abortion ban, the new Roberts Supreme Court, in a 5-4 decision, upheld the federal abortion ban, undermining a core principle of *Roe v. Wade*: that women's health must remain paramount, and overturning *Stenberg v. Carhart* (Carhart I), issued seven years earlier. Writing for the majority, Justice Kennedy said lawmakers could overrule a doctor's medical judgment, and the "state's interest in promoting respect for human life at all stages in the pregnancy" outweighs a woman's interest in protecting her health.[328, 329]

2014: The Supreme Court declined to hear an appeal from Arizona officials seeking to revive a state law that barred most abortions after twenty weeks of pregnancy. The ruling did not affect similar laws passed in other states except the law in Idaho, which is under the jurisdiction of the same appeals court.[330]

2015: The Supreme Court agreed to hear a Texas case that would have closed all but a handful of abortion clinics. The case, *Whole Woman's Health v. Cole*, centered on a series of far-reaching restrictions on Texas abortion providers and clinics, which led to the closure of about half of the state's abortion facilities. The law was struck down by the Roberts Court in 2016 as imposing an "undue burden."

2019: The Supreme Court in a 5-4 decision blocked a Louisiana law similar to *Whole Woman's Health* that could have left the state with only one doctor in a single clinic authorized to provide abortions. The temporary stay did not end the case. The Court is likely to hear a challenge to the law on the merits in its next term, with a decision by June 2020.

2020: More than twenty lawsuits that have the potential to overturn *Roe* are in various stages of judicial review.

APPENDIX III

The Political Parties and Their Platforms

Party platforms are revisited in presidential election years, and voted on at the national party conventions. They remain in effect until the next presidential election (e.g. the 2016 platforms remain in effect until the political conventions in Summer 2020). While there are some changes every four years, the general philosophy is highly consistent from one election to the next, and the wording is often nearly identical to the previous platform.

Platforms serve as "blueprints" for the parties, articulating their political philosophies as well as specific promises and plans for what the party will accomplish if it has control. Platforms can be dozens of pages long; we have included only those topics and points most relevant to women and discussed in this book. Issues (our captions) are in alphabetical order, with platform page numbers noted in parentheses. Categories and captions between the two platforms are not a perfect match, since platforms differ slightly on issues they address.

All quotes below are verbatim, and are presented without comment. In a very few cases, words in square brackets [ ] have been added for clarity. Administrative actions and bills most relevant to women promised in the platforms that have been signed into law since the platforms were adopted in 2016 are noted in curly brackets { }. We have tried not to burden the reader with platform content that is pure rhetoric, pronouncements against the other party, or self-congratulation for past accomplishments. We include only what the parties clearly state they stand for, and what they plan to do.

We encourage readers to review the platform statements that follow carefully, and use them to hold elected officials and candidates alike accountable. Have they adhered to their promises and positions? If not, why not? If not yet, when? What have they done specifically to advance a particular position or promise?

Republican Platform 2016

Abortion, Family Planning, Sex Education

We assert the sanctity of human life and affirm that the unborn child has a fundamental right to life which cannot be infringed. We support a human life amendment to the Constitution and legislation to make clear that the Fourteenth Amendment's protections apply to children before birth. (13)

We oppose the use of public funds to perform or promote abortion or to fund organizations, like Planned Parenthood, so long as they provide or refer for elective abortions or sell fetal body parts rather than provide health care. (13)

We urge all states and Congress to make it a crime to acquire, transfer, or sell fetal tissues from elective abortions for research, and we call on Congress to enact a ban on any sale of fetal body parts. We call on Congress to ban the practice of misleading women on so-called fetal harvesting consent forms. (13)

We will not fund or subsidize health care that includes abortion coverage. (13)

We support the appointment of judges who respect traditional family values and the sanctity of innocent human life. (13)

We salute the many states that now protect women and girls

through laws requiring informed consent, parental consent, waiting periods, and clinic regulation. (14)

We condemn the Supreme Court's activist decision in *Whole Woman's Health v. Hellerstedt.* (14)

Over a dozen states have passed Pain-Capable Unborn Child Protection Acts prohibiting abortion after twenty weeks, and we call on Congress to enact the federal version. (14)

We call on Congress to ban sex-selection abortions and abortions based on disabilities. (14)

We oppose embryonic stem cell research. We oppose federal funding of embryonic stem cell research. (14)

We oppose school-based clinics that provide referral or counseling for abortion and contraception. (34)

We renew our call for replacing "family planning" programs for teens with sexual risk avoidance education that sets abstinence until marriage as the responsible and respected standard of behavior. (34)

We call for a permanent ban on federal funding and subsidies for abortion and health care plans that include abortion coverage. (37)

Affirmative Action

We reject unfair preferences, quotas, and set-asides as forms of discrimination. (9)

Affordable Care Act / Health Care

Improving health care must start with repeal of the dishonestly named Affordable Care Act of 2010: Obamacare. (36)

We will not fund or subsidize health care that includes abortion coverage. (33)

We respect the states' authority and flexibility to exclude abortion providers from federal programs such as Medicaid and other health care and family planning programs so long as they continue to perform or refer for elective abortions or sell the body parts of aborted children. (24)

We will reduce mandates and enable insurers and providers of care to increase health care options and contain costs. (36)

We will promote price transparency so consumers can know the cost of treatments before they agree to them. (36)

We propose to end tax discrimination against the individual purchase of insurance and allow consumers to buy insurance across state lines. (37)

We support state and federal legislation to cap non-economic damages in medical malpractice lawsuits (37)

We call for a permanent ban on federal funding and subsidies for abortion and health care plans that include abortion coverage. (37)

We respect the rights of conscience of health care professionals, doctors, nurses, pharmacists, and organizations, especially the faith-based groups. (37)

Children

Traditional marriage and family, based on marriage between one man and one woman, is the foundation for a free society and has for millennia been entrusted with rearing children and instilling cultural values. (11)

We especially support the innovative financing mechanisms that make options available to all children: education savings accounts (ESAs), vouchers, and tuition tax credits. (34)

We do not support the U.N. Convention on Women's Rights, the Convention on the Rights of the Child, the Convention on the Rights of Persons with Disabilities, and the U.N. Arms Trade Treaty, as well as various declarations from the U.N. Conference on Environment and Development. (51)

We support measures such as the First Amendment Defense Act to ensure [private entities which facilitate adoption] do not face government discrimination because of their views on marriage and family. (31)

Education/Title IX

We endorse the First Amendment Defense Act, [which] would protect the nonprofit tax status of faith-based adoption agencies, the accreditation of religious educational institutions, the grants and contracts of faith-based charities and small businesses, and the licensing of religious professions. (11)

We renew our call for replacing "family planning" programs for teens with sexual risk avoidance education that sets abstinence until marriage as the responsible and respected standard of behavior. (34)

We especially support the innovative financing mechanisms that make options available to all children: education savings accounts (ESAs), vouchers, and tuition tax credits. (34)

The [Obama Administration's Title IX regulations] must be halted. (35)

The federal government should not be in the business of originating student loans. (35)

Accreditation should be decoupled from federal financing, and states should be empowered to allow a wide array of accrediting and credentialing bodies to operate. (35)

Equal Rights

We oppose discrimination based on race, sex, religion, creed, disability, or national origin and support statutes to end such discrimination. (9)

We endorse the First Amendment Defense Act, Republican legislation in the House and Senate which will bar government discrimination against individuals and businesses for acting on the belief that marriage is the union of one man and one woman. (11)

We assert the First Amendment right of freedom of association for religious, private, service, and youth organizations to set their own membership standards. (11)

We reaffirm the existing protections that provide all employees of the federal government the opportunity to pursue their desire to serve their country free from discrimination. (26)

We urge marriage penalties to be removed from the tax code and public assistance programs. (31)

Global Women's Rights

We do not support the U.N. Convention on Women's Rights, the Convention on the Rights of the Child, the Convention on the Rights of Persons with Disabilities, and the U.N. Arms Trade Treaty, as well as various declarations from the U.N. Conference on Environment and Development. (51)

LGBTQ Rights

We condemn the Supreme Court's ruling in *United States v. Windsor*. We also condemn the Supreme Court's lawless ruling in *Obergefell v. Hodges* [which defined] marriage as the union of one man and one woman. (10)

We endorse the First Amendment Defense Act, Republican legislation in the House and Senate which will bar government discrimination against individuals and businesses for acting on the belief that marriage is the union of one man and one woman. (11)

We do not accept the Supreme Court's redefinition of marriage and we urge its reversal, whether through judicial reconsideration or a constitutional amendment returning control over marriage to the states. (32)

We oppose government discrimination against businesses or entities which decline to sell items or services to individuals for activities that go against their religious views about such activities. (31)

Medicaid

We respect the states' authority and flexibility to exclude abortion providers from federal programs such as Medicaid and other health care and family planning programs so long as they continue to perform or refer for elective abortions or sell the body parts of aborted children. (24)

We propose . . . the dynamic compassion of work requirements [for food stamps, Medicaid and Children's Health Insurance Program benefits]. (32)

We propose to block grant Medicaid and other payments and to assist all patients, including those with pre-existing conditions, to obtain coverage in a robust consumer market. (36)

Medicare

We propose these reforms: Impose no changes for persons 55 or older. Give others the option of traditional Medicare or transition to a premium-support model . . . Guarantee to every enrollee an income-adjusted contribution toward a plan of their choice, with catastrophic protection. Without disadvantaging present retirees or those nearing retirement, set a more realistic age for eligibility in light of today's longer life span. (24)

Republican legislation now allows Medicare Part D and Medicare Advantage plans to limit patients to a single pharmacy. (40)

Military Women

We support the all-volunteer force and oppose unnecessary policy changes, including compulsory national service and Selective Service registration of women for a possible future draft. We reiterate our support for both the advancement of women in the military and their exemption from direct ground combat units and infantry battalions. (43)

Social Security

Current retirees and those close to retirement can be assured of their benefits. Of the many reforms being proposed, all options should be considered to preserve Social Security. (24)

Democratic Platform 2016

Abortion, Family Planning, and Sex Education

We will appoint judges who defend the constitutional principles of liberty and equality for all, and will protect a woman's right to safe and legal abortion. (23)

We will fight Republican efforts to roll back the clock on women's health and reproductive rights, and stand up for Planned Parenthood. (31)

We will continue to oppose, and seek to overturn, federal and state laws and policies that impede a woman's access to abortion, including by repealing the Hyde Amendment. (33)

We condemn and will combat any acts of violence, harassment, and intimidation of reproductive health providers, patients, and staff. (33)

We will defend the ACA, which extends affordable preventive health care to women, including no-cost contraception, and prohibits discrimination in health care based on gender. (33)

We recognize that quality, affordable comprehensive health care, evidence-based sex education and a full range of family planning services help reduce the number of unintended pregnancies and thereby also reduce the need for abortions. (33)

We strongly and unequivocally support a woman's decision to have a child, including by ensuring a safe and healthy pregnancy and childbirth, and by providing services during pregnancy and after the birth of a child, including adoption and social support services, as well as protections for women against pregnancy discrimination. (34)

We will support sexual and reproductive health and rights around the globe. We support the repeal of harmful restrictions that obstruct women's access to health care information and services, including the "global gag rule" and the Helms Amendment that bars American assistance to provide safe, legal abortion throughout the developing world. (41)

Affordable Care Act

We will defend the ACA, which extends affordable preventive health care to women, including no-cost contraception, and prohibits discrimination in health care based on gender. (33)

Democrats will empower the states . . . to use innovation waivers under the ACA to develop unique locally tailored approaches to health coverage. (31)

We will keep fighting until the ACA's Medicaid expansion has been adopted in every state. (31)

Children/Childcare

We will increase investments to make quality childcare more affordable, boost wages for childcare workers. (4)

Democrats will protect proven programs like the Supplemental Nutrition Assistance Program (SNAP). (18)

The Child Tax Credit (CTC) should be expanded by making more of it refundable, or indexed to inflation to stem the erosion of the credit. (18)

The Indian Child Welfare Act is critical to the survival of Indian culture, government, and communities and must be enforced with the statutory intent of the law. (20)

Democrats will invest in early childhood programs like Early Head Start and provide every family in America with access to high-quality childcare and high-quality preschool programs. (29)

We support efforts to ensure that early childhood educators are experienced and high-quality. (29)

Education

We will help people grow their skills through jobs and skills training opportunities. (18)

We will make community college free, while ensuring the strength of our Historically Black Colleges and Universities and Minority-Serving Institutions. (27)

Democrats will fight to bring an end to sexual assault on campuses. We will provide comprehensive support to survivors, and ensure a fair process for all on-campus disciplinary proceedings and in the criminal justice system. (34)

We will increase sexual violence prevention education programs that cover issues like consent and bystander intervention, not only in college, but also in secondary school. (34)

Employment

We should raise the federal minimum wage to $15 an hour over time and index it, give all Americans the ability to join a union regardless of where they work. (3)

We will fight to secure equal pay for women. (4)

Democrats will make sure that the United States finally enacts national paid family and medical leave by passing a family and medical leave act. (4)

We will fight to allow workers the right to earn at least seven days of paid sick leave. (4)

We will support efforts to limit the use of forced arbitration clauses in employment and service contracts. (4)

We will combat biases across economic, political, and social life that hold women back and limit their opportunities and also tackle specific challenges facing women of color. (17)

The Earned Income Tax Credit (EITC) program should be expanded for low-wage workers not raising children, including extending the credit to young workers starting at age 21. (18)

Equal Rights

After 240 years, we will finally enshrine the rights of women in the Constitution by passing the Equal Rights Amendment. (17)

Democrats will fight for the continued development of sex discrimination law to cover LGBT people. We will also fight for comprehensive federal nondiscrimination protections for all LGBT Americans, to guarantee equal rights in areas such as housing, employment, public accommodations, credit, jury service, education, and federal funding. (17)

We commit ourselves to insuring fair treatment for LGBT veterans, including by proactively reviewing and upgrading discharge records for veterans who were discharged because of their sexual orientation. (37)

Global Women's Rights

We will urge US ratification of the Convention on the Elimination of All Forms of Discrimination Against Women. (17)

We will support sexual and reproductive health and rights around the globe. (41)

We will stop the scourge of human trafficking and modern slavery of men, women, boys, and girls. (41)

We will continue to support the United States National Action Plan on Women, Peace, and Security. We will work to end the epidemic of gender-based violence around the world. (41)

We support the repeal of harmful restrictions that obstruct women's access to health care information and services, including the "global gag rule" and the Helms Amendment that bars American assistance to provide safe, legal abortion throughout the developing world. (41)

Democrats will push for more inclusive governance in Iraq and Syria that respects the equal rights of all citizens. (44)

We will help our African partners improve their capacity to respond to crises and protect citizens, especially women and girls. (45)

Medicare/Medicaid

Democrats will fight any attempts by Republicans in Congress to privatize, voucherize, or "phase out" Medicare as we know it. (31)

We will oppose Republican plans to slash funding and block grant Medicaid and SNAP, which would harm millions of Americans. (31)

We will keep fighting until the ACA's Medicaid expansion has been adopted in every state. (31)

Democrats will fight to make sure that Medicare will negotiate lower prices with drug manufacturers. (32)

Military Women

We must also look for more ways to make certain the VA provides veteran-centric care, such as providing women with full and equal treatment, including reproductive health services. (36)

We commit ourselves to insuring fair treatment for LGBT veterans, including by proactively reviewing and upgrading discharge records for veterans who were discharged because of their sexual orientation. (37)

We are proud of the opening of combat positions to women.

Social Security

Democrats will expand Social Security so that every American can retire with dignity and respect, including women who are widowed or took time out of the workforce to care for their children, aging parents, or ailing family members. (6)

We will fight every effort to cut, privatize, or weaken Social

Security, including attempts to raise the retirement age, diminish benefits by cutting cost-of-living adjustments, or reducing earned benefits. (5-6)

Democrats will expand Social Security so that every American can retire with dignity and respect, including women who are widowed or took time out of the workforce to care for their children, aging parents, or ailing family members. (6)

Violence Against Women

We will continue to support the United States National Action Plan on Women, Peace, and Security. We will work to end the epidemic of gender-based violence around the world. We will urge ratification of the Convention for the Elimination of All Forms of Discrimination Against Women. (41)

We will continue to support the Violence Against Women Act to provide law enforcement with the tools it needs to combat this problem. We will support comprehensive services for survivors of violence and increase prevention efforts in our communities and on our campuses. Democrats will fight to bring an end to sexual assault, wherever it occurs, including on campuses. We will provide comprehensive support to survivors, and ensure a fair process for all on-campus disciplinary proceedings and in the criminal justice system. We will increase sexual violence prevention education programs that cover issues like consent and bystander intervention, not only in college, but also in secondary school. (34)

Endnotes

1. Pieklo, Jessica Mason. "Republicans Get Another Win in Their Fight to Gut Title X." *Rewire.News,* Jul 11, 2019. Retrieved August 3, 2019 from https://rewire.news/article/2019/07/11/republicans get another win in their fight to gut title x/

2. Sherr, Lynn. *Failure is Impossible: Susan B. Anthony in Her Own Words.* New York: Times Books, Random House, 1995.

3. Flexner, Eleanor. *Century of Struggle: The Woman's Rights Movement in the United States.* Cambridge, Massachusetts: The Belknap Press of Harvard University Press, 1959, 1975.

4. Gender Differences in Voter Turnout, Fact Sheet. Center for American Women and Politics, Rutgers University, New Brunswick, N.J. 2005. Retrieved January 15, 2008 from http://www.cawp.rutgers.edu/Facts/genderdiff.pdf

5. "The 2008 Presidential Election and Trends in Opinions on Education." Celinda Lake, Lake Research Partners, Public Education Network Annual Conference, November 16, 2008. Retrieved from http://www.docstoc.com/docs/5507993/The 2008 Presidential Election and Trends in Opinions on Education

6. Mohdin, Aamna "American women voted overwhelmingly for Clinton, except the white ones" citing Edison National Election

poll, Quartz, November 9, 2016. Retrieved May 28, 2019 from https://qz.com/833003/election 2016 all women voted over-whelmingly for clinton except the white ones/

7.   "Women in the 2006 Elections." Washington, D.C.: Lake Research Partners, November 17, 2006.

8.   "Women Voters Made the Difference in 2006 Election." *Ms. Magazine* press release, November 17, 2006.

9.   "2008 Election Gender Gap." Arlington, Va. Feminist Majority.

10. "2010 Exit Polls, U.S. House." CNN Election Center. Retrieved October 3, 2011 from http://www.cnn.com/ELECTION/2010/results/polls/#val=USH00p1

11. Kile, Jocelyn. "As GOP celebrates win, no sign of narrowing gender, age gaps." Washington, D.C.: Pew Research Center, November 5, 2014. Retrieved October 15, 2015 from http://www.pewresearch.org/fact tank/2014/11/05/as gop celebrates win no sign of narrowing gender age gaps/

12. "Gender Gaps in Voting Evident in all 2016 U.S. Senate Races." Center for American Women in Politics, November 10, 2016. Retrieved May 27, 2019 http://www.cawp.rutgers.edu/sites/default/files/resources/post election gg release senate 2016.pdf

13. Velencia, Janie. "The 2018 Gender Gap Was Huge" *FiveThirtyEight*, Nov. 9, 2018. Retrieved May 27, 2019 from https://fivethirty eight.com/features/the 2018 gender gap was huge/

14. "The Independents," *The Washington Post*. Retrieved February 15, 2008 from http://www.WashingtonPost.com

15. "Women More Likely to Be Democrats, Regardless of Age," Gallup poll, June 12, 2009.

16. "Partisan Polarization Surges in Bush, Obama Years." Washington, D.C.: Pew Research Center, June 4, 2012. Retrieved February 21, 2014 from http://www.people press.org/2012/06/04/section 9 trends in party affiliation/

17. "A Deep Dive Into Party Affiliation," Washington, D.C.: Pew Research Center, April 7, 2015. Retrieved October 15, 2015

from http://www.people press.org/2015/04/07/a deep dive into party affiliation/

18. "Party Identification Table" Washington, D.C.: Pew Research Center, Jan–Aug 2016. Retrieved May 27, 2019 from https://assets.pewresearch.org/wp content/uploads/sites/5/2016/09/09 13 16 Party ID Combined Detailed Tables.pdf

19. "Women in the House." *National Journal.* Retrieved Dec. 31, 2007 from http://nationaljournal.com/voteratings/pdf/06women minorities.pdf

20. U.S. Senate, roll call votes, 108th Congress, 1st session. Retrieved December 15, 2007 from http://www.senate.gov

21. Sullivan, Patricia. "Anne Gorsuch Burford, 62, Dies; Reagan EPA Director." *Washington Post,* July 22, 2004: B06.

22. Sydell, Laura. "Clarence the Credible, How Journalists Blew the Thomas Story." *Fairness and Accuracy in Reporting, Extra!, 1992: Special Issue on Women.*

23. U.S. Department of Human Services. Donna E. Shalala, Ph.D., Secretary of Health and Human Services. Retrieved November 15, 2007 from http://www.surgeongeneral.gov/library/youthvio lence/shalala.htm

24. Barnes, Robert. "Over Ginsburg's Dissent, Court Limits Bias Suits." *The Washington Post,* May 30, 2007: A01.

25. Lee, Christopher. "Birth Control Foe To Run Office on Family Planning." *The Washington Post,* October 17, 2007: A15.

26. Berkowitz, Bill. "Wade Horn Cashes Out." Media Transparency, April 25, 2007. Retrieved December 1, 2007 from http://www.mediatransparency.org/story.php?storyID=190

27. Barnes, Robert. "Roberts Court Moves Right, But With a Measured Step." *The Washington Post,* April 20, 2007: A03.

28. Longman, Martin. "Trump Has Assembled the Worst Cabinet in History," *Washington Monthly,* May 17, 2019. Retrieved June 24, 2019 from https://washingtonmonthly.com/2019/05/17/trump has assembled the worst cabinet in history/

29. Ibid.

30. Dzikiy, Phil. "Trump's EPA finalizes new rule to replace Clean Power Plan in desperate attempt to 'save' coal." *electrek*, June 19, 2019. Retrieved June 24, 2019 from https://electrek.co/2019 /06/19/epa new rule save coal/

31. Chu, Simone C. and Lewis, Iris M. "What Happens Next with Title IX: DeVos's Proposed Rule, Explained." *The Harvard Crimson*, February 27, 2019. Retrieved June 24, 2019 from https://www.thecrimson.com/article/2019/2/27/titleixexplainer/ Note: Rules were not finalized as of mid-2019, but some schools had already adopted them.

32. Risen, James. "White House Is Subpoenaed on Wiretapping." *The New York Times*, June 28, 2007.

33. "DOJ Flinches, Skirts Drone Strike Subpoena Fight." *Legal Times*, April 17, 2013. Retrieved February 22, 2014 from http://legaltimes.typepad.com/blt/2013/04/doj flinches skirts subpoena fight with congress.html

34. Wolfe, Jan and Stauffer, Caroline. "Factbox: Clash between Trump, U.S. House Democrats shifts into courts." Reuters, June 19, 2019. Retrieved June 21, 2019 from https://www.reuters .com/article/us usa trump congress investigations fac/factbox clash between trump us house democrats shifts into courts idUSKCN1TK141

35. Roberts, John, Tobacco Executive Goes Public Over Company Lies. February 3, 1996. Retrieved December 1, 2007 from http://www.bmj.com/cgi/content/full/312/7026/267/a

36. Milbank, Dana. "Sweeteners for the South." *The Washington Post*, Sunday, November 22, 2009.

37. "Burwell v. Hobby Lobby Stores, Inc." Washington, D.C.: Supreme Court of the United States SCOTUS Blog. Retrieved September 1, 2015 from http://www.scotusblog.com/case files/ cases/sebelius v hobby lobby stores inc/

38. "Women in the 2006 Elections" Washington, D.C.: Lake

Research Partners, November 13,2006. Retrieved February 23, 2014 from http://www.lakeresearch.com/polls/pdf/Women%20 in%20the%202006%20Elections%20_%20Lake%20Research .pdf

39. January 2011 political survey, Washington, D.C.: Pew Research Center for The People & The Press. Personal correspondence.

40. Winston, David. "Placing Priority: How Issues Mattered More than Demographics in the 2016 Election." Democracy Fund Voter Study Group, December 2017. Retrieved June 27, 2019 from https://www.voterstudygroup.org/publication/placing priority #introduction

41. "Gender Gap on Importance of Abortion, Birth Control, Inequality, Environment." Pew Research Center, September 29, 2014. Downloaded November 2, 2015 from http://www.people -press.org/2014/09/12/wide-partisan-differences-over -the-issues-that-matter-in-2014/9-12-2014_07/

42. Langer, Gary and Siu, Benjamin. "Election 2018 exit poll analysis: Voter turnout soars, Democrats take back the House, ABC News projects." *ABC News*, Nov 7, 2018. Retrieved June 27, 2019 from https://abcnews.go.com/Politics/ election-2018-exit-poll-analysis-56-percent-country/ story?id=59006586

43. "American women are more likely to identify as feminists now than in 2016." *YouGov* poll, RealTime Research August 9, 2018. Retrieved June 28, 2019 from https://today.yougov .com/topics/lifestyle/articles-reports/2018/08/09/feminism -american-women-2018

44. "A Ms. Foundation for Women Survey." PerryUndem Research for the Ms. Foundation for Women, August, 2015. Retrieved June 27, 2019 from https://forwomen.org/wp-content/uploads /2015/10/Ms-National-Survey-Executive-Summary.pdf

45. Menasce, Horowitz, Juliana, Parker, Kim and Stepler, Renee. "Wide Partisan Gaps in U.S. Over How Far the Country Has

Come on Gender Equality." Pew Research Center, October 18, 2017. Retrieved June 28, 2019 from https://www.pewsocial trends.org/2017/10/18/wide-partisan-gaps-in-u-s-over-how-far -the-country-has-come-on-gender-equality/

46. Opinion Research Corporation, national poll commissioned by the ERA Campaign Network, July 6-9, 2001.

47. Brenan, Megan. "Record-Low 46% of Women Pleased With Society's Treatment." Gallup, January 17, 2019. Retrieved June 29, 2019 from https://news-gallup-com.proxyau.wrlc.org/poll/246056 /record-low-women-pleased-society-treatment.aspx?g_ source=link_newsv9&g_campaign=item_246560&g_ medium=copy

48. "Legality of Abortion, 2018-2019 Demographic Tables." Gallup, May, 2019. Retrieved July 18, 2019 from https://news .gallup.com/poll/244097/legality-abortion-2018-demographic -tables.aspx?g_source=link_NEWSV9&g_ medium=TOPIC&g_campaign=item_&g_content=Legality %2520of%2520Abortion%2c%25202018-2019%2520Demogra phic%2520Tables

49. Montanaro, Domenico. "Poll: Majority Want To Keep Abortion Legal, But They Also Want Restrictions." NPR, June 7, 2019. Retrieved July 27, 2019 from https://www.npr. org/2019/06/07/730183531/poll-majority-want-to-keep -abortion-legal-but-they-also-want-restrictions

50. Gallup tracking results, polling on abortion, 1975B2015. Retrieved November 2, 2015 from http://www.gallup.com/ poll/1576/abortion.aspx

51. "Abortion Survey, May 2019." College Pulse. Retrieved August 3, 2019 from https://collegepulse.com/wp-content/ uploads/2019/05/Abortion-topline.pdf

52. Newport, Frank. "For the First Time, Majority of Americans Favor Legal Gay Marriage." Gallup Organization, May 20, 2011. Retrieved October 3, 2011 from http://www.gallup.com/

poll/147662/First-Time-Majority-Americans-Favor-Legal-Gay-Marriage.aspx

53. "Changing Attitudes on Gay Marriage." Pew Research Center, July 29, 2015. Retrieved November 2, 2015 from http://www.pewforum.org/2015/07/29/graphics-slideshow-changing-attitudes-on-gay-marriage/

54. "Attitudes on Same-Sex Marriage." Pew Research Center, May 14, 2019. Retrieved June 20, 2019 from https://www.pewforum.org/fact-sheet/changing-attitudes-on-gay-marriage/

55. Swift, Art. "Most Americans Say Same-Sex Couples Entitled to Adopt." Gallup, May 30, 2014. Downloaded November 2, 2015 from http://www.gallup.com/poll/170801/americans-say-sex-couples-entitled-adopt.aspx

56. Cooperman, Rosalyn. "Men and Women Voters' Different Positions on Guns Matter in Midterm Elections." Rutgers University, Center for American Women in Politics, July 2, 2018. Retrieved July 21, 2019 from http://www.genderwatch2018.org/men-women-voters-guns/

57. "A Step Forward in the Fight Against Gun Violence." Editorial Board, *Bloomberg*, November 9, 2018. Retrieved July 21, 2019 from https://www.bloomberg.com/opinion/articles/2018-11-09/midterm-elections-2018-gun-safety-a-winning-issue

58. Hart Research Poll for Everytown for Gun Safety, October 28, 2018. Retrieved July 21, 2019 from https://everytown.org/documents/2018/10/guns-and-the-2018-election.pdf/?utm_source=newsletter&utm_medium=email&utm_campaign=sendto_newslettertest

59. Jones, Jeffrey M. "New High in U.S. Say Immigration Most Important Problem." Gallup, June 21, 2019. Retrieved August 1, 2019 from https://news.gallup.com/poll/259103/new-high-say-immigration-important-problem.aspx. References Gallup 190621Immigration.pdf

60. *The Global Gender Gap Report 2018.* Geneva, Switzerland: World

Economic Forum, 2018. Retrieved May 29, 2019 from http://www3.weforum.org/docs/WEF_GGGR_2018.pdf

61. Shingler, Randy. "Women's Rights: Our Unfinished Business." *Medium*, Mar 8, 2018. Retrieved May 29, 2019 from https://medium.com/@trshingler/womens-rights-our-unfinished -business-ddf61d8ec224

62. "Female heads of state and government around the world as of March 31, 2019." *EWN Eyewitness News*. Retrieved May 29, 2019 from https://ewn.co.za/2019/03/31/female -heads-of-state-and-government-around-the-world

63. Thornton, Alex. "These countries have the most women in parliament." Geneva, Switzerland: World Economic Forum, February 12, 2019. Retrieved May 30, 2019 from https://www. weforum.org/agenda/2019/02/chart-of-the-day-these-coun- tries-have-the-most-women-in-parliament/

64. *Gender Quota Database*. Stockholm, Sweden, International Institute for Democracy and Electoral Assistance (International IDEA), 2019. Retrieved May 30, 2019 from https://www.idea. int/data-tools/data/gender-quotas/quotas

65. Polochek, Soloman and Jun Xiang. *The Gender Pay Gap: A Cross-Country Analysis*. State University of New York at Binghamton, 2006. Retrieved November 2, 2011 from http://www.rand. org/content/dam/rand/www/external/labor/seminars/adp/ pdfs/2006_polachek.pdf

66. Anderson, Sarah. "Five Charts that Show Why We Need to Tackle Gender Justice and Poverty Together." Washington, D.C.: Institute for Policy Studies, May 17, 2018. Retrieved May 30, 2019 from https://ips-dc.org/five-charts-show-need- tackle-gender-justice-poverty-together/

67. "Income and Poverty in the United States: 2017." Washington, D.C.: U.S. Census Bureau, September 12, 2018. Retrieved May 30, 2019 from https://www.census.gov/library/publica- tions/2018/demo/p60-263.html

68. Scheil-Adlung, Xenia and Sandner. Lydia. "The Case for Paid Sick Leave." *World Health Report (2010) Background Paper 9.* Geneva, Switzerland, World Health Organization. Retrieved November 2, 2011 from http://www.who.int/healthsystems/ topics/financing/healthreport/SickleaveNo9FINAL.pdf

69. "Fast Facts: Maternity Leave Policies Across the Globe." *Vital Record,* Texas A&M University, January 2018. Retrieved May 30, 2019 from https://vitalrecord.tamhsc.edu/fast-facts-maternity-leave-policies-across-globe/

70. Toossi, Mitra. "Labor force projections to 2020." Washington, D.C.: Bureau of Labor Statistics, January, 2012. Retrieved June 25, 2019 from https://www.bls.gov/opub/mlr/2012/01/ art3full.pdf

71. Glynn, Sarah Jane. "Breadwinning Mothers Continue to Be the U.S. Norm." Washington, D.C.: Center for American Progress, May 10, 2019. Retrieved June 24, 2019 from https://www.amer-icanprogress.org/issues/women/reports/2019/05/10/469739/ breadwinning-mothers-continue-u-s-norm/

72. Pettibone, Richard. "Top 100 Federal Contractors FY2017." Forecast International, July 12, 2018. Retrieved June 24, 2019 from https://dsm.forecastinternational.com/wordpress/2018/07/12/ top-100-federal-contractors-fy2017/

73. Moore, Emily. "The huge issue students don't learn about: The college major gap." *NBC News,* September 6, 2018. Retrieved June 25, 2018 from https://www.nbcnews.com/know-your -value/feature/huge-issue-students-don-t-learn-about-college -major-gap-ncna906736

74. "Analysis: Women Hold Two-Thirds of Country's $1.4-Trillion Student Debt." Washington, D.C.: American Association of University Women, May 21, 2018. Retrieved June 24, 2019 from https://www.aauw.org/article/women-hold-two-thirds-of-college-student-debt/

75. Barillas, Joshua. "AACSB and AAUP Faculty Salary Comparative

Analysis." Association to Advance Collegiate Schools of Business, May 30, 2018. Retrieved June 24, 2019 from https://aacsbblogs. typepad.com/dataandresearch/gender/

76. Gu, Jackie. "Women Lose Out to Men Even Before They Graduate From College," *Bloomberg*, March 15, 2018. Retrieved June 24, 2019 from https://www.bloomberg.com/graphics/2018 -women-professional-inequality-college/

77. "Parents and the High Cost of Child Care 2013 Report." Arlington, VA: National Association of Child Care Resource and Referral Agencies. Retrieved January 28, 2014, from http://www .naccrra.org

78. Livingston, Gretchen. "About one-third of U.S. children are living with an unmarried parent," Pew Research Center, April 27, 2018. Retrieved April 18, 2019 from https://www.pewresearch .org/fact-tank/2018/04/27/about-one-third-of-u-s-children- are-living-with-an-unmarried-parent/

79. "The Affordable Care Act is Working." U.S. Department of Health and Human Services, June 24, 2015. Retrieved October 30, 2015 from http://www.hhs.gov/healthcare/facts-and-features/ fact-sheets/aca-is-working/index.html

80. *Deadly Delivery: The Maternal Health Care Crisis in the USA*. London: Amnesty International, 2010, updated 2013. Retrieved January 28, 2014, from http://www.amnestyusa.org/sites/default /files/pdfs/deadlydelivery.pdf

81. Hooyman, Nancy R. "Social and Health Disparities in Aging: Gender Inequities in Long-Term Care." American Society on Aging, May 24, 2019, citing earlier research. Retrieved June 1, 2019 from https://www.asaging.org/blog/social-and-health- disparities-aging-gender-inequities-long-term-care

82. Ibid.

83. "The State of Abortion and Contraception Attitudes in All 50 States." PRRI, August 13, 2019. Retrieved August 13, 2019 from

https://www.prri.org/research/legal-in-most-cases-the
-impact-of-the-abortion-debate-in-2019-america/

84. "Social Security Programs Throughout the World: Europe, 2018." Washington, D.C.: U.S. Social Security Administration Office of Policy, Retrieved May 29, 2019 from https://www.ssa.gov/policy/docs/progdesc/ssptw/2018-2019/europe/france.html

85. Ibid.

86. "The National Intimate Partner and Sexual Violence Survey 2015 Data Brief." Washington, D.C.: Center for Disease Control. Retrieved June 25, 2019 from https://www.cdc.gov/violenceprevention/pdf/2015data-brief508.pdf. Gun Violence information from *A Surveillance for Violent Deaths—National Violent Death Reporting System, 27 States, 2015*. CDC. Retrieved June 25, 2019 from https://www.cdc.gov/mmwr/volumes/67/ss/ss6711a1.htm

87. Diamond, Dan and Pradhan, Rachana. "Trump administration rolls back health care protections for LGBTQ patients." *Politico*, May 24, 2019. Retrieved July 11, 2019 from https://www.politico.com/story/2019/05/24/transgender-patients-protections-health-care-1343005?utm_campaign=KHN%3A%20First%20Edition&utm_source=hs_email&utm_medium=email&utm_content=73092098&_hsenc=p2ANqtz-8WubMlFc2_cZC-fArOZ5iDCfsmeAG4Ri5G6nUaqe-2AeJJNHMSobeER-cuLZqOFuAEYJsiBkKlF3a7CcKp6Fbd8oITmsrw&_hsmi=73092098

88. Allyn, Bobby. "Judge Blocks Trump Rule Requiring Pharma Companies to Disclose Drug Prices in TV Ads." *NPR*, July 9, 2019. Retrieved July 11, 2019 from https://www.npr.org/2019/07/09/739770699/judge-blocks-trump-rule-requiring-pharma-companies-to-say-price-of-drugs-in-tv-a

88. Alkon, Cheryl. "The Biggest Healthcare Changes Under Trump." *The Paper Gown*, April 3, 2019. Retrieved June 30, 2019 from

https://thepapergown.zocdoc.com/the-biggest-healthcare-changes-under-trump/

90. *Voters Real Health Care Agenda.* Justice.org. Retrieved January 8, 2008 from http://justice.org/pressroom/CJSPollMe

91. Lowen, Linda. "How Health Care Reform Benefits Women." About.com, December 16, 2010. Retrieved February 10, 2010 from http://womensissues.about.com/od/womensbodiesminds/a/HealthCareReformWomen.htm

92. "National Report: Women's Access to Health Care Services." Washington, D.C.: National Women's Law Center, 2007.

93. Ibid.

94. Burk, Martha. "Astroturf War." *Ms. Magazine*, Fall, 2009.

95. U.S. Department of Commerce, Bureau of the Census, Current Population Survey, 2007, 2008, and 2009 Annual Social and Economic Supplement (ASEC); and U.S. Department of Commerce, Bureau of the Census, "State Single Year of Age and Sex Population Estimates: April 1, 2000 to July 1, 2008 RESIDENT," at http://www.census.gov/popest/states/asrh/files/SCBEST2008BAGESEXBRES.csv. Calculations by Children's Defense Fund, Washington, D.C. November 29, 2009 from http://childrensdefensefund.org

96. *Child Health.,* U.S. Center for Disease Control, National Center for Health Statistics (2006). Retrieved January 4, 2008 from http://www.cdc.gov

97. "Obamacare Enrollment Numbers, Q1 2015" Obamacare Facts, citing GallupHealthways Well-Being Index, Retrieved August 3, 2015 from http://obamacarefacts.com/sign-ups/obamacare-enrollment-numbers/

98. "National Health Expenditure Projections 2018-2027." Center for Medicare and Medicaid Services, 2019.

99. "U.S. Health Care Spending Highest Among Developed Countries." *Hopkins Bloomberg Public Health Magazine*, Summer, 2019. Downloaded July 1, 2019 from https://www.jhsph.

edu/news/news-releases/2019/us-health-care-spending-high-est-among-developed-countries.html

100. Sherman, Erik. "U.S. Health Care Costs Skyrocketed to $3.65 Trillion in 2018." *Fortune*, February 21, 2019. Retrieved July 2, 2019 from https://fortune.com/2019/02/21/us-health-care-costs-2/

101. *Definition of Socialized Medicine.* Retrieved January 8, 2008 from http://Medicinenet.com

102. Luhby, Tami. "Here's what the GOP plans for health care look like." *CNN*, March 29, 2019. Retrieved July 3, 2019 from https://www.cnn.com/2019/03/28/politics/republican-health-care-proposals/index.html

103. Richtman, Max. "GOP's proposed Medicare voucher program would lead to demise of the system." *The Hill*, March 5, 2018. Retrieved July 3, 2019 from https://thehill.com/opinion/health-care/376767-gops-voucher-system-for-medicare-would-lead-to-the-programs-demise

104. Kevles, Daniel J. "The Secret History of Birth Control." *The New York Times*, July 22, 2001.

105. "Trump Administration Releases Final Text of Domestic Gag Rule Restriction on Title X," *Rewire News*, February 22, 2019. Retrieved April 12, 2019 from https://rewire.news/article/2019/02/22/trump-administration-releases-final-text-of-domestic-gag-rule-restriction-on-title-x

106. Ranji, Usha, Yali Bair, and Alina Salganicof. "Medicaid and Family Planning: Background and Implications of the ACA." Kaiser Family Foundation, Jul 08, 2015. Retrieved October 16, 2015 from http://kff.org/womens-health-policy/issue-brief/medicaid-and-family-planning-background-and-implications-of-the-aca/

107. Go, Alison. "Spending Bill Reduces Cost of Birth Control Pills on Campus." *U.S. News & World Report* online, March 11, 2009. http://www.usnews.com/blogs/paper-trail/2009/03/11/

spending-bill-reduces-cost-of-birth-control-pills-on-campus.
html

108. Rachel Benson Gold. "Federal Authority to Impose Medicaid Family Planning Cuts: A Deal States Should Refuse." *Guttmacher Policy Review,* Spring 2006: Volume 9, Number 2.

109. "Trump Administration Cuts Off All UNFPA Funding," *Feminist Newswire*, Feminist Majority Foundation, April 18, 2017. Retrieved April 10, 2019 from https://womendeliver.org/press/trump-administration-cuts-off-unfpa-funding/

110. Jackson, David and Kennedy, Kelly. "Obama backs restrictions on morning-after pill." *USA Today*, December 8, 2011. Retrieved February 16, 2012 from http://yourlife.usatoday.com/health/story/2011-12-08/Obama-Morning-after-pill-decision-common-sense/51745132/1

111. Neergaard, Lauran. "FDA Approves Morning After Pill Over-the-counter Sales After Court Order." *The Huffington Post*, June 20, 2013. Retrieved February 18, 2014 from http://www.huffingtonpost.com/2013/06/20/fda-morning-after-pill_n_3475178.html

112. Stein, Rob. "Pharmacists' Rights at Front of New Debate." *The Washington Post*, March 28, 2005: A01.

113. Platner, John. *Planned Parenthood, Bush and Birth Control.* (2005). Retrieved February 18, 2008 from http://www.plannedparenthood.org/issues-action/birth-control/bc-bush-6516.htm

114. Kliff, Sarah. "The Future of Abstinence." *Newsweek* magazine online, Oct 27, 2009 http://newsweek.com

115. U.S. Social Security Act, '510(b)(2).

116. "Abstinence Only Sex Ed Ineffective." *ABC News*, April 2007. Retrieved February 18, 2008 from http://abcnews.go.com/Health/Sex/story?id=3048738

117. Mike Stobbe. "Teen Birthrate Makes Rare Rise." Associated Press, Thursday, Dec. 6, 2007.

118. Lampen, Claire. "It isn't required in 19 states to teach teens

about condoms," *The Daily Dot*, July 31, 2018. Retrieved April 13, 2019 from https://www.dailydot.com/irl/abstinence-only-education/

119. Meckler, Laura. "Budget Widens Teen-Pregnancy-Prevention Efforts." *Wall Street Journal* online, May 7, 2009. http://online.wsj.com/article/SB124171750523696797.html

120. Meyer, Elizabeth J. "Funding Abstinence: The War on Sex Ed," *Psychology Today*, December 11, 2108. Retrieved April 13, 2019 from https://www.psychologytoday.com/us/blog/gender-and-schooling/201812/funding-abstinence-the-war-sex-ed

121. Ibid.

122. *History of Abortion in the U.S.* Boston: Our Bodies, Ourselves Health Resource Center. Retrieved December 22, 2007 from http://www.ourbodiesourselves.org/book/excerpt.asp?id=27

123. *History of Abortion.* National Abortion Federation, Washington, D.C. Retrieved December 22, 2007 from http://www.pro-choice.org/about_abortion/history_abortion.html

124. Ibid.

125. *NAF Violence And Disruption Statistics: Incidents of Violence & Disruption Against Abortion Providers in the U.S. & Canada.* Downloaded February 17, 2012 from http://www.prochoice.org

126. "National Clinic Violence Survey." *Feminist Majority*, January 2019. Retrieved April 10, 2019 from https://www.feminist.org/anti-abortion-violence/facts.html

127. Montanaro, Domenico. "Poll: Majority Want To Keep Abortion Legal, But They Also Want Restrictions." *NPR*, June 7, 2019. Retrieved July 27, 2019 from https://www.npr.org/2019/06/07/730183531/poll-majority-want-to-keep-abortion-legal-but-they-also-want-restrictions

128. "Ashcroft Seeks Hospital Abortion Records." *Democracy Now*, February 13, 2004. Retrieved December 22, 2007 from http://www.democracynow.org

129. "Court Battle Over Oklahoma's Strict Abortion Law." Associated Press, October 23, 2009

130. Guttmacher Institute, April 2019. Retrieved April 10, 2019 from http://www.guttmacher.org

131. "Abortion Access in the United States." *Choice Voices*, Planned Parenthood of New York City, February, 2007.

132. Koeninger, Kevin. "Sixth Circuit Lifts Block of Kentucky Ultrasound Abortion Law," Courthouse News Service, April 4, 2019. Retrieved April 18, 2019 from https://www.courthousenews. com/sixth-circuit-lifts-block-of-kentucky-ultrasound-abortion-law

133. "Ohio governor signs ban on abortion after 1st fetal heartbeat," *PBS News Hour*, April 11, 2019. Retrieved April 12, 2019 from https://www.pbs.org/newshour/politics/ohio-governor-signs-ban-on-abortion-after-1st-fetal-heartbeat

134. Vagianos Alanna. "Texas Lawmakers are Considering the Death Penalty for Women Who Get Abortions" *Huffington Post*, April 10, 2019. Retrieved April 18, 2019 from https://www.huffpost. com/entry/texas-lawmakers-are-considering-the-death-penalty-for-women-who-get-abortions_n_5cade41ae4b0d6eb 63c26324

135. "America's Women and the Wage Gap 2019." Washington, D.C.: National Partnership for Women and Families citing U.S. Census Bureau. (2018). Current Population Survey, Annual Social and Economic (ASEC) Supplement: Table PINC-05: Work Experience in 2017—People 15 Years Old and Over by Total Money Earnings in 2017, Age, Race, Hispanic Origin, Sex, and Disability Status. Retrieved 20 March 2019, from https:// www.census.gov/data/tables/time-series/demo/income-poverty/cps-pinc/pinc-05.html (Unpublished calculation based on the median annual pay for all women and men who worked full-time, year-round in 2018)

136. "The Wage Gap: The Who, How, Why, and What To Do 2019."

"Fair Pay for Women Requires a Fair Minimum Wage 2015." Washington, D.C.: National Women's Law Center, Retrieved May 13, 2019 from https://nwlc.org/resources/the-wage-gap-the-who-how-why-and-what-to-do/

137. Rose, Stephen J. and Hartmann, Heidi I. "Still a Man's Labor Market: the Long-term Earnings Gap." Washington, D.C.: Institute for Women's Policy Research, May, 2004.

138. *Behind the Pay Gap*, Washington, D.C: American Association of University Women, April, 2007.

139. Turner, Coby. "Google It: Pay Equity Class Action Complaint Dismissed," Seyfarth Shaw. December 11, 2017. Retrieved May 15, 2019 from https://www.calpeculiarities.com/2017/12/11/google-it-pay-equity-class-action-complaint-dismissed/

140. Levin, Sam. "Oracle systematically underpaid thousands of women, lawsuit says," *The Guardian*, US Edition, January 18, 2019. Retrieved May 15, 2019 from https://www.theguardian.com/technology/2019/jan/18/oracle-women-workers-lawsuit-salaries-pay

141. Blumberg, Peter. "Nike Women Clear First Hurdle in Lawsuit Over Gender Pay Gap." *Bloomberg*, February 27, 2019. Retrieved May 15, 2019 from https://www.bloomberg.com/news/articles/2019-02-27/nike-loses-initial-challenge-to-gender-bias-class-action-lawsuit

142. "Minimum Wage: Facts at a Glance." Washington, D.C.: Economic Policy Institute, April, 2007.

143. Filion, Kai. "Fact sheet for 2009 minimum wage increase: Minimum Wage Issue Guide." Washington, D.C.: Economic Policy Institute, July 20, 2009.

144. Pramuk, Jacob "House passes bill to hike the federal minimum wage to $15 per hour." *CNBC*, July 18, 2019. Retrieved July 21, 2019 from https://www.cnbc.com/2019/07/18/house-passes-raise-the-wage-act-15-per-hour-minimum-wage-bill.html

145. Gould, Elise and McNicholas, Celine. "Unions help narrow the

gender wage gap," Washington, D.C.: Economic Policy Institute. April 3, 2017. Retrieved May 15, 2019 from https://www.epi. org/blog/unions-help-narrow-the-gender-wage-gap/

146. *US Mortgage Defaults Leveling Off but Repos Rising.* Retrieved February 17, 2008 from http://www.researchrecap.com/index. php/2007/11/29/us-mortgage-defaults-leveling-off-but -repos-rising/

147. Aversa, Jeannine. "Majority Believe US in Recession." Associated Press, Feb. 10, 2008.

148. Weisman, Jonathan. "Congress Approves Stimulus Package." *The Washington Post*, February 8, 2008: Page A01.

149. Paletta, Damian and Long, Heather. "Trump may be about to face his biggest test yet on the economy." *The Washington Post*, June 17, 2019. Retrieved July 19, 2019 from https://www.washington post.com/business/economy/trump-is-about-to-face-his-biggest-test-yet-on-the-economy/2019/06/17/ec9d00a6-911b-11e9-b 570-6416efdc0803_story.html?utm_term=.d28e5979c587

150. Dwight D. Eisenhower, speech, American Society of News-paper Editors, April 16, 1953.

151. *Statement on the Treasury Surplus–Brief Article.* Weekly Compilation of Presidential Documents. (September 21, 2000). Retrieved January 2, 2008 from http://findarticles.com

152. Belasco, Amy. *The Cost of Iraq, Afghanistan, and Other Global War on Terror Operations Since 9/11.* Washington, D.C.: Congressional Research Service March 29, 2011.

153. Brennan, David "How Much Higher are Trump's Budget Deficits than Obama's?" *Newsweek*, August 18, 2018. Retrieved June 17, 2019 from https://www.newsweek.com/how-much-higher-are-trumps-budget-deficits-obamas-1069476

154. Amadeo, Kimberly. "Cost of Iraq War, its Timeline, and the Economic Impact." *The Balance*, June 18, 2019. Retrieved June 18, 2019 from https://www.thebalance.com/cost-of-iraq-war-timeline-economic-impact-3306301

155. Agiesta, Jennifer and Cohen, Jon. "Public Opinion in U.S. Turns Against Afghan War." *The Washington Post*, August 20, 2009.

156. Victor, Daniel. "Need a Refresher on the War in Afghanistan? Here Are the Basics." *The New York Times*, January 28, 2019. Retrieved June 17, 2019 from https://www.nytimes.com/2018/12/21/world/asia/afghanistan-war-explainer.html?login=email&auth=login-email

157. "U.S. military stops releasing information tracking progress in Afghanistan." *CBS News*, May 1, 2019. Retrieved August 3, 2019 from https://www.cbsnews.com/news/us-military-stops-releasing-information-tracking-progress-in-afghanistan/

158. Foster, Sarah. "Here's how much Trump's tariffs on China could cost American consumers." *Bankrate*, May 24, 2019. Downloaded July 17, 2019 from https://www.bankrate.com/personal-finance/trump-trade-war-tariffs-china-cost-american-consumers/

159. Estes, Ralph. *Who Pays, Who Profits?* Washington, D.C.: IPS Books, 1993.

160. "Europe's Welfare States." *The Economist*, Apil 1, 2004.

161. Ibid.

162. Office of Management and Budget, "Budget of the United States Government, Fiscal year 2020" February 2019. Retrieved April 15, 2019 from https://www.pgpf.org/budget-basics/who-pays-taxes

163. Gardner, Matthew, Wamhoff, Steve, Martellotta, Mary and Roque, Lorena. "Corporate Tax Avoidance Remains Rampant Under New Tax Law," April 11, 2019. Institute on Taxation and Economic Policy, April 11, 2019.

164. Bunn, Daniel and Fornwalt, Daniel. "A Comparison of the Tax Burden on Labor in the OECD, 2018," Washington, D.C.: The Tax Foundation, September 27, 2018. Retrieved April 15, 2019 from https://taxfoundation.org/comparison-tax-burden-labor-oecd-2018/

165. Gardner, Matt. "A Tax Rate for Richest 400 People at Its

Second Lowest Level Since 1992." Citizens for Tax Justice Tax Tax Blog, January 29, 2015. Retrieved September 28, 2015 from http://www.taxjusticeblog.org/archive/2015/01/tax_rate_for_top_0001_is_at_it.php#.VgnGYpcpUZM

166. "Republican Myths about Costs of the Affordable Care Act." Congressional Budget Office figures cited by U.S. Senate Democratic Policy Committee, March 2011. Retrieved November 30, 2011 from http://dpc.senate.gov/dpcdoc.cfm?doc_name=fs-112-1-11

167. "Estimated War-Related Costs: Iraq and Afghanistan." Center for Defense Information. Retrieved November 30, 2011, from http://www.infoplease.com/ipa/A0933935.html

168. Amadeo, Kimberly. "Trump's Tax Plan and How It Affects You," *Balance.com*, April 12, 2019. Retrieved April 18, 2019 from https://www.thebalance.com/trump-s-tax-plan-how-it-affects-you-4113968

169. Estes. *Who Pays, Who Profits?*

170. Table T10-0269 Taxable Estates, Estate Tax Liability, and Average Estate Tax Rate, By Size of Gross Estate, 2011. Washington, D.C.: Tax Policy Center. Retrieved October 3, 2011 from http://taxpolicycenter.org/numbers/Content/PDF/T10-0269.pdf

171. Burk, Martha. "A Feminist Tea Party?" *Ms. Magazine*, Spring, 2007.

172. Cox, Daniel and Kamboj, Harmeet. "How Social Contact with LGBT People Impacts Attitudes on Policy." *PRRI*, June, 2017. Retrieved July 11, 2019 from https://www.prri.org/spotlight/lgbt-pride-month-social-contact-gay-lesbian-transgender-individuals/

173. "Discharges Under the Don't Ask/Don't Tell Policy: Women and Racial/Ethnic Minorities." The University of California School of Law Williams Institute, September, 2010. Retrieved February 11, 2014 from http://williamsinstitute.law.ucla.edu/wp-content/uploads/Gates-Discharges2009-Military-Sept-2010.pdf

174. "Gays In The Military Should Be Allowed To Come Out." Quinnipiac University poll, April 2009. Retrieved November 20, 2015 from http://www.quinnipiac.edu/news-and-events/quinnipiac-university-poll/national/release-detail?ReleaseID=1292

175. Condon, Stephanie. "Supreme Court Strikes Down Key Part of DOMA, Dismisses prop. 8 Case." *CBS News*, June 26, 2013. Retrieved February 10, 2014 from http://www.cbsnews.com/news/supreme-court-strikes-down-key-part-of-doma-dismisses-prop-8-case/

176. "Marriage." Gallup Trends, May 2015. Retrieved October 8, 2015 from http://www.gallup.com/poll/117328/marriage.aspx

177. Newport, Frank. "Americans Favor Rights for Gays, Lesbians to Inherit, Adopt." Princeton, N.J.: Gallup, December 17, 2012. Retrieved February 20, 2014 from http://www.gallup.com/poll/159272/americans-favor-rights-gays-lesbians-inherit-adopt.aspx

178. Greenberg, Daniel et al. "Americans Show Broad Support for LGBT Nondiscrimination Protections." *PRRI,* March 12, 2019. Downloaded July 19, 2019 from https://www.prri.org/research/americans-support-protections-lgbt-people/

179. Bruni, Frank. "The Gay Truth About Trump." *The New York Times,* June 23, 2019.

180. "Trump's record of action against transgender people." National Center for Transgender Equality, July, 2019. Retrieved July 11, 2019 from https://transequality.org/the-discrimination-administration

181. "HRC Map." Washington, D.C.: Human Rights Campaign, Retrieved May 31, 2019 from hrc.org

182. "Status of the Social Security and Medicare Programs: A Summary of the 2019 Annual Reports." Office of the Chief Actuary Social Security and Medicare Boards of Trustees,

2019. Retrieved May 20, 2019 from https://www.ssa.gov/oact/ TRSUM/

183. Ibid.

184. *The 2013 Annual Report of the Board of Trustees of the Federal Old-age and Survivors Insurance and Federal Disability Insurance Trust Funds.* Washington, D.C.: Social Security Administration, Retrieved December 3, 2013 from http://www.ssa.gov/oact/tr/2013/tr2013.pdf

185. "Polling Memo: Americans' Views on Social Security." Washington, D.C.: *Social Security Works*, October, 2016. Retrieved May 20, 2019 from https://socialsecurityworks.org/2019/03/26/social-security-polling/

186. United States Social Security Administration. *Social Security is Important to Women.* (August, 2019). Retrieved May 20, 2019 from https://www.ssa.gov/news/press/factsheets/women-alt.pdf

187. Ibid.

188. United States Social Security Administration. *Social Security is Important to Women.*

189. Romig, Kathleen. "Social Security Lifts More Americans Above Poverty Than Any Other Program." Washington, D.C.: Center on Budget and Policy Priorities, November 5, 2018. Retrieved May 21, 2019 from https://www.cbpp.org/research/social-security/social-security-lifts-more-americans-above-poverty-than-any-other-program

190. United States Social Security Administration. *Social Security is Important to African Americans.* (August, 2018). Retrieved May 20, 2019 from https://www.ssa.gov/news/press/factsheets/africanamer-alt.pdf

191. Gould, Elise. "Latina workers have to work 10 months into 2018 to be paid the same as white non-Hispanic men in 2017." Washington, D.C.: Economic Policy Institute, October 31, 2018. Retrieved May 21, 2019 from https://www.epi.org/blog/latina-

workers-have-to-work-10-months-into-2018-to-be-paid-the-s
ame-as-white-non-hispanic-men-in-2017/

192. Olorunnipa, Toluse. "Bolton Calls National Debt Economic Threat to U.S." *Bloomberg*, October 31, 2018. Retrieved May 21, 2019 from https://www.bloomberg.com/news/articles/2018-10-31/bolton-calls-u-s-national-debt-economic-threat-to-society-correct

193. Jones, Chuck. "Trump's Additional Budget Deficit was Largely Due To The Corporate Tax Cut." *Forbes*, Oct. 31, 2018. Retrieved May 21, 2019 from https://www.forbes.com/sites/chuckjones/2018/10/31/trumps-additional-budget-deficit-was-largely-due-to-the-corporate-tax-cut/#593d611358f7

194. "Social Security Policy Options." Washington, D.C., Congressional Budget Office, July, 2010. Retrieved December 3, 2013 from http://www.cbo.gov/sites/default/files/cbofiles/ftpdocs/115xx/doc11580/07-01-ssoptions_forweb.pdf

195. Williams, Sean. "Raising the Payroll Tax by This Much Would Fix Social Security." *The Motley Fool*, June 23, 2018. Retrieved May 21, 2018 from https://www.fool.com/retirement/2018/06/23/raising-the-payroll-tax-by-this-much-would-fix-soc.aspx

196. *Strengthening Social Security for Women*. Washington, D.C.: National Task Force on Social Security and Women, National Council of Women's Organizations and The Institute for Women's Policy Research, 1999.

197. "Expanding Social Security Benefits for Financially Vulnerable Populations." National Council of Women's Organizations and Center for Community Change, Washington, D.C.: October, 2013.

198. Williams, Sean. "Donald Trump on Social Security: 9 Things You Should Know." *The Motley Fool*, June 7, 2019. Retrieved July 18, 2019 from https://www.fool.com/retirement/2019/06/07/donald-trump-on-social-security-9-things-you-shoul.aspx

199. "The National Intimate Partner and Sexual Violence Survey 2015 Data Brief." Washington, D.C.: Center for Disease Control. Retrieved June 25, 2019 from https://www.cdc.gov/violen-ceprevention/pdf/2015data-brief508.pdf. Gun Violence infor-mation from "Surveillance for Violent Deaths—National Violent Death Reporting System, 27 States, 2015." CDC. Retrieved June 25, 2019 from https://www.cdc.gov/mmwr/volumes/67/ss/ss6711a1.htm

200. Smith, S.G., Zhang, X., Basile, K.C., Merrick, M.T., Wang, J., Kresnow, M., Chen, J. "The National Intimate Partner and Sexual Violence Survey (NISVS): 2015 Data Brief Updated Release." Atlanta, GA: National Center for Injury Prevention and Control, Centers for Disease Control and Prevention, 2018. Retrieved July 7, 2019 from https://www.cdc.gov/violencepre-vention/pdf/2015data-brief508.pdf

201. "National Statistics." Washington, D.C.: National Coalition Against Domestic Violence. Retrieved October 15, 2015 from http://www.ncadv.org/learn/statistics

202. "NY Group, University To Study Rape Kit Backlog." Associated Press, Sept. 19, 2011. Retrieved November 4, 2011 from http://www.foxnews.com/us/2011/09/19/ny-group-university-to-study-rape-kit-backlog/

203. "Test Rape Kits. Stop Serial Rapists." ENDTHEBACKLOG, 2019. Retrieved July 7, 2019 from http://www.endthebacklog.org/backlog-why-rape-kit-testing-important/test-rape-kits-stop-serial-rapists

204. "Put Volunteer Attorneys to Work for Domestic Violence Survivors." Washington, D.C.: National Organization for Women. Retrieved January 21, 2008 from http://www.capwiz.com/now/issues/alert/?alertid=10543461

205. "Paid Sick Days, State Laws March 2019/Paid Sick Days City and County Laws October 2018," National Partnership for Women and Families, Washington, D.C. Retrieved April 14,

2019 http://www.nationalpartnership.org/our-work/resources/workplace/paid-sick-days/paid-sick-days-statutes.pdf

206. American Public Health Association, cited in HR 1784, Healthy Families Act, introduced by Rep. Rosa DeLauro, 116th Congress of the United States, March 14, 2019.

207. Williams Claudia, Drago, Robert Ph.D., and Miller, Kevin Ph.D. "44 Million U.S. Workers Lacked Paid Sick Days in 2010: 77 Percent of Food Service Workers Lacked Access." Briefing paper, Institute for Women's Policy Research, Washington, D.C. January 2011.

208. Heymann, Jody, Earle, Alison, and Hayes, Jeffrey. "How Does the United States Measure Up?" Institute for Health and Social Policy, McGill University, 2007.

209. Nagele-Piazza, Lisa J.D. "States Push Back on Local Paid-Sick-Leave Laws," Society of Human Resource Management, October 22, 2018. Retrieved April 13, 2019 from https://www.shrm.org/resourcesandtools/legal-and-compliance/state-and-local-updates/pages/states-push-back-on-local-paid-sick-leave-laws.aspx

210. "Maternity and Paternity at Work: Law and Practice Across the World." International Labor Organization, Geneva, Switzerland, 2014. Retrieved August 5, 2015 from http://www.ilo.org/wcmsp5/groups/public/dgreports/dcomm/documents/publication/wcms_242617.pdf

211. "Chart PF2.1.A. Paid maternity leave, 2016," Paris, France. OECD Social Policy Division. Retrieved April 14, 2019 from https://www.oecd.org/els/soc/PF2_1_Parental_leave_systems.pdf

212. Jeffrey A. Mello. *Defining Hours of Service Under the Family and Medical Leave Act in Employment Disputes.* Retrieved February 16, 2008 from http://64.233.167.104/search?q=cache:Bmjax8tzhEsJ:www.cba.csus.edu/Partner/media/journal/FMLA%2520paper%2520for%2520Journal.doc+Family+Medical+

Leave+Jeffrey+A.+Mello+Towson&hl=en&ct=clnk&cd=1&gl
=us

213. "Fast Facts: Maternity leave policies across the globe," Texas A&M Health Science Center, January 23, 2018. Retrieved April 14, 2019 from https://vitalrecord.tamhsc.edu/fast-facts -maternity-leave-policies-across-globe/

214. "Swedish Policy Supports Stay-at-home Dads." *Albuquerque Journal*, November 13, 2011. p. E4.

215. "State Family and Medical Leave Insurance Laws, February 2019," Washington, D.C.: National Partnership for Women and Families. Retrieved April 14, 2019 from http://www.nation-alpartnership.org/our-work/resources/workplace/paid-leave/ state-paid-family-leave-laws.pdf

216. Heyman et. al.

217. "Voters Views on Paid Family + Medical Leave. October 2018," Washington, D.C.: National Partnership for Women and Families. Retrieved April 14, 2019 from http://www.nation-alpartnership.org/our-work/resources/workplace/paid-leave/ voters-views-on-paid-family-medical-leave-survey-find-ings-august-2018.pdf

218. Helburn, Suzanne W. and Barbara R. Bergmann. *America's Child Care Problem*. New York: Palgrave, 2002.

219. Ibid.

220. "Factsheet: Estimates of Child Care Eligibility and Receipt for Fiscal Year 2013," U.S. Department of Health and Human Services, November 2, 2017. Retrieved April 19, 2019 from https:// aspe.hhs.gov/pdf-report/factsheet-estimates-child-care-eligibil-ity-and-receipt-fiscal-year-2013

221. Bornfreund, Laura. "FY11 Budget Finally Passed Brings Good News for Early Ed," Washington, D.C.: New America Foundation, April 19, 2011. Retrieved September 26, 2011 from http://ear-lyed.newamerica.net/node/48826

222. Taxin, Amy. "State child care cuts force hard choice on parents,"

Associated Press, December 29, 2011. Retrieved February 23, 2012 from http://www.newsvine.com/_news/2011/12/29/98 06039-state-child-care-cuts-force-hard-choice-on-parents

223. "Congress Approves Spending for FY 2014: Sequester Cuts Partly Replaced, but Many Programs Still Below Their FY 2010 Levels," Washington, D.C.: Coalition for Human Needs, January 24, 2014. Retrieved February 18, 2014 from http://www.chn.org/human_needs_report/chn-congress-approves-spending-fy-2014-sequester-cuts-partly-replaced-many-programs-still-fy-2010-levels/

224. Malik, Rasheed. Hamm, Katie, Schochet, Novoa, Leila, Workman, Simon, and Jessen-Howard, Cristina and Steven. "America's Child Care Deserts," Washington, D.C.: Center for American Progress, December 6, 2018. Retrieved April 19, 2019 from https://www.americanprogress.org/issues/early-childhood/reports/2018/12/06/461643/americas-child-care-deserts-2018/

225. Renzulli, Kerri Anne. "Trump's 2020 budget proposal promises paid parental leave, $1 billion childcare investment." *CNBC*, March 12 2019. Retrieved Ausgust 3, 2019 from https://www.cnbc.com/2019/03/11/trumps-2020-budget-proposal-promises-1-billion-childcare-investment.html

226. "U.S. Child Care Seriously Lags Behind that of Europe." *American Sociological Association News*, November 18, 2002.

227. "Employment Characteristics of Families Summary," U.S. Department of Labor, Bureau of Labor Statistics, April 18, 2019. Retrieved April 18, 2019 from https://www.bls.gov/news.release/famee.nr0.htm

228. Livingston, Gretchen. "About one-third of U.S. children are living with an unmarried parent," Pew Research Center, April 27, 2018. Retrieved April 18, 2019 from https://www.pewresearch.org/fact-tank/2018/04/27/about-one-third-of-u-s-children-are-living-with-an-unmarried-parent/

229. Organisation for Economic Co-operation and Development. "Out-of-Pocket Child Care Costs for a Couple Family: full-time care at a typical child care center," 2016. Retrieved April 19, 2019 from https://read.oecd-ilibrary.org/social-issues-migra-tion-health/society-at-a-glance-2016/childcare-costs-are -around-15-of-net-family-income-across-the-oecd_soc_ glance-2016-graph14-en#page1

230. Ceder, Jill LMSW, JD. "Childcare Costs." *VeryWell Family*, February 05, 2018. Retrieved April 18, 2019 from https://www .verywellfamily.com/affording-child-care-4157342

231. Workman, Simon and Jessen-Howard, Steven. "Understanding the True Cost of Child Care for Infants and Toddlers," Washington, D.C.: Center for American Progress, November 15, 2018. Retrieved April 18, 2019 from https://www.americanprogress .org/issues/early-childhood/reports/2018/11/15/460970/ understanding-true-cost-child-care-infants-toddlers/

232. "National Parent Polling Results," Arlington, VA: National Association of Child Care Resource & Referral Agencies, September, 2011. Retrieved February 18, 2014 from http:// www.naccrra.org/sites/default/files/default_site_pages/2011/ parent_polling_one_pager_healthsaf_sept_2011_0.pdf

233. Helburn, Suzanne W. and Barbara R. Bergmann. *America's Child Care Problem*. New York: Palgrave, 2002.

234. *The State of Preschool 2018*, The National Institute for Early Education Research, Rutgers University Graduate School of Education. Retrieved April 18, 2019 from http://nieer.org/ state-preschool-yearbooks/2018-2

235. "Average Salary of Child Care Worker Jobs," ZipRecruiter, April 15. 2019. Retrieved April 22, 2019 from https://www .ziprecruiter.com/Salaries/Child-Care-Worker-Salary

236. Malik et. al. "America's Child Care Deserts."

237. U.S. Department of Health and Human Services, National Clearinghouse for LongBterm Care Information, 2011. http://

www.longtermcare.gov/LTC/Main_Site/Paying/Public_
Programs/Veterans.aspx

238. Tolchin, Martin. "Other Countries Do Much More for Disabled."
     The New York Times, March 29, 1990.

239. "The Turnover Challenge in Skilled Nursing Facilities."
     HealthStream, September 11, 2017. Retrieved May 20,
     2019 from https://www.healthstream.com/resources/blog/
     blog/2017/09/11/the-turnover-challenge-in-skilled-nursing-
     facilities

240. Efstathiou, Jim Jr. "Obama Extends Minimum Wage to 2
     Million Home Health Aides." *Bloomberg Politics*, September 17,
     2013. Retrieved February 18, 2014 from http://www.
     bloomberg.com/news/2013-09-17/obama-extends-mini-
     mum-wage-to-2-million-home-health-aides.html

241. "Nursing Home Costs in 2019 by State and Type of Care"
     SeniorLiving.org. Retrieved May 20, 2019 from https://www.
     seniorliving.org/nursing-homes/costs/

242. Foss, Kimberly, and Gertie, Bob. "7 Ways Women Can Cut
     The Cost Of Long-Term Care Insurance." *Forbes*, Jan 10, 2017,
     Retrieved July 11, 2019 from https://www.forbes.com/sites/
     nextavenue/2017/01/10/7-ways-women-can-cut-the-cost-of-
     long-term-care-insurance/#6f8d6b415ebb

243. Rau, Jordan. "Nursing Home Fines Drop As Trump
     Administration Heeds Industry Complaints." *Kaiser Health
     News*, March 15, 2019. Retrieved May 20, 2019 from
     https://khn.org/news/nursing-home-fines-drop-as-trump-
     administration-heeds-industry-complaints/

244. Carrns, Ann. "Checking the Details on Gender for Long-Term
     Care Insurance." *The New York Times*, February 15, 2014.

245. Musil, Caryn McTigue. "Scaling the Ivory Towers." *Ms. Maga-
     zine*, Fall 2007.

246. "Digest of Education Statistics." National Center for Education

Statistics, 2018. Retrieved July 8, 2019 from https://nces. ed.gov/programs/digest/d18/tables/dt18_303.70.asp

247. "Distribution of Medical School Graduates by Gender 2018." Henry J. Kaiser Family Foundation. Retrieved July 7, 2019 from https://www.kff.org/other/state-indicator/medical-school-graduates-by-gender/?currentTimeframe=0&sortModel=%7B %22colId%22:%22Location%22,%22sort%22:%22asc%22%7D

248. "High School Participation Increases for 29th Consecutive Year." September 11, 2018. National Federation of State High School Associations. Retrieved July 7, 2019 from https://www .nfhs.org/articles/high-school-sports-participation-increases-for-29th-consecutive-year/

249. Klein, Sue. "Tracking Deliberate Sex Segregation in U.S. K-12 Public Schools." Washington, D.C.: Feminist Majority Foundation, 2018. Retrieved July 9, 2019 from http://feminist.org/education/pdfs/SexSegReport2018.pdf

250. Ibid.

251. Klein, 2018.

252. Klein, 2018.

253. "Obama Administration Warns Schools to Follow Sex Crime Protocol." *Campus Safety Magazine*, April 5, 2011. Retrieved October 27, 2015 from http://www.campussafetymagazine .com/article/Obama-Administration-Kicks-Off-Sexual-Violence-Awareness-Effort

254. Brown, Sarah and Mangan, Katherine. "What You Need to Know About the Proposed Title IX Regulations." *The Chronicle of Higher Education*, November 16, 2018. Retrieved July 9, 2019 from https://www.chronicle.com/article/What-You-Need-to-Know-About/245118

255. "Trends in Political Values and Core Attitudes: 1987-2007." Washington, D.C.: Pew Research Center for People and the Press. Retrieved March 13, 2014 from http://www.people-press.

org/2007/03/22/trends-in-political-values-and-core-atti-tudes-1987-2007/

256. Associated Press-GfK Poll conducted by GfK Roper Public Affairs & Media. May 28-June 1, 2009. Retrieved November 24, 2009 from http://www.pollingreport.com/race.htm

257. *USA Today* poll conducted by Princeton Survey Research Associates International. June 27-30, 2013 as reported by PollingReport.com. Retrieved February 20, 2014 from http://www.pollingreport.com/race.htm

258. "Affirmative Action." summary of polls. Ballotpedia. Retrieved August 10, 2015 from http://ballotpedia.org/Affirmative_action

259. Norman, Jim. "Americans' Support for Affirmative Action Programs Rises." *Gallup*, February 27, 2019. Retrieved June 2, 2019 from https://news.gallup.com/poll/247046/americans-support-affirmative-action-programs-rises.aspx

260. "More History of Affirmative Action Policies from the 1960s." American Association for Access, Equity, and Diversity. Retrieved June 3, 2019 from https://www.aaaed.org/aaaed/history_of_affirmative_action.asp

261. *Adarand Construction v. Pena.* The Supreme Court ruled that the most rigorous type of constitutional review, "strict scrutiny," must be applied to federal affirmative action programs. At the same time it ruled that affirmative action programs are both legal and needed.

262. Jackson, Abby. "The Supreme Court just ruled in favor of affir-mative action in college admissions." *Business Insider*, June 23, 2016. Retrieved June 3, 2019 from https://www.businessinsider.com/supreme-court-ruling-on-fisher-v-texas-2016-6

263. Moore, Mary and Jennifer Hahn. "Contracting Connerly." *Ms. Magazine*, Winter 2008.

264. Walker, Blair S. *Washington's Anti-Affirmative Action Vote Thrust Into Spotlight.* (July 13, 1999). Retrieved December 29, 2007 from http://Stateline.org

265. Ibid.

266. Moore and Hahn.

267. News of the Nation. *Affirmative Action Setbacks* (1997). Retrieved December 29, 2007 from Infoplease.com

268. Ocampo, Carmina. "Prop 209: Ten Long Years." *The Nation*, December 11, 2006.

269. "UC Berkeley Fall Enrollment Data." UC Berkeley Office of the CFO, 2014. Retrieved February 12, 2014 from http://opa. berkeley.edu/statistics/enrollmentdata.html

270. Asimov, Nanette. AUC Minority Enrollment Among Lowest in Nation." SFGate.com, January 14, 2010. Retrieved November 16, 2011 from http://articles.sfgate.com/2010-01-14/ bay-area/17828191_1_uc-berkeley-flagship-schools-latino-students

271. "Fall Enrollment at a Glance." University of California, 2018. Retrieved June 3, 2019 from https://www.universityofcalifornia.edu/infocenter/fall-enrollment-glance

272. Wilfore, Kristina. "Take the Initiative: A Feminist Guide to Ballot Measures That Will Impact Women's Lives." *Ms. Magazine*, Fall 2006.

273. Goldberg Day, Judy and Hill, Catherine. *Behind the Pay Gap*, Washington, D.C.: American Association of University Women Educational Foundation, 2007.

274. "Missing Pieces Report: The 2018 Board Diversity Census of Women and Minorities on Fortune 500 Boards." Deloitte, 2019. Retrieved June 3, 2019 from https://www2.deloitte. com/us/en/pages/center-for-board-effectiveness/articles/missing-pieces-fortune-500-board-diversity-study-2018.html?id=us :2el:3pr:diversity:eng:boardef:011619

275. Zwahlen, Cyndia. ASBA Effort for Women Owners Stirs Outrage." *Los Angeles Times*, January 3, 2008.

276. "Women-Owned Small Businesses." Washington, D.C.: U.S. Small Business Administration. Retrieved February 12, 2014

from http://www.sba.gov/content/contracting-opportunities-women-owned-small-businesses

277. Froelings, Lisa. "U.S. Government Hits Goal for Women Owned Small Businesses." *Small Business Trends*, Dec 26, 2018. Retrieved June 3, 2019 from https://smallbiztrends.com/2016/03/us-government-goal-women-owned-small-businesses.html

278. Williams, Terry. "Small Businesses Owners Lose $30B as Federal Contracting Falls Short of Required Spending with Small Businesses in FY2008." August 24, 2009. Retrieved November 6, 2009 from http://www.nasbc.org/magazine

279. *Women in the Military: Where They Stand. 10th Edition, 2019.* Service Women's Action Network. Retrieved May 22, 2019 from https://www.servicewomen.org/wp-content/uploads/2019/04/SWAN-Where-we-stand-2019-0416revised.pdf

280. Tyson, Ann Scott. "For Female GIs, Combat Is a Fact," *The Washington Post*, Friday, May 13, 2005.

281. Jelinek, Pauline. "Report: Too Many Whites, Men Lead U.S. Military." Associated Press, March 7, 2011. Retrieved November 27, 2011 from http://www.msnbc.msn.com/id/41955329/ns/us_news-life/t/report-too-many-whites-men-lead-us-military/#

282. "Broad Support for Combat Roles for Women." Washington, D.C.: Pew Research Center, January 29, 2013. Retrieved October 3, 2015 from http://www.people-press.org/2013/01/29/broad-support-for-combat-roles-for-women/

283. Steinhauer, Jennifer. "Elite Units in Military to Admit Women." *The New York Times*, June 18, 2013.

284. Dao, James. "Servicewomen File Suit Over Direct Combat Ban." *The New York Times*, Nov. 27, 2012. Retrieved August 3, 2019 from https://www.nytimes.com/2012/11/28/us/servicewomen-file-suit-over-direct-combat-ban.html

285. "Confronting Rape in the Military." *The New York Times*, March 12, 2004.

286. Crawfore, Jamie. "Military Sexual Assaults Increase Sharply, Pentagon Report Finds." *CNN*, May 2, 2019. Retrieved May 23, 2019 from https://www.cnn.com/2019/05/02/politics/us-military-sexual-assault-report/index.html

287. Harkins, Gina. "Sailors Created 'Rape List' Aboard Navy's 2nd Sub to Integrate Women." Military.com, May 17, 2019. Retrieved May 23, 2019 from https://www.military.com/daily-news/2019/05/17/sailors-created-rape-list-aboard-navys-2nd-sub-integrate-women.html

288. McGreal, Chris. "Rape Case To Force US Defence Firms Into the Open." *The Guardian*, October 15, 2009. Retrieved November 27, 2011 from http://www.guardian.co.uk/world/2009/oct/15/defence-contractors-rape-claim-block

289. "Give Military Women the Health Care Coverage They Deserve." Washington, D.C.: National Women's Law Center, May 12, 2012. Retrieved March 12, 2014 from http://www.nwlc.org/resource/give-military-women-health-care-coverage-they-deserve

290. *Penalized for Serving Their Country: The Ban On Abortion for Women in the Military,* Washington, D.C.: Center for Reproductive Rights, June 2003. Retrieved January 2, 2008 from http://www.reproductiverights.org

291. "RAND Study Finds Divorce Among Soldiers Has Not Spiked Higher Despite Stress Created By Battlefield Deployments." The RAND Corporation, April 12, 2007.

292. "Child Custody Considerations for Members of the Military." Military OneSource, November 28, 2018. Retrieved May 27, 2019 from https://www.militaryonesource.mil/family-relationships/relationships/relationship-challenges-and-divorce/child-custody-considerations-for-members-of-the-military

293. "Veteran Population." National Center for Veterans Analysis and Statistics. May 3, 2019. Retrieved May 27, 2019 from https://www.va.gov/vetdata/docs/Demographics/VetPop_Infographic_2019.pdf

294. "New Report Spotlights Continuing Challenges Facing Women Veterans." Disabled American Veterans, September 12, 2018. Retrieved May 27, 2019 from https://www.dav.org/learn-more/news/2018/new-report-spotlights-continuing-challenges-facing-women-veterans/

295. "Female Veterans are Fastest Growing Segment of Homeless Veteran Population." Military.com, March 28, 2018. Retrieved May 27, 2019 from https://www.military.com/militaryadvantage/2018/03/28/female-veterans-are-fastest-growing-segment-homeless-veterans.html

296. Ibid.

297. Steinhauer, Jennifer. "Treated Like a 'Piece of Meat': Female Veterans Endure Harassment at the V.A." *The New York Times*, March 12, 2019. Retrieved May 27, 2019 from https://www.nytimes.com/2019/03/12/us/politics/women-veterans-harassment.html

298. "The U.S. Government and International Family Planning & Reproductive Health: Statutory Requirements and Policies." Kaiser Family Foundation, Mar 12, 2015. Retrieved November 9, 2015 from http://kff.org/global-health-policy/fact-sheet/the-u-s-government-and-international-family-planning-reproductive-health-statutory-requirements-and-policies/

299. *Global Gag Rule: A Flawed Policy That Sacrifices Women's Lives.* Washington, D.C.: NARAL Pro-Choice America, January 22, 2007. Retrieved December 15, 2007 from http://www.prochoiceamerica.org

300. "What is the Global Gag Rule?" Planned Parenthood Action Fund, May 2019. Retrieved May 15, 2019 from https://www.plannedparenthoodaction.org/communities/planned-parenthood-global/end-global-gag-rule

301. "Taliban Attacks on Afghan Girls' Schools Increase." *Feminist Daily News Wire*, July 12, 2006.

302. Starkey, Jerome. "Karzai's Secret U-Turn On Afghan Rape Law." London: *The Independent*, August 15, 2009.

303. Rubin, Alissa. "For Afghan Woman, Justice Runs Into Static Wall of Custom." *The New York Times*, December 2, 2011. A1.

304. Gibbons-Neff, Thomas and Barnes, Julian E. "Under Peace Plan, U.S. Military Would Exit Afghanistan Within Five Years," *The New York Times*, February 28, 2019. Retrieved May 15, 2019 from https://www.nytimes.com/2019/02/28/us/politics/afghanistan-military-withdrawal.html

305. Mengli, Ahmed, Yusufzai. Mushtaq and Bruton. F. Brinley. "Taliban official says comments on women at Afghan peace talks were 'misconstrued'." *NBC News*, April 16, 2019. Retrieved May 15, 2019 from https://www.nbcnews.com/news/world/taliban-official-says-comments-women-afghan-peace-talks-were-misconstrued-n994886

306. Rahim, Najim and Zucchino, David "Attacks on Girls' Schools on the Rise as Taliban Make Gains." *The New York Times*, May 21, 2019.

307. "Iraqi Women: Prostituting Ourselves to Feed Our Children." CNN.com, August 16, 2007. Retrieved December 31, 2007 from http://www.cnn.com/2007/WORLD/meast/08/15/iraq.prostitution/index.html

308. Kaya Zeynep. "Gender equality in Iraq and Iraqi Kurdistan." London School of Economics and Political Science, January, 2018. Retrieved July 11, 2019 from https://blogs.lse.ac.uk/mec/2018/01/05/gender-equality-in-iraq-and-iraqi-kurdistan/

309. "US Stance at UN a Backward Step on Women's Rights." Human Rights Watch, April 25, 2019. Retrieved May 20, 2019 from https://www.hrw.org/news/2019/04/25/us-stance-un-backward-step-womens-rights

310. "The Trump Administration's Draft Executive Order on Treaties." WTO@20 Conference 2017, New Delhi. Retrieved May 15, 2019 from https://worldtradelaw.typepad.com/ielpblog/

2017/02/the-trump-administrations-draft-executive-order-on-treaties.html

311. Rassekh Milani, Leila (ed.). *Human Rights for All, CEDAW.* Washington, D.C.: Working Group on Ratification of the U.N. Convention on the Elimination of All Forms of Discrimination Against Women, 2001.

312. "Treaty Status" International Campaign to Ban Land Mines. Retrieved May 15, 2019 from http://www.icbl.org/en-gb/the-treaty/treaty-status.aspx

313. Mehta, Sarah. "There's Only One Country That Hasn't Ratified the Convention on Children's Rights: US," ACLU Human Rights Program, November 20, 2015. Retrieved May 15, 2019 from https://www.aclu.org/blog/human-rights/treaty-ratification/theres-only-one-country-hasnt-ratified-convention-childrens

314. Mousin, Craig B. JD, MDiv "Rights Disappear When US Policy Engages Children as Weapons of Deterrence." *AMA Journal of Ethics,* January, 2019. Retrieved May 31, 2019 from https://journalofethics.ama-assn.org/article/rights-disappear-when-us-policy-engages-children-weapons-deterrence/2019-01

315. Burk, Martha. *Cult of Power: Sex Discrimination in Corporate America and What Can Be Done About It.* New York: Scribner, 2005, p. 83.

316. Tripp, Aili Marie. "Debating Women's Rights and Customary Law in Africa Today." Conference paper, Indiana University School of Law, March 2007.

317. *Lawmakers are Seeking Legislation That Addresses Medicare Part D Problems.* August, 2006. Retrieved January 8, 2008 from NeedyMeds.com

318. *2008 Part D Coverage: Major Changes Are Coming,* Washington, D.C.: Center for Medicare Advocacy. Retrieved November 1, 2007 from http://www.medicareadvocacy.org

319. *Medicare Advantage Coverage*. Financial Web. Retrieved January 8, 2008 from http://www.finweb.com

320. Markey, Jeanne A. and Sarola, Raymond M. "'Cloud of secrecy' in Medicare Advantage plans can create an environment for fraud." *STAT*, February 8, 2019. Retrieved July 2, 2019 from https://www.statnews.com/2019/02/08/secrecy-medicare-advantage-plans-fraud/

321. Herman, Bob. "Medicaid is a major source of insurance coverage for childbirths." *Axios*, September 1, 2018. Retrieved July 2, 2019 from https://www.axios.com/medicaid-as-a-source-for-childbirth-93f4aff2-1cb2-4972-990e-cbd214b990c2.html

322. Norris, Louise. "Medicaid coverage in your state." healthinsurance.org, February, 2019. Retrieved July 2, 2019 from https://www.healthinsurance.org/medicaid/

323. Lambrew, Jeanne M., Ph.D. "The State Children's Health Insurance Program: Past, Present, and Future." *The Commonwealth Fund*, February 9, 2007, Volume 49.

324. Mallaby, Sebastian. "Bush's Unhealthy Veto." *The Washington Post*, Monday, October 1, 2007: A19.

325. "Over 2,200 Veterans Died in 2008 Due to Lack of Health Insurance." Press Release from Physicians for a National Health Program, November 10, 2009. November 29, 2009 from http://www.pnhp.org/news/2009/november/over_2200_veterans_.php

326. Caruso, David B. "VA makes little headway in fight to shorten waits for care." *Military Times*, April 9, 2015. Retrieved August 3, 2015 from http://www.militarytimes.com/story/military/benefits/veterans/2015/04/09/va-wait-times-continue/25422103/

327. "Timeline of Important Reproductive Freedom Cases Decided by the Supreme Court." American Civil Liberties Union. Retrieved December 31, 2007 from http://www.aclu.org/reproductiverights/gen/16463res20031201.html

328. Ibid.

329. Tillman, Laura and John Schwartz. "Texas Clinics Stop Abortions After Court Ruling." *The New York Times*, November 1, 2013. Retrieved February 18, 2014 from http://www.nytimes.com/2013/11/02/us/texas-abortion-clinics-say-courts-ruling-is-forcing-them-to-stop-the-procedures.html?

330. Ertelt, Steven. "Supreme Court: Arizona Can't Enforce Ban on Abortions After 20 Weeks." Washington, D.C.: LifeNews.com, January 13, 2014. Retrieved February 18, 2014 from http://www.lifenews.com/2014/01/13/supreme-court-arizona-cant-enforce-ban-on-abortions-after-20-weeks/

Index